JOHN HENRY NEWMAN

Reason, Rhetoric and Romanticism

JOHN HENRY NEWMAN

Reason, Rhetoric and Romanticism

Edited by
David Nicholls and Fergus Kerr, OP

The Bristol Press

The front cover illustration is based on a picture from the Bloxham MSS in Magdalen College, Oxford. We are grateful to the President and Fellows of Magdalen College for permission to reproduce the picture.

A CIP catalogue record of this book is available from the British Library

ISBN 1 85399 147 3

First published in 1991 by:
The Bristol Press
226 North Street
Bedminster
Bristol BS3 1JD

The Bristol Press is an imprint of Bristol Classical Press

Printed and bound in Great Britain by
Billing and Sons Ltd, Worcester

CONTENTS

INTRODUCTION — 1
David Nicholls and Fergus Kerr, OP

1 DEMYTHOLOGISING NEWMAN — 13
Valerie Pitt

2 OXFORD, TRACT 90 AND THE BISHOPS — 28
Peter Nockles

3 NEWMAN AND KINGSLEY — 88
P.J. FitzPatrick

4 NEWMAN'S *GRAMMAR* AND THE CHURCH TODAY — 109
P.J. FitzPatrick

5 DID NEWMAN ANSWER GLADSTONE? — 135
Fergus Kerr, OP

6 IMPEDED WITNESS: NEWMAN AGAINST LUTHER ON JUSTIFICATION — 153
Joseph S. O'Leary

7 INDIVIDUALISM AND THE APPEAL TO AUTHORITY — 194
David Nicholls

8 NEWMAN'S MID-VICTORIAN DREAM — 214
Elisabeth Jay

9 DANGEROUS CONCEITS OR CONFIRMATIONS STRONG? — 233
Valentine Cunningham

CONTRIBUTORS — 253

INDEX — 255

INTRODUCTION

David Nicholls and Fergus Kerr, OP

John Henry Newman died in 1890. His life had spanned almost the whole of the nineteenth century and his influence went far beyond the confines of the ecclesiastical communities to which he belonged. He was indeed an eminent Victorian. Newman's life divides neatly into two by his reception into the Roman Catholic Church in 1845.

After having been raised as a fairly conventional Anglican he came, as a young man, under the sway of an evangelical clergyman, some of whose ideas made a permanent impression on the future cardinal. As a fellow of Oriel College, and then Vicar of St Mary's university church in Oxford, Newman was at the centre of the Tractarian movement, whose beginning he dated from John Keble's famous Assize sermon of 1833. With Keble, E.B. Pusey and others Newman reasserted the Catholic doctrines and practices of the Church of England against the strongly Erastian tendencies of the time. The Anglican Church was part of the one Catholic and apostolic church; it should not be seen as a department of state whose future could be determined by Act of Parliament. From the pulpit of St Mary's Newman preached to a church packed with undergraduates and dons; these *Parochial Sermons* were soon published. From 1826 to 1843 he preached a series of fifteen university sermons which centred on the relation between faith and reason. He also lectured, in St Mary's, on *The Prophetical Office of the Church* where he argued that the Anglican Church represented a *via media* between the errors of Rome on the one hand and those of popular Protestantism on the other. At this time he published his most systematic theological work, the *Lectures on the Doctrine of Justification*, considered in some detail by Joseph O'Leary in chapter 6.

The position of Newman and the Oxford Movement (as it came to be called) was proclaimed with great confidence in a series of *Tracts for the Times*, with the motto 'If the trumpet give an uncertain sound, who shall prepare himself to the battle?'. The series culminated in the notorious Tract 90, in which Newman claimed that the Thirty-Nine Articles of the Church of England could be interpreted in a Catholic sense and even seemed to be suggesting that they were not generally incompatible with the decrees of the Council of Trent. Peter Nockles, in chapter 2, looks at Newman's role in these events, concluding that his somewhat romanticised account of the story, which has become the generally accepted version, needs qualifying in important respects. The critical, not to say hostile, reception which Tract 90 received appears to have shocked its author. Yet Nockles shows that the Tract, like the *Remains* of Hurrell Froude, which Newman co-edited in 1838, was in certain respects *intended* to shock; the author was fully aware of what he was doing.

From 1841 onwards Newman adopted a lower profile and eventually withdrew from Oxford to the village of Littlemore, which was part of the parish of St Mary's. There he first ministered to the people as parish priest and, after resigning as Vicar in 1843, lived with a group of close followers as a lay member of the Church of England, until his reception into the Roman Catholic Church in 1845. It was at this time that he wrote his influential *Essay on the Development of Christian Doctrine*.

After a period of study he was ordained in the Roman Catholic Church and set about founding the Birmingham Oratory. In this post-conversion period he published *Certain Difficulties felt by Anglicans in Catholic Teaching* – lectures addressed to the Anglican party of 1833 – and his remarkable novel *Loss and Gain*. In chapter 9 Valentine Cunningham shows how no clear line can be drawn between Newman's fictional work and his other writings; they share a fascination with words, stories and images. By confusing appeals to the classical origins of English words, and other sleights of hand, he skilfully imposed his own peculiar meaning on a text. He was bewitched by language, especially by his own writings.

In 1851 Newman accepted the rectorship of the new Catholic university in Dublin, where he remained, on and off, until 1858. He encountered a certain resistance to his plans from some Irish bishops who viewed with suspicion his attempt to plant a kind of replica of Oxford in the emerald isle. On returning to England he was involved in the editorship of the *Rambler*, a Catholic journal which was critical of reactionary and ultramontane tendencies in the Church. It was in this journal that Newman published his essay 'On Consulting the Faithful in Matters of Doctrine', in 1859. In response to some remarks in a book review by Charles Kingsley, Professor of History at Cambridge, Newman penned his most celebrated work, the *Apologia pro Vita Sua*, in 1864. P.J. FitzPatrick discusses this controversy in chapter 3, while for Valerie Pitt in chapter 1 it is the classical text for understanding Newman's conception of the drama in which he was the principal actor. In the following year he published the *Dream of Gerontius* which forms the focus of Elisabeth Jay's essay (chapter 8).

Most of Newman's liveliest writing was produced in the heat of controversy; he thrived on combat and was most effective in the cut and thrust of debate. He took on Luther, Peel, Pusey, Kingsley and in 1875 responded to Gladstone's 'Expostulation' on the Vatican Decrees. The statesman had argued that the decrees on papal infallibility and the universal jurisdiction of the pope called into question the loyalty of Roman Catholic citizens; how could they recognise a double sovereignty? Gladstone's position was in certain respects flawed, but some of the legitimate arguments went unanswered. Fergus Kerr, OP considers some facets of this controversy in chapter 5 and in chapter 7 David Nicholls looks more generally at the way Newman's ecclesiastical authoritarianism is related to his basic individualism.

In his last major publication, *An Essay in Aid of a Grammar of Assent*, published in 1870, Newman returned to themes which he had followed in his *Oxford University Sermons*. He attempted in this essay to defend the reasonableness of assent to religious propositions, on the ground that many of our everyday judgments, which none of us is prepared to doubt, are also based on an accumulation of probabilities rather than on demonstrative proof. He distinguished between real and notional assent and postulated an 'illative sense', as the faculty of perceiving the truth of a proposition by an immediate practical judgment. P.J. FitzPatrick subjects the argument of the *Grammar* to a philosophical critique in chapter 4.

The publication of the *Apologia* marks the beginning of a period in which Newman achieved increasing recognition and acceptance in England. He was made honorary fellow of Trinity College, Oxford, where he had been an undergraduate, and two years later in 1879, was appointed Cardinal by the recently elected Pope Leo XIII.

Newman was very much a man – indeed a gentleman – of his time, a point emphasised by Valerie Pitt. Newman and his fellow Tractarians were but part of a whole Romantic movement in literature, art and architecture which was rooted in the past. His use of historical types in his discussion of contemporary controversy does not, however, always convince. What Arius, Nestorius, or Eutyches were in the early Church, 'such are Luther and Calvin now [*sic*]'; the position of the Anglican bishops he identified with the Eusebians or Monophysites. 'Ancient history is not dead', he cried, 'it lives; it prophesies of what passes before our eyes...we see ourselves in it as in a glass, and if the *via media* was heretical then, it is heretical now'. His was a generation absorbed by the past; not a dead past but a living, legendary past, vitally connected to the present. It was a generation inspired by the novels of Walter Scott, 'who turned men's minds in the direction of the middle ages', and by the poetry of Coleridge, Wordsworth and Southey. It was a generation which consciously turned its back on the eighteenth century, an age 'when love was cold'. Indeed the huge impact on the religious and cultural life of England made by Newman and the Oxford Movement is due largely to the fact that they were men of their time. But does Newman also have something true and important to say to the modern world? Most authors in the present collection would doubt it. Nevertheless, there are some today who look to Newman for guidance and inspiration. The Second Vatican Council was said by many to be 'Newman's Council', and his works were frequently quoted by the Fathers of the Council. Others, however, would see the recent remark by Pope John Paul II, 'we feel Newman to be our spiritual contemporary' as saying more about the Pope than about the Cardinal.

The attempt to make an objective assessment of Newman's significance is to some degree hampered by the movement for his canonisation. Conferences and other gatherings on Newman, to all appearances of an academic nature, frequently turn out to be part of a quasi-political campaign where any criticism of Newman's life or thought is resented as a betrayal of 'the cause'.

Until recently, at least in England, there has been a good deal of hesitancy and scepticism about canonising Newman. To some extent, no doubt, Newman's reputation remained tainted in many people's minds, and perhaps especially the clergy's, by his alleged influence on the modernists – not that anyone had any clear idea of who *they* were, except that they were a bad thing. A figure who was supposedly as remotely intellectual and almost neurotically introspective as Newman did not appeal much to the generation who favoured Belloc, Chesterton and Frank Sheed. Newman seemed altogether too subtle and refined, even over-delicate and old-maidish, to nourish that bluff kind of militant apologetics. On the whole, Roman Catholics in England (if they had to choose) would surely have preferred Henry Edward Manning to John Henry Newman. In popular iconography at least, Newman seemed an introverted and feline character compared with Manning, the manly if authoritarian pastor who mediated in the London Dock Strike of 1889 (the only fact about him that most people knew).

The rediscovery of Newman by his fellow Catholics began slowly after the First World War, curiously enough in Germany, as his works were translated and diffused by such enthusiasts as Erich Przywara and Theodor Haecker (through *Hochland*, the periodical which he edited with such distinction for so many years). By the 1950s Newman had been co-opted into the efflorescence of French Catholic theology, promoted especially by such leading theologians as Louis Bouyer and Yves Congar. Finally, in the English-speaking world, in the 1960s, a series of books by Newman scholars reaffirmed his standing as a major Christian thinker. From being at best an important figure in Victorian literature and in the history of ecclesiastical controversies, Newman emerged with quasi-'patristic' authority. While there is a growing Newman cult and increasingly frequent appeals to his intercession for miraculous conversions and cures, particularly in places hallowed by association with him (such as Littlemore, Maryvale and the Oratory in Birmingham), there is little doubt that it would be as a 'doctor of the Church' that Newman would be (as they say) 'raised to the altar'.

Once great thinkers in the history of the Church – Augustine and Thomas Aquinas come immediately to mind – receive the status of 'holy doctors' our perception and presentation of their work, perhaps inevitably, become over-simple and even something of a caricature. Their complexity, the necessarily fragmented and lacunary character of their work, even what is interestingly inchoate and ambiguous, all such features too often fade from our attention. What we have sought to do, in this set of essays, is to trace some of the ways in which Newman's rhetoric may conceal from us, as it no doubt concealed from *him*, what his subtext, the silent omissions and the unconscious evasions, nevertheless disclose.

Newman certainly offers us some memorable images: once read they can never be forgotten. The interesting difficulty lies in deciding how far he himself understood them. Consider, for instance, the chapter in his novel, *Loss and Gain*, written in Rome during the summer vacation in 1847, after his ordination and novitiate as an Oratorian. The young hero, Charles Reding, having finally decided to leave the Church of England, stops over in Bath and visits a bookshop to buy some of the essential Roman Catholic works of devotion. (*The Garden of the Soul* is on his list: at that date still the best example of traditional English Catholic piety before more Italian forms of devotion became popular):

> [He] heard the shop-door open, and, on looking round, saw a familiar face. It was that of a young clergyman, with a very pretty girl on his arm, whom her dress pronounced to be a bride. Love was in their eyes, joy in their voice, and affluence in their gait and bearing. Charles had a faintish feeling come over him; somewhat such as might beset a man on hearing a call for pork-chops while he was sea-sick. He retreated behind a pile of ledgers and other stationery, but they could not save him from the low, dulcet tones which from time to time passed from one to the other.

The rest of this chapter (part 3, chapter 2) is entirely taken up with the conversation between the newly wed couple which Reding, from his concealment behind the ledgers, is forced to overhear – a conversation which shows how trivially minded the pair are but in particular how her worldliness unfits the young woman for her position as a clergyman's wife. In effect, the message is that a wife must always degrade a man's priestly ministry. The reference to 'affluence' and 'dulcet tones' presage the rest of the chapter: as readers, we are expected to share the hero's repugnance at the couple for being so much in love but also, and *a fortiori*, at the church in which a married man might be a priest. The young clergyman, White by name, entered the novel at an early stage – at a breakfast party in an Oxford don's rooms, in which boiled eggs stimulate him to admire the ancient Easter liturgy and a dish of hot sausages fails to interrupt the theological flow, much to Reding's disgust. At this stage White (an Irishman, for some reason) is the Romewards-leaning undergraduate. He was also, at this stage, a passionate advocate of clerical celibacy, of 'sacerdotal purity', 'angelic blessedness', and so on. Celibacy of the clergy is, indeed, one of the principal issues in the book.

The unforgettable thought is, of course, the thought or rather the *smell*, when one is suffering from sea-sickness, of pork chops: succulent, greasy, nauseatingly glutinous. This is how married love, or anyway a clergyman's marriage, feels to the hero of *Loss and Gain*.

Celibates, especially celibate clergy, are rather prone nowadays to romanticise married love. Perhaps St Paul, if he was unmarried, was saner and more realistic when he said that it is better to marry than to burn. But to react to the sight of married love as a sea-sick man would react to the smell of pork chops surely betrays a deeply unsatisfactory conception of priestly celibacy (even if it may express a lamentably common one). It might be expected to discredit Newman's hero completely. In fact, in the story, Newman's attitude to his hero is by no means entirely uncritical and unambiguous. But it does not seem, from the rest of the narrative, that, as readers, we are expected to condemn or even ridicule Reding's celibate queasiness at the sight of a married clergyman. On the contrary, Newman, as author, seems to invite us to accept his hero's attitude as perfectly normal.

We have space to cite only one more instance of Newman's apparently innocent captivation by, and captivity in, his own powerful rhetoric. Consider his famous account of 'Catholic Christendom' in the *Apologia* (chapter 5). After describing the Catholic Church as 'an arena' for an 'awful, never-dying duel' between authority and private judgment, the exercise of infallibility and the reaction of reason against it – 'It is necessary for the very life of religion, viewed in its large operations and its history, that the warfare should be incessantly carried on' (itself an astounding image for the Church) – Newman went on as follows:

> it is a vast assemblage of human beings with wilful intellects and wild passions, brought together into one by the beauty and the Majesty of a Superhuman Power, – into what may be called a large reformatory or training-school, not as if into a hospital or into a prison, not in order to be sent to bed, not to be buried alive, but (if I may change my metaphor) brought together as if into some moral factory, for the melting, refining, and moulding, by an incessant, noisy process, of the raw material of human nature, so excellent, so dangerous, so capable of divine purposes.

Of course, these words were dashed off in Birmingham in 1864, and Newman was clearly well aware of the metaphorical charge of his rhetoric ('if I may change my metaphor'). It may be argued that, as a metaphor for the Church, this is no more bizarre that St Paul's vision of a body which consists of no more than a surrealistic eye or ear. It is certainly an extremely modern, mid-Victorian image: the Church as a Birmingham smelting works. Parkhurst Reformatory in the Isle of Wight was established in 1843. The very idea of a reformatory as a penal institution for allegedly incorrigible juvenile offenders dates from the late 1830s. This metaphor for the Church must have seemed novel in the 1860s. It is an exhilarating picture: how often are we likely to think nowadays of the 'wilful intellects and wild passions' of church-going people? Newman's view of the Church is a powerful challenge to the bland consensus which sometimes seems the ideal of loving neighbourliness. But the Church as a reformatory is a daringly violent image which prompts many questions about Newman's personal experience of living (or suffering) in a particular ecclesiastical institution which, as his rhetoric surely shows, he felt as a punishment as well as a rehabilitation. The question once again, in this unforgettable image, is whether what Newman wants to say is not contradicted by his own metaphors.

The Church as a reformatory, clerical celibacy as prone to nausea at the sight of a married priest – immensely powerful and deeply disturbing as these metaphors plainly are, do they not, in their ambivalence, raise questions about Newman's orthodoxy as well as about his common sense and sanity? Great as Newman is, do not his writings often invite readings which run against the grain of his rhetoric? The essays in this book seek to explore, in various ways, some of the crucial ambiguities in Newman's work.

Newman was a controversialist and rhetoric was his mode of discourse. His writings were designed to refute criticism and to persuade. Almost everything he wrote was *ad hominem* and must be understood in the context of the debate in which he was engaged at the time. It is therefore difficult to find in Newman a coherent position from one work to another or indeed within a single work. Frequently he hints and suggests without making clear exactly what he is claiming. This is perhaps particularly evident in his *Essay on Development*. Newman's favourite tactic is the one adopted by Bishop Joseph Butler in his controversy with the deists. The Bishop had argued that to accept revelation is as rational as to accept natural religion. The deists should either advance to orthodoxy or retreat to atheism. To Anglicans Newman said: you accept developments in the early Church, how can you reject the later Roman developments? To unbelievers he said: religious judgments are indeed made on the basis of probabilities, but so are your common sense judgments; it is illogical to accept the latter with certitude but deny the possibility of certitude in the former. This *tu quoque* argument can, of course, have an effect which is unintended. As Leslie Stephen observed:

> An argument, according to Boyle's familiar illustration, is like a crossbow; because...it has a force independent of the arm that wields it. But has also the peculiarity that it frequently goes off backward.[1]

On reading Newman's *Essay on Development*, F.D. Maurice glumly remarked, 'Of all the books I ever read, it seems to me the most sceptical; much more calculated to make sceptics than Romanists, though probably it will make some of each class.'[2]

His rhetorical method and his desire to persuade led Newman to adopt manifestly contradictory positions. In one place, for example, he waxed eloquently on the opposition of the Church to the world. There is between the two a total lack of comprehension:

> The world believes in the world's ends as the greatest of goods; it wishes society to be governed simply and entirely for the sake of this world...The Church moves in a simply opposite direction...Oh, most tender loving Mother, ill-judged by the world, which thinks she is, like itself, always minding the main chance.[3]

Yet in asserting the identity of the Roman Catholic Church in the nineteenth century with the Church in the first age, he appealed precisely to the world as arbitrator. 'Say there is no Church at all, if you will,' he declaimed, 'and at least I shall understand you, but do not meddle with a fact *attested by mankind.* I am,' he continued, 'almost ashamed to insist upon so plain a point!'[4]

This collection of essays makes no attempt to cover the whole of Newman's life and works. There are several aspects of his work about which we say little or nothing. For example, there is nothing in this volume about the important contribution he made both to the development of educational institutions in the British Isles and to educational theory. The authors deal rather with selected facets of his thought. They are concerned to place him in his historical context at the same time as considering whether he has significance for the present day. Newman has, however, become 'all things to all men'.

While ecumenists see in his ideas on the development of doctrine the possibility of an escape from rigid formularies and the way forward to a new unity among Christians, others (particularly in England) view his conversion as a model for future relations between the Anglican and Roman Catholic Churches: individual conversion as the principal way to unity. Addressing those of the Oxford Movement who remained in the Church of England, Newman saw his own path to 'the true home of your souls and the valley of peace' as one which they should follow. If some of them did they would 'suddenly be filled with yearnings deep and passionate, for the salvation of those dear friends whom you have outstripped...you will weary heaven with your novenas for them, and you will be ever getting Masses for their conversion...and you will not rest till the bright morning come, and they are yours once again.'[5]

Just as the Anglican Newman could not resist making malicious attacks on Rome, so the Catholic convert could not desist from vindictive remarks on the Church of England as 'barren, unmeaning, and baseless'. Elsewhere he wrote of 'such counterfeits as the Anglican Church'; her members 'she holds in bondage, separated from that faith and that Church in which alone is salvation. If I can do aught', he went on, 'towards breaking their chains, and bringing them into the Truth, it will be an act of love towards their souls, and of piety towards God.'[6] In the following pages he heaped contempt on the Church of England as 'commonplace or worthless':

> We see in the English Church...nothing more nor less than an Establishment, a department of Government...it has no real identity of existence in distinct periods...It has no traditions; it cannot be said to think...It has no love for its members...[7]

The canonisation of Newman would be interpreted in many quarters as giving official support to a 'triumphalist' ecclesiology and would be seen as something of a blow to the work of the Anglican-Roman Catholic International Commission (ARCIC) and to the cause of Christian unity.

While liberals welcome the 'existentialist' emphasis of Newman's philosophy as a release from the scholastic strait-jacket within which theologians were forced to work for so long, conservatives appeal to his attacks on theological liberalism and to the basically Aristotelian foundation of his thought. It should also be recognised that Newman's existentialism is a two-sided weapon; it may cut down scholastic rationalism, but it may also be seen as the source of a menacing and irrational authoritarianism. It became a central feature of Italian fascism and it is no coincidence that the French syndicalist, Georges Sorel, whose ideas inspired the young Mussolini, quoted Newman's *Grammar* with approbation.[8] Fortunately Newman's article on the Tamworth Reading Room did not fall into the Frenchman's hands;

he and his Italian disciples would have been very much at home with such sentiments as: 'life is for action' and 'whereas man is born for action, action flows not from inferences, but from impressions, – not from reasonings, but from Faith.'[9]

Newman's significance for the Church today is perhaps above all in his attempt to understand the proper role of reason in Christian life, and to explore its variety of modes. In his most sceptical moods Newman appealed to reason, attempting to defend the limits of its legitimate sphere by argument. Even in his own religious life he claimed to be guided 'not by my imagination, but by my reason'. 'Had it not been for this severe resolve,' he went on, 'I should have been a Catholic sooner than I was.'[10] He was, however, rightly critical of rationalism, or as he called it 'liberalism', which is 'the exercise of thought upon matters, in which, from the constitution of the human mind, thought cannot be brought to any successful issue, and therefore is out of place.'[11] Whether these matters can be specified in advance in quite the way he believed is questionable. Nevertheless the issues he explored in his *Oxford University Sermons* are with us still and his words are able to shed light even today on the complex problem of the appropriate role of reason in religious belief.

NOTES

1. Leslie Stephen, 'Cardinal Newman's Scepticism', *Nineteenth Century*, February 1891, p. 179. The image of the bow, from which Newman fired his quill pen, is the central theme of the 'Newmania' window on the front cover of this book.

2. F. Maurice, *The Life of Frederick Denison Maurice* (London, 1884), i, p. 422.

3. *Certain Difficulties felt by Anglicans in Catholic Teaching* (London, 1895), i, pp. 235-7.

4. *Difficulties*, i, p. 369 (our italics). In the *Essay on Development* he also asserted that external and superficial similarities between the early Church and the modern Roman Catholic Church was good evidence for their identity. This led one critic to remark: 'Do you really mean that there have been the greatest possible changes taking place in the form and doctrine of Christianity, and that the one thing which has remained permanent, is just the external appearance which it presents to the world?', F.D. Maurice, *The Epistle to the Hebrews*

(London, 1846), p. lvi.

5. *Difficulties*, i. pp. 360-1.

6. *Discourses to Mixed Congregations* (1871), p. 193; *Difficulties*, i. pp. 5, 315.

7. *Difficulties*, i. pp. 6-7.

8. Georges Sorel, *Réflexions sur la violence* (Paris, 1910), pp. 6n, 38n.

9. *Discussions and Arguments on Various Subjects* (London, 1872), pp. 295, 304. We are not, of course, suggesting that Newman himself would have had a great deal of sympathy with Italian fascism or French syndicalism; he was much too conservative.

10. *Apologia pro Vita Sua* (London, 1895), p. 119.

11. *Apologia*, p. 288.

1

DEMYTHOLOGISING NEWMAN

Valerie Pitt

There is a spectacular happening in the *Acts of the Apostles* which perhaps should serve as an anchor for these discussions. It is the episode at Lystra when the mob set Paul and Barnabas up as gods and prepared to sacrifice to them. The saints, of course, behaved like saints, or, rather, like decent and sensible men: they 'ran in' among the people trying to persuade them that they were not gods but mortal creatures, 'men of like passions with you'. They had some difficulty, apparently, even then in restraining the crowds.

The incident is a salutary comment on the absurd deferences given to, and expected by, 'personalities' both in the Church and in secular society, a warning not so much to the objects of this hyperdulia (very few people can seriously take themselves for gods and goddesses, or not for long) as to the worshippers. It is the admiring mobs who are the worry: the unthinking crowds lost in the thrill of myth who glamorise and divinise almost any public character. I once heard a youngster cry out in excitement 'I touched *him*!' as though he had entered into the mana of some Sacred Being. The *him* in this instance was, however, a man disguised for an advertising stunt as a Womble of Wimbledon Common. It was a moment to savour and to confirm a distrust of the charismatic. That these are men – not to say Wombles or even women – of like passions with us is a useful reminder.

What, it may be asked, has this to do with John Henry Newman? Well, if any Church figure ever carried about with him the delicious miasma of myth it was Newman – and not only for his contemporaries. The young men who flocked to his preaching, and to Littlemore to agonise over their doubts, obviously felt themselves to be, because of their contact with him, actors, however minor, in some marvellous romance of faith. Indeed, even those uninfluenced by his religion felt the romance of those high years of the Oxford Movement. Kingsley himself admired Newman's 'calm eloquence', Jowett considered reading the Fathers to see if he ought to become a Puseyite, and after all, it was a shocking liberal, Matthew Arnold, the son of his Anglican *bête noire*, who wrote the classic description of the Vicar of St Mary the Virgin, gliding like an enchanter to his pulpit. You can't get more charismatic than that, even at Earls Court with choirs and cheer leaders. His fellow dons recognised the phenomenon when they altered the dinner hour in their colleges so that it coincided with the hour of Mr Newman's Sunday Service. It says something about those services that some of the young men preferred them to their food.

It is not evident that Newman had, or was allowed to have, anything like this effect on Roman Catholic congregations, not at least until after the publication of the *Apologia pro Vita Sua.* That, of course, did it. All the prophylactics of the Hierarchy against that terrifying charm (like the Oxford dons, Manning and others knew what they were dealing with) went for nothing. For the *Apologia* set out precisely the romance of faith and, what's more, presented its hero in another, yet more appealing guise: not only the young Anglican but the venerable Catholic still persecuted in his old age. We haven't recovered from all that for it was not only his contemporaries who wandered, enchanted, in the sea-wood of Newman's myth. It was almost every generation of the religious-minded since his time; we ourselves aren't yet out of the mists. The question, then, is 'How to dispel this enchantment?'. Some, seduced by these illusions, may wish to ask 'Why?'.

The Pauline argument, of course, dominates. Our gospel forbids it. Ordinary human *nous* does too. It is dangerous to all parties to treat a man as even a half-god: to give over 'our capability and use of reason' to the authority of sanctity or of charisma (which is not the same thing) any more than to the authority of office. Newman never really understood the dangers of his own magnetism, indeed, he struggled at times not to recognise its existence, but he would surely have St Paul's mind in this matter. There is, however, another argument. The disadvantage of yielding our minds to the specious enchantments of human gods is, leaving aside its blasphemy, that it imprisons all of us in a fantasy world, shut out from the light of common day. If we are to enquire about Newman's significance, his reality, we need precisely to fetch him into that daylight. For instance, there are two familiar eikons of the hero as *Hagios*: Richmond's drawing of the don as an intense young man, and Millais' Cardinal, all scarlet and lace, painted in 1881. Both, interestingly, show the man without his glasses though the evidence is that he was helpless without them. Richmond's Newman is etherealised, with a far away expression, and although all Richmond's sitters have that look to them, there's no doubt that it is a striking evocation of the Magus of St Mary's. It needs, however, to be compared with the many small drawings of the man in company with his family and his friends, or with the more formal miniature painted by Sir William Ross in 1845 which shows him as donnish, getting to be gaunt in the face and extremely tense: in fact, as human not mythological. The Millais is even more interesting. Millais aroused some disapproval in Newman's entourage because he wasn't in awe of the occasion or the personage. He addressed his eminent sitter as 'dear old boy' and talked to him with his pipe in his mouth. Still he knew how to earn his thousand pounds and it is a magnificent portrait: of a prince of the Church: not an old man of eighty with brittle bones and a pronounced stoop. It is the many photographs which, even though obviously posed, convey that reality to us, and not only the photographs of his old age but those of his middle, half-forgotten years. It's the Newman of the Oratory which comes across in these, faintly shabby and sometimes creased, in the unEnglish, half-fancy dress of his Order, biretta and all, and always with the worry lines tightening his jaw and his hands.

What was he like, then, in the world of the sketches and the photographs, in the light of common Victorian day? There must be, and there was, a human being behind the *Hagios*: a man who had trouble with his teeth and his digestion, wrote to Dean Church's children about *The Hunting of the Snark* and played Beethoven on his 'fiddle'; more importantly, a man, though he struggled against it, who was very much of his own generation. More than most, Newman's mind was a 'social and cultural fact', formed within the discourse of his own society, in his own period. It was incurably, even sentimentally, romantic and paradoxically constrained, in the very vehemence of his resistance, by the strains in that discourse which he most loathed and rejected. His Roman Catholicism, his elevation of dogma, may seem to run counter to the *Zeitgeist*, but it develops in a symbiosis with the nineteenth-century liberalism he could neither defeat nor avoid. Besides, he was what Oxford made him: a 'scholar and a gentleman', an early Victorian gentleman, with all that that then implied in terms of culture, place, peer group and common assumptions.[1] He 'belonged': it was the great asset that he brought to his adopted Church – and one which it half resented.

Now the defining characteristic of a Victorian gentleman was that he had no visible means of support: no trade requiring his diligence, no apparent obligation to set his hand, his own hands, to the provision of his daily needs, food and fire and so on. He simply existed, and they existed around him. It was not a question so much of income[2] as of domestic infrastructure. A gentleman did not cook his own meals, do his own washing or make his own shirts.[3] No more did Newman. There is no evidence that he had the necessary skills and he certainly did not allow himself the time. The formidable schedule devised for his life at Littlemore, nine hours of study, umpteen hours of prayer, scarcely allowed him space to clean his teeth, let alone to get the housework done. For that they got someone in from the village. Later, when he was established as an Oratorian, the Rule required the Fathers to take on some of their own domesticities, but there were, at times, servants and lay brothers. They had (Newman told the Pope) a 'widow woman' in for the cooking. The truth is that though Newman chose to work diligently in what he conceived to be his vocation, he had that choice. He had, as a member of a highly privileged class, something denied to the great mass of his contemporaries, leisure to think, and for long stretches of time he used it principally to think about his own soul. All his achievements, including the construction of his own religious *persona* were, as was normal in persons of his class and background, built on the anonymous and probably underpaid[4] labour of other men or, more probably, women. That is a criticism of Newman, though not more than it would be of any other Victorian cleric of any denomination. It remarks his context and, more especially, its unrealised dangers. Any 'gentleman' is, inevitably, cocooned from the coarser demands of the world of work: a celibate clergyman, an Oxford don, a religious living within the protection of an ordered, exclusively male community, is positively insulated, isolated, doubly damned to an introverted perception of life unless he takes steps to deal with the problem. Newman did not take those steps. Instead, he aspired to a religious pitch, which even if endowed with common sense, which I doubt, was massively privileged. He had, unfortunately for himself, time and the mental space to fidget about the state of his faith. Most of us must leave ours to God.

The unreality of Newman's way of life was, if anything, reinforced by an exposure, at least in his youth, to secular, literary, culture. He was the child not only of the Evangelical but, like the other Tractarians, of the Gothic and Romantic revivals. If nothing else Keble nourished his disciples not only on the pure milk of the nonjuring word but on the Wordsworth and water of *The Christian Year* in which the created world ('There is a book who runs may read') appears as a shadowplay only of the divine. And Newman himself treats the Lake Poets, and Scott, as forerunners, formative if not quite of the theology of the Movement, certainly of its spiritual culture. So it was: the sense of the material world as the symbol and veil of the divine enabled Newman and the Tractarians, to evade much of the hard reality of their times (rural poverty as well as golden harvest), to live in a dream, certainly to give themselves to charitable activity, but not to ask the necessary and difficult questions about the demands of the Kingdom of God which their successors[5] found imperative. It fostered, too, the cultivation of an over-refined spirituality. The intensity of Newman's interest in his inner life, his careful watching of the movements of his own mind, was the habit of his early evangelical discipline yet also of literary convictions about affective sensibility and the creative mind. But more insidious, much more insidious for a young man of Newman's stamp, was the Romantic poet's tendency to make himself the hero of his own myth. Newman, in the *Apologia*, describes the moment, in Rome, when he yielded to this temptation: 'Now too – Southey's beautiful poem of Thalaba, for which I had an immense liking, came forcibly to my mind. I began to think I had a mission.' *Thalaba the Destroyer,*[6] published in 1801, is an oriental Gothic fantasy. Its hero, Thalaba, with whom Newman seems to identify, has such a 'mission': to destroy a wizard king and his sea dominion. Could it be that Newman fantasised the Whig Cabinet into a nest of sorcerers? At any rate, in an imagination excited by the idea of 'mission', he clearly aligns himself with Thalaba as a vengeance figure, a destroyer of evils and evil men: in his case, of the Liberal Establishment. He is set apart for the task, and driven: if not quite in a true *Sturm und Drang* mode, certainly under the oppression of divine command. That would be an oppression, for though it's not usually remarked, Newman's apprehension of God is, often, altogether 'uncheerful'.[7] His preaching indicates over and over again that the Lord will indeed 'be extreme to mark what is done amiss' and *serve us all right*. His personal records make it clear that he applied the message to himself, that his sense of God's work in and through him was troubled with fear and guilt. He saw his original conversion, at fifteen, as the deliverance of one 'more like a devil' than a wicked boy and thought his illness a judgment on his forwardness in following his own will. He was afraid that he might die before he could submit to the Roman obedience where his soul would be safe. All that is religious extravagance: we may reasonably ask where a schoolboy, or even a Fellow of Oriel, found the opportunity for satanic corruptions? But then guilt and gloom were the literary fashion in Newman's youth. While he was figuring himself as destroyer and deliverer it was easy to slip into the common Gothic/Byronic role of the noble but sin-haunted exile.

Indeed, there's more than a trace of the Byronic habit in Newman; the habit of making a drama out of a spiritual crisis, of seeing the phases of one's own development as episodes on a cosmic stage. The 'distant scene' he did not ask to see is wonderfully wild, like a landscape by Salvador Rosa, or a stage set for *Freischütz*:

> So long Thy power hath blest me, sure it still
> Will lead me on,
> *O'er moor and fen, o'er crag and torrent, till*
> *The night is gone.*

It is the conventional setting, of course, for the Gothic hero under trial and is, in this case, a metaphor for the troubles, his sister's death, his own dangerous illness in Sicily, through which 'Thy power' was leading Newman to the ardours of the Tractarian campaign. The metaphor was transmuted, perilously, into real time in the famous, crucial episode, of Newman's reception into the Roman Church, as Fr Dominic Barberi, the Passionist, recounted it to his superiors. Here is Newman who for months has been writing agonised letters to his friends and has clearly painted himself into a Roman corner, within walking distance of a Roman Catholic church in St Clements, or of a train to London[8] where, at any time in that long limbo, he might have been quietly received, 'begging' Fr Dominic, still sopping wet from a night journey through a great storm, to hear his confession and receive his submission. It's a marvellously melodramatic scene, and indeed the whole history of Newman's conversion was conducted with precisely that degree of self-conscious awareness which, inevitably, makes for psychological theatre: the sort of thing which made a fateful moment of the awful discovery, recorded in the *Apologia*, 'I was a Monophysite!' and, incidentally, prevented the self-absorbed self-spectator from attending to a number of historical and other questions not irrelevant to the problem of doctrinal consensus.

I am not asserting that Newman was insincere: the phenomenon is common to many accounts of conversion. What I am suggesting is that half-consciously, creatively, he was shaping and moulding the material of his own experience to present a particular interpretation, and a wider application, of that experience to the world. Of course he meant to do that at the merely controversial level: as a tactic against Kingsley's attack on his integrity he presents the history of his mind – the appealing and dramatic picture of Fr Newman the spiritual pilgrim – which was to block out Kingsley's caricature. There was, however, more to it than that. Wordsworth had, in *The Prelude*, presented his own imaginative history as archetypally the growth of the poet's mind. The *Apologia* is a parallel, the history of a religious mind, a particular religious mind in the process of conversion perceived perhaps by Newman himself, certainly taken by too many papalising Anglicans as having not merely a personal but an archetypal, that is a mythical, force. This, we are expected to read in Newman's story, is how the Almighty manages events; how, like an experienced stage producer he conjures the high spectacle of this salvation. In such a scenario a quiet visit to a local priest would have been an aesthetic error of a kind to which the divine producer is not usually prone. Fr Barberi had to arrive in a gothic rain storm to make the climax and the point.

In this drama all the princes of the world, Lord John Russell and the Bishop of Oxford, all were the Almighty's means to drive John Henry Newman to the haven where he would be the bosom of a Church that he thought had uniquely historic authority. Let's not make the mistake of refusing to believe what he tells us. To him it was a haven: calm water in spite of Faber and Manning and everything. Too calm: he hadn't really solved the great problem of which his own history was no more than an example, the problem of an old faith in a new world. In his absorption in his own history, the high theatre not merely of his conversion but of the Catholic Revival, both he and certainly his Anglican friends mistook or did not perceive the real nature of their religious problem, which is also ours, or of Newman's potential insight into it. Keble might carry on about National Apostasy and look to the apostolic past or to Stuart Divines for a guarantee of their beliefs, but neither Keble nor his disciples had much idea of what was happening in their own world. Something was, but they set their minds against it: political and social upheaval, still more the threat of revolution, were the sin of rebellion against divine order. That was all there was to it. Yet they, like their contemporaries, were caught in uncertainties of a cultural change so profound that even the models and the language of rationality were no longer adequate to the understanding of the world. How could they in that situation – how can we – sustain in ourselves a faith in revelation all of whose forms and models were created for what is, increasingly, an alien culture? The Oxford Fathers chose to define their unease in terms of the Christian's relation to historic authority. The First Vatican Council made the same kind of mistake, out of the same blinkered vision, when it committed the Roman Church to the doctrine of an infallible *magisterium* vested in the See of Rome. It wasn't so much that the reasoning is wrong: if you start from the premise that truth is seated in institutions that, I suppose, is where the logic gets you. It's the premise itself which is shaky, for the concept of an eternal verity faithfully and consistently reflected in an organisation directed by mortal and mutable men, belongs, precisely, to that culture whose slow dying creates the problem for faith.

The Tractarian mind was set, as some religious minds still are, against the recognition of that creeping mortality. Change there certainly was, but to acquiesce, much more to promote, to accelerate it, was a sin. That's nowhere more evident, or more bizarre, than in the Movement's political attitudes. It was to be expected that an Oxford Tory would resist the Whig reforms of the 1830s and even the new conservatism of Sir Robert Peel, but that young men brought up in the Regency, faced with the actual regalities of George IV and William IV, should argue for the divine right of kings is another thing. Yet Newman says that he believed in it even in the middle of 'the great Reform agitation':

> Shortly before there had been a revolution in France; the Bourbons had been dismissed: and I believed it was unchristian for nations to cast off their governors and, much more, sovereigns who had the divine right of inheritance.

That, of course, is the nonjuring position and it sometimes seems that Newman, Keble and all their bright young men were unable to make the transition from the seventeenth to the eighteenth century, let alone into their own restless times. It's an inability which incapacitates them in matters more serious than politics. In 1832, for instance, the British Association met in Oxford and the University, surprisingly, conferred honorary doctorates on some of its members. Keble expressed the alarm and anger of his friends: the University had 'truckled to the spirit of the times'. Newman was away at the time, but there's no doubt he shared the feeling. Science, as he indicated in a sermon on the dangers inherent in the gift of reason, is a very suspicious activity:

> All these inducements to live by sight and not by faith are greatly increased, when men are engaged in any pursuit which properly *belongs* to the intellect. Hence sciences conversant with experiments on the material creation tend to make men forget the existence of spirit and the Lord of spirits.

It's a fair comment on that, that one of the new Doctors of Civil Law was Michael Faraday – and Faraday, as it happened, was a faithful Christian, though not in a denomination which the Tractarians would recognise. He was besides a genius (as Keble was not) and, because of his work on electricity, a founding father of modern physics and (as Keble was not, as Newman was not) a maker of our present world. It's as if the Movement had calmly opted out, not only of their own present, but of any future and much of the past. Behind the sermon I have just quoted lies Newman's theorising about the activity of angels which he considered to be:

> the real causes of motion, light, and life, and of those elementary principles of the physical universe, which, when offered in their developments to our senses, suggest to us the notion of cause and effect, and of what are called the laws of nature.

Did he really suppose, for instance, that Stephenson had harnessed the seraphim to Locomotive One? After all, this was the 1830s, the age of the steam loom and the railway, and more than a hundred and fifty years after the publication of the *Principia Mathematica*. Yet Newman confronts all that that implies, the very crisis of traditional order, with what? With the left-overs of pre-Newtonian thinking: the doctrine of the divine right of kings and the metaphysics of the alchemists. He had simply shut the doors of his mind against what was happening in the intellectual no less than in the material life of his society.

Now we are not dealing here with the 'simple faithful', but with the flower of a great university at a time of astonishing intellectual advance. In fact, what we have is a man who, on the evidence, was especially concerned to confront the problem of faith and reason and might well have contributed a Christian insight to that advance if he had not, paradoxically, distrusted intelligence and, worse, thought that God himself distrusts the very brains he gave us. Even Coleridge, who was not exactly a raving theological radical, comes under Newman's condemnation because he took his speculations beyond what is 'permitted'. The remark is a clue to Newman himself; he does not allow himself to speculate. 'One step enough for me.' The *Apologia* derives its considerable power not from the originality of its theological thinking but from its author's personality and his genius for friendship. The *History of My Religious Opinions* is a history of influences, of Newman's friends and of the books he read. In that he is like a mediaeval scholar: when he wants to decide a question he looks at what the *auctores* say.

Other writers, telling the story of their inner lives, struggle to understand and explain what happened to them. J.S. Mill, Newman's contemporary, develops in his *Autobiography*, a theory about the psychological mechanisms at work in his personal history. St Augustine in his *Confessions*, which like the *Apologia*, is a conversion narrative, speculates about everything, the nature of evil, the behaviour of babies, the mystery of time. They ask questions: Newman does not, and that is neither a strength nor, as he saw it, a duty. There is no Christian obligation not to see, or try to see 'the distant scene'.

It is not a strength: on the contrary, Newman's shuddering from 'our weak and conceited reason', the block he placed on his own mind, meant that, in the end, he can't and doesn't speak to our condition in any way which might have been warranted by his continuing concern with the conditions which make for faith.[9] That, of course, was the real substance of his quarrel with Kingsley. The oddity of that was that both men assumed what we should now call a 'social construction of reality', an ideology. Roman Catholics, Kingsley says, are conditioned to an ingrained dishonesty of mind because they submit to the doctrinal authority of the Roman See. That's what their cultural formation does to them. Newman would not admit to the dishonesty but he does say, indeed, insists, it is precisely because they have a 'Catholic' mind that Catholics find no difficulty in those beliefs which Kingsley finds distasteful. A Protestant, on the other hand, would not be in a state to accept, for instance, those miracle stories in the lives of saints about which Newman himself was notoriously credulous and Kingsley demanded evidence. Neither controversialist, of course, articulated the basic assumption, but Newman was a good deal more conscious of what he was about; for while Kingsley was skating along on the inherited no-popery of a healthy Englishman, Newman, under Keble's guidance, and with the aid of the Tractarian's guru, Bishop Butler, had worked himself out a useful theory of rational 'assent' to religious belief on the grounds of 'probability'. For Newman, however, probability by itself is scarcely enough: it is the condition of mind through which it is perceived which gives it its power:

> It is faith and love which give to probability a force which it has not in itself. Faith and love are directed towards an object; in the vision of which object they live; it is that object, received in faith and love, which renders it reasonable to take probability as sufficient for internal conviction. Thus the argument from probability, in the matter of religion, became an argument from personality, which in fact is one form of the argument from authority.

It is on this premise, Newman blandly argues, that he was able to believe anything (transubstantiation was his example) which might be so was so because authority, that is the Pope, had said it was so. There are, one may think, a good many questions begged here.

No matter: the problem of assent lies almost at the source of Newman's Christian life and, in spite of his best endeavours to shut himself away from the common concerns of his time, that is where it belongs. He was *not* a proxy Monophysite but a nineteenth-century scholar. The substance of his dilemma was a nineteenth-century phenomenon: he shared it with many of his contemporaries. What bothered him in the first place, as it bothered them, was not so much a question about authority as a question of guarantee. How does the condition of faith come about in the believing mind in the first place and how can we authenticate it either in the individual believer or in the believing community?

That, of course, was the nub of the Oxford concern with 'probability' and its need to assert the apostolic character of the Church of England: continuity guarantees. Newman never entirely escapes those debates: as late as 1870 in the *Grammar of Assent* he is still peddling probability, but the work has a *post hoc* feel to it. It is a manual to show that assent to Roman Catholic positions can be intellectually respectable and that propaganda purpose, among other things, meant that it was dead born.[10] His instinct was truer, in spite of the dramatics, when he presented the problem, in the *Apologia*, through his own long dialogue with himself, his own soul's struggle to assure itself in an uncertain world. Apart from anything else the Victorian mind was conditioned to an awareness that rational argument was not the only way to truth. That, after all, is what John Stuart Mill explains in the *Autobiography*. The Romantic poets had retreated from the treacherousness of Enlightenment rationality to something like the condition of faith, or at least to that feel for the reality of things which grows in the interaction of the mind and its world:

> Dust as we are the immortal spirit grows
> Like harmony in music...

Something like that, some growth, or so the conversion stories indicate, occurs when we come to the condition of faith. Something like that is Newman's account of his own mind in the *Apologia*. The trouble is that though this happens, and to many people, it is essentially a private not a common experience and provides no cast iron guarantee against the possibilities of delusion. That Newman was aware of this 'dark invisible workmanship' in his own development is evident in one of the more improbable episodes in that most improbable novel *Loss and Gain* in which our young hero on his way to the Passionists to be received into the Roman Communion encounters a Roman priest (but of course) in a railway carriage and discourses with this perfect stranger on the nature of faith, on the exact date of ripening, the readiness at which the recognition of probability triggers the psychological mechanism of assent and submission to authority. That of course is a speculation about Newman's own experience: unlike the dramatics of the *Apologia* – it attends to and indicates the shifts of mind and situation which brought John Henry Newman to his submission. It also explains what surprised and upset his friends, the long will-he-won't-he period at Littlemore when his reason had consented to the claims of Rome, but he could not be sure that it was not deluded. He could not move: the moment of ripeness, the conviction of the whole man, had not arrived.

What he experienced then was a cultural spasm: the break-up and reforming of an inherited mind-set and that is something about which, in Newman's case, we ought to be a little wary. That new wholeness of his perception is not, for us, a warrant against his suffering from delusion. The man had isolated himself at Littlemore, away from his peers and the ordinary activities of his profession, and had given himself up not only to a regimen of study and obsessive self-questioning on the one issue but to ascetic practices, watching or sleeping on the ground, fasting and so on. This, but for the element of external compulsion, was a brain-washing regimen, calculated, as we now know, to disorient the personality, to shatter and remake a mind-set and induce docility. It is surprising that Newman survived at all in any state of mental balance, but that is not to say that his experience in any way demonstrates his doctrine. For the fascinating, if horrid, truth is that the story of this soul tells us a great deal which is at odds with its own high drama. Newman is in quest, so the scenario instructs us, for authority and historic continuity – but when we examine his account more closely, his understanding of faith, of the psychological condition of faith in the individual, doesn't apparently sustain anything like a traditional or even his personal view of authority. Faith isn't commanded, *can't* be commanded: it grows, it evolves out of the experience and the reflection on experience of the individual. Newman did not accept the truths of Christianity because the Church had the authority of the Apostles (whatever that may mean). He came to believe that the Church of Rome had apostolic authority because he worked and had lived through a complex process of psychological need and rational enquiry of a kind we should now call 'cultural'. Or rather I should say he set, almost hypnotised, himself to believe it. What is more, one could say, or rather, *I* shall say he cheats a bit on apostolic authority which is, on his own showing, anything but immutable. The personal and cultural history of the individual which brings her or him to a saving faith is paralleled, is it not, by 'development' in the Church, a concept Newman virtually invented to save his own appearances. For, being an English gentleman, he could not fulfil his own conversion to Rome without somehow managing the rococo accretions of theological centuries which happily are now (or are they?) chipped away from the great edifices of Christian belief. However, once again the man is undermining his own apparent foundation. The faith of the Church is not, once one begins to entertain the idea of development, a 'faith once delivered to the Saints': not in the sense of its being a precious deposit locked in the formulae of the Church like bones in a reliquary to be displayed at intervals, incorrupt and unchanged. Once we admit of development – as we must – the faith of the Church cannot be defined in terms of the dogmas propagated by its central authorities and institutions. In a sense it cannot be defined at all, though it can be proclaimed, for what we are dealing with is the solitary and shared experience of generations of Christians in their separate encounters, with the saving mystery of God. As the faith of the individual is shaped in experience so is the faith of the Church. It is not to be identified by or with its institutions and authorities, but, down the ages, with its people, Christ's faithful members.

It is difficult to be altogether sympathetic to the dramatics of Newman's situation. In the conditions of Victorian England they were a luxury for a Christian and still are. Besides, though he clearly knew otherwise in his bones and being, he defined the problem of faith too abstractly, in terms of dogma and institutions, and so made a strait-jacket for his own thinking and, even now, for the more excitable churchmen of both his denominations. But, paradoxically, while fidgeting for objective dogmatic authority he had begun to feel away from the institution to the Church 'which is the blessed company of all faithful people' and from authority to consensus. Both his native and his adopted communion might do well to try to complete his unfinished thoughts.

NOTES

1. 'I do but wish' Newman writes to Macmillan about Kingsley's review of Froude 'to draw the attention of yourselves, *as gentlemen*, to a grave and gratuitous slander'. 'I have done' Kingsley says, after Newman had cavilled at his apology 'as much *as one English gentleman can expect from another*.' The freemasonry is explicit even in hostility.

2. Newman was not a rich man. His income, however, was always genteel: once he had resigned his fellowship and his benefice it derived, principally, from his books. A gentleman might not live by trade, nor, strictly, by scribbling, but selling sermons was respectable and in Newman's case reasonably lucrative.

3. The wives, sisters and daughters of eminent Victorians sewed endless shirts for their menfolk – and cravats and handkerchiefs and slippers. It was an unpaid and largely unacknowledged support service.

4. Victorian domestics were badly paid and, since social justice was not a question to which Newman addressed his mind, one supposes he went along with current practice.

5. Henry Scott Holland, for instance, and Charles Gore who did not identify 'Catholic' and 'Tory'.

6. It's a pleasing irony that *Thalaba* was a revolutionary poem. Shelley, who knew it by heart, took it as a model for the still more revolutionary *Queen Mab*.

7. The description is Austin Farrer's and perceptive. See, amongst others, a sermon on Christmas Day, on *Religious Joy*: 'For one day we may put off the burden of our polluted consciences, and rejoice in the perfections of our Saviour Christ, without thinking of

ourselves, without thinking of our own miserable uncleanness…'.

8. The Oxford branch of Brunel's Great Western Railway was completed in the spring of 1844. Presumably the news reached Littlemore.

9. I am indebted to the Revd A.D. Kirkwood for reminding me that, when all is said and done, Newman did, and others didn't, confront the problem of faith and reason.

10. The deadness of the *Grammar of Assent* is, in a way, the nemesis of Newman's obstinate withdrawal from anything which smacked of infidelity in the intellectual life of his time. It reaches back to the epistemological problems posed by Locke (whom Newman read when young) and the eighteenth-century empiricists, and is altogether innocent even of Kant, let alone the German idealists, and that at a time when T.H. Green was the current Oxford guru. And, of course, it had no truck with the problems historiography created for theology. In short, it did not address itself to the condition of that generation – nor of this.

2

OXFORD, TRACT 90 AND THE BISHOPS

Peter Nockles

For many, the claim of John Henry Newman to fame and greatness rests on that period of his Anglican career when he was the acknowledged inspiration and leader of a well-known High Church revival of religious life and thought within the Church of England which emanated from within the University of Oxford during the period 1833 to 1845. This revival was known, due to its place of origin, as the Oxford Movement, or Tractarianism after the series called 'Tracts for the Times' which the Movement's leaders, Keble, Froude and Pusey as well as Newman, produced as a medium for the dissemination of its teaching and influence. It was a movement which was to leave an indelible mark on the faith and practice of the Church of England. Although he was to secede to the Church of Rome in 1845, Newman's role in the profound impact of the Oxford Movement on the Church of England was crucial. Any reconsideration or reappraisal of Newman cannot afford to overlook this vital portion of his life when for at least twelve years he was virtually centre-stage in the history of the Church of England, and when the history of Oxford University almost becomes his own personal religious history. Above all, such a reappraisal cannot avoid focusing on the climactic episode in the history of the Oxford Movement and Newman's Anglican career – the controversy surrounding his notorious Tract 90, the last in the series 'Tracts for the Times'. The impact of Tract 90 can scarcely be overestimated. According to a contemporary observer, 'with perhaps, the exception of Burke's *Reflections on the Revolution in France*, no pamphlet ever created a sensation so wide, so deep, so enduring'.[1] In fact, within a fortnight of its publication in January 1841, 2,500 copies of Tract 90 had been sold.[2] London as well as Oxford was stirred up, and the newspapers were full of the ensuing row. Clearly, there are good grounds for a consideration of Tract 90 as a key element in any re-evaluation of Newman's thought, his personality and his place in religious history.

The wider story of Newman and Oxford has been often told, and little more than an outline as a necessary background to understanding the Tract 90 controversy and what Newman was striving to achieve, need be repeated here. Yet, something of a reconsideration is necessary, precisely because of the distorting lens that has been provided by an almost inevitable concentration on the Oxford Movement as viewed through Newman's eyes. One reason for the pervasiveness and influence of the Newmanite perspective is easy to discern. A rich and fertile quarry for historians has been provided by that magnificent personal literary record of his religious odyssey, which Newman has left posterity, in his *Apologia pro Vita Sua*, first published in 1864. The result has been that an historiography has grown up, that focuses almost exclusively on Newman, with lesser attention devoted to other Tractarian leaders. The Movement has come to be viewed through Newman's eyes, its opponents judged from his point of view. For instance, Newman has been allowed to set the very dates of both the dawn and apparent conclusion of the Oxford Movement – the Assize Sermon by Keble on 14 July 1833,[3] and the condemnation of W.G. Ward by the Oxford Heads of Houses in February 1845, respectively. In fact, a good case can be made out for predating the origin of the Movement back to 1829 with the University's rejection of Sir Robert Peel as its MP in protest at Catholic Emancipation.[4] At the same time, the fact that Newman was removed effectively from any further direct part in the Tractarian controversy in 1845 is not sufficient ground for considering that that in itself marked the end of the Oxford Movement.

In a real sense then, it seems that our historical understanding of the Oxford Movement has come to be coloured and shaped by the personal drama of Newman's peculiar religious odyssey. It has been essentially as a landmark in the unfolding of this religious journey that the merits of Tract 90 and the official Anglican reaction to it have been viewed and judged. The result has been the gradual emergence of a distinctive historiography of the Movement in many ways moulded by Newman's immediate followers such as Dean Church, the author of a classic and highly influential historical account. In this historiography, the official negative reaction to Tract 90 has pride of place as the cathartic, bitter experience that broke Newman's supposedly meek spirit and made his position in the Church of England intolerable. Newman and those of his followers who seceded with him to the Church of Rome, were portrayed as innocent victims of an 'anti-

Catholic' vendetta or persecution, led by Anglican bishops, whom we are informed, should have known better. As Church put it, the authorities 'treated as absurd, mischievous, and at length traitorous, an effort, than which nothing could be more sincere'.[5] Yet, there is another side to this story which must be examined. Some have recently begun to question various aspects of the account given by Newman in the *Apologia*. Attention has been drawn to what has been called Newman's 'subjectivism' in his portrayal of his dealings with the Anglican authorities.[6] However, there is now room for a wider revision of some long accepted viewpoints.

In his famous *Lectures on Anglican Difficulties* published in 1850, Newman was to argue that the whole direction of the Oxford Movement ever since its formal inauguration in 1833 had always inevitably pointed in the direction of the Church of Rome.[7] Thus, the ultimate submission of Newman and some of his followers to Rome in 1845 and subsequent years, could plausibly be presented as the Movement's true and fitting fulfilment. Yet, as Christopher Dawson once argued, this view was not shared by any other leader of the Movement, with the possible exception of Hurrell Froude,[8] whose early death in 1836 makes what might have been his final outlook a matter for mere conjecture. Pusey and Keble certainly did not view the destiny of the Oxford Movement in these terms, still less that large, amorphous mass of Anglican High Churchmen who rallied to the Movement in 1833 and retained varying degrees of sympathy with it for a number of years. For these, so-called 'old High Churchmen', not only Newman's eventual secession, but the twists and turns of the Oxford Movement under his leadership from 1838 onwards and certainly after Tract 90, would be tantamount to a betrayal of what they conceived to have been the original principles of 1833. For such early supporters of the Movement, these principles were none other than those traditional High Church Anglican principles which the Church of England had never ceased to uphold, albeit at times haltingly and ambivalently. These principles had flourished in the seventeenth century. They had been expressed in the writings of the Caroline Divines and early Nonjurors. Moreover, contrary to the view of many historians, and not least the Tractarians themselves, these same principles had continued to be upheld by numerous eighteenth- and early nineteenth-century Churchmen, variously described and classified as old High Church or Orthodox.[9]

Of course, when the Oxford Movement commenced, Newman

along with Keble and then Pusey, insisted that they intended but to restate and follow out these traditional Anglican High Church principles. Yet, change and flux were always latent in Newman's approach. Behind the façade of the initial apparent unanimity among conservative Churchmen in 1833 against the perceived liberal threat posed by Whig expropriation of Church property and Erastian interference in matters spiritual, there lay concealed intrinsic inner differences that time would widen and expose. Any definition of the Oxford Movement must take into account the fact that it was not a static phenomenon, but rather, one which developed and underwent modifications in response to the flux of ideas and changing circumstances. The party of 1845 was manifestly not the party of 1833. There was to be a definite evolution of theological principles. In this evolution, Tract 90 was indeed to prove a landmark.

The Oxford Movement increasingly was to diverge, especially from 1841 and Tract 90 onwards, from the classic High Anglican tradition to which the University of Oxford had remained broadly loyal since the seventeenth century. Of course, a theological consensus was provided by a common belief in such doctrines as the Apostolical Succession, Baptismal Regeneration and the Eucharistic Sacrifice. However, on questions as fundamental as the rule of faith, the merits of the Reformation and attitude to the Church of Rome, and the relationship between Church and State, the Tractarians would come to differ markedly from the bulk of High Churchmen who at first tended to support the Movement but who eventually, albeit often reluctantly, came to express their unease and disagreement. An awareness of this divergence is vital for a true understanding of the history of the Oxford Movement and its relationship to the older High Church traditions in the Church of England, as I have made clear elsewhere.[10] Moreover, it is a conclusion supported by some recent scholarship. For my view that the Tractarians came to challenge, then shatter, the doctrinal consensus of earlier High Church Anglicanism, seeming to dissolve the Church of England into its constituent parts as never before, has been corroborated by the recent work of Paul Avis.[11] It is then in the historical context of the revolutionary potential and impetus of the Oxford Movement and of its breach as well as elements of continuity with pre-Tractarian *High* Churchmanship, that Newman's Tract 90 and the response elicited to it, needs to be set.

For a period, it was simply the need for all conservative forces in Church and State to unite in the face of what then seemed like a common enemy, that helps explain the wide early appeal of the Movement at Oxford.[12] Clearly, the times were ripe for the message of the early numbers of the 'Tracts for the Times'. In a period of apparent danger to the Church, the unfettered but simple High Church message they conveyed struck a chord with many who would soon be disillusioned when the immediate external danger to the Church relaxed and ebbed away. Moreover, many High Churchmen would continue to sympathise with, if not support, the Movement, out of what was to prove to be a quite mistaken notion of its essentially conservative tendency. An example of this type of support was represented by that important group which in 1833 actually formed one wing of the original Movement and which formed an association in defence of the Church. Signatures were collected, the Archbishop of Canterbury and the King were petitioned. Stalwarts of this group included such learned but lesser known Oxford figures as William Palmer of Worcester College, Charles Ogilvie of Balliol College and Vaughan Thomas of Corpus Christi College. In Hurrell Froude's idiosyncratic parlance, Churchmen such as Palmer, for all their detestation of liberalism and dissent and for all their rigid High Churchmanship, were nonetheless what he called 'Z's'.[13] By the epithet 'Z', Froude referred to a conservative, protestant High Churchmanship, which he sharply distinguished from Tractarianism. For the Tractarians proper, Froude claimed the title of 'Apostolicals' and the code label, 'Y's'. This, in turn, marked them out from the 'X's' represented by 'ultra-Protestants' or Evangelicals. A follower and later annalist of the Oxford Movement, William Copeland, rightly argued that it was 'extremely important to keep the Movement, which was from within, as clear as possible from the external circumstances, with which it came into contact'. As Copeland pointed out, 'Froude certainly had as much dreaded the calm of the church, as Palmer was frightened at the storm raised against it.'[14] Almost from the start, Palmer was nervous about the publication of the Tracts as potentially prejudicial to the Movement's acceptance, and he repeatedly advised caution and recommended a committee of revision to avoid 'unguarded expressions'.[15] In their turn, Newman, Froude and Keble grew increasingly impatient with Palmer's cautious line. Froude counselled that the Tractarians should 'throw the 'Z's' overboard'.[16]

Newman and his followers certainly were happy to avail themselves of the tacit support of the 'Z's' in the early phase of the Movement. In particular, they owed much to the moral support of one

'Z' who went further than many in collaboration, Hugh James Rose. Yet, even Rose was suspected of being a 'mere conservative' at heart, by Froude. Froude kept up pressure on Newman to maintain his distance, and to set the Movement on a more dynamic course. Froude succeeded. The always uneasy coalition between the two elements in the original Movement was doomed to break down, with differences becoming ever more apparent. These differences were as much psychological as theological. They consisted in what Newman described as 'the principle of personality'. For Newman, 'Z's' such as Palmer lacked,

> any insight into the force of personal influence and congeniality of thought in carrying out a religious theory, a condition which Froude and I considered essential to any true success in the stand which had to be made against liberalism.[17]

Significantly, Newman considered that Palmer had too many establishment connections among 'high church dignitaries, archdeacons, London rectors, and the like'.[18] In contrast, the Tractarians prided themselves on their relative freedom from ties of high office in the Church that might have inhibited their room for manoeuvre. In Oxford itself, the Tractarians tended to represent the grass-roots feelings of younger members of the University as opposed to 'men of rank and station'. Part of their moral strength and religious influence derived from their sense of detachment from the University of the seniors as represented by that close-knit but aloof oligarchy, the Heads of Houses. The dealings of the Tractarian leaders with the Heads confirmed them in their wariness of committees of what Newman disparagingly called 'sound, safe men'. Of the utmost significance in this context, was Newman's later avowal in the *Apologia*, that 'deliverance is wrought not by the many, but by the few, not by bodies but by persons'.[19] In fact, Newman insisted on the intensely personal medium of much of the Movement's growing influence among the junior ranks of the University in the years after 1833. Although no longer himself a tutor at Oriel after 1830, Newman rightly stressed the extent to which the spread of ideas and principles was fostered through the agency of the pedagogical relationship between college tutor and pupil as personalised by himself and his followers.[20]

It was these factors of temperament, ethos and circumstance, that help explain the almost total want of fixedness in the Movement. It was a lack of direction which Newman readily admitted and was almost proud of. As he later put it, 'I was not the person to take the lead of a party; I never was, from first to last, more than a leading member of a school'.[21] Even more candidly, he later confessed that 'the Movement, viewed with relation to myself, was but a floating opinion; it was not a power. It never would have been a power, if it had remained in my hands'. He freely applied to himself what was said by St Gregory Nazianzen, 'I could'st a people raise, but could not rule'.[22] Yet there was an attempt here to evade responsibility, and something akin to false modesty. The Movement was a power because of Newman's advocacy. He may not have sought leadership but it was thrust upon him. Followers hung on his every word, even imitating his very gait and gestures. 'Credo in Newmannum' was to become the watchword of a whole generation of undergraduates and younger MAs.[23] Newman could not have been altogether unconscious of the immense power which he exercised through personal friendship and discipleship, moral example and, above all, through the spiritual impact of his preaching in St Mary's.[24] At times, he acted in a way that showed that he was conscious of this power and force to mould and influence. What the younger members of the University who were vulnerable to Newman's spell required was guidance and direction. In his sermons, he certainly inculcated the ideal of holiness but the limits and parameters of Anglican teaching Newman seemed almost constitutionally incapable of providing.

Traditional High Churchmen knew where they stood. However, their essentially static theological position not unnaturally had less appeal to the younger Oxford generation than the more inspirational vision of catholicity provided by Newman. Yet, at the same time they were drawn down a path to which there was no obvious end or object in view. Moreover, High Churchmen and others on whose support the Movement relied in the early stages, were provoked rather than always conciliated or put at ease. Much blame can be laid on Newman here. His behaviour seemed designed to narrow rather than broaden the confines of support and would ultimately confer an essentially 'party', extraneous and sectarian character on the Oxford Movement. As Newman later candidly admitted,

> it came to pass at that time, that there was a double aspect in my bearing towards others...My behaviour had a mixture in it both of fierceness and of sport; and on this account, I dare say, it gave offence to many; nor am I here defending it.

Newman enlarged further on what he meant, admitting that,

> I was not unwilling to draw an opponent on step by step to the brink of some intellectual absurdity, and to leave him to get back as he could. I was not unwilling to play with a man, who asked me impertinent questions. I was reckless of the gossip which was circulated about me; and, when I might easily have set it right, did not deign to do so. Also I used irony in conversation, when matter-of-fact men would not see what I meant...This kind of behaviour was a sort of habit with me.[25]

It would seem that friends and early supporters such as the 'Z' Palmer of Worcester were almost as much victims of this 'fierce' behaviour as open opponents such as the editor of the evangelical *Christian Observer* and the 'high and dry' Margaret Professor of Divinity, Godfrey Faussett.[26] A later, albeit hostile reviewer of Newman's *Apologia* was not altogether unfair in suggesting that in such behaviour there was perhaps more 'of the "knowledge" that "puffeth up" than of the "charity" which "edifieth"'.[27]

Newman's almost arrogant self-confidence in his mature Anglican years perhaps inevitably came to blight his judgment. Again, in the *Apologia* many years later, Newman was prepared to admit almost as much. As he then explained,

> This absolute confidence in my cause, which led me to the imprudence or wantonness which I have been instancing, also laid me open, not unfairly, to the opposite charge of fierceness in certain steps which I took, or words which I published.[28]

Newman had in mind instances of extravagant and highly coloured language as in *Lyra Apostolica*, when he maintained that before learning to love, we must 'learn to hate'.[29] However, one of the more glaring instances of seemingly misguided steps that he took as a consequence of this self-confidence, was one which he never admitted to having been rash or mistaken. This was the decision to publish the *Remains* of Richard Hurrell Froude in 1838.

The controversial publication of Froude's *Remains* represented a landmark and turning-point in the history of the Oxford Movement. The publication provoked bitter reaction, and exposed latent, hitherto largely hidden differences between the traditional High Churchmen and Tractarians. Prior to this, there had existed a degree of outward unison between Tractarians, traditional High Churchmen and many conservative Evangelicals, exemplified by the triple alliance forged at Oxford in February 1836 to protest against the Whig government's appointment of the allegedly heterodox, Renn Dickson Hampden to the Regius Professorship of Divinity. The publication of Froude's *Remains* dashed this tentative alliance apart, and brought into the open the first rumblings of official disapproval of the Movement. It was probably inevitable that the revelations of Froude's unguarded and sometimes immature railings against the English Reformers and Reformation, should have provoked widespread offence. Many High Churchmen no less than Evangelicals were outraged.[30] As editors of the *Remains*, Newman and Keble were responsible. Why had they allowed the publication of such controversial matter? It might have been thought that the storm raised would have made them realise that publication had proved a grave mistake. Yet, far from being apologetic or contrite over the furore and regretting the potential damage done to the progress of the Movement, Newman rejoiced in what he felt was the blow struck for Catholic principles by the publication. As Piers Brendon has aptly put it, Newman almost welcomed the hostile reaction from High Churchmen and Evangelicals, as conclusive proof of his 'theorem that wide unacceptability was the best test of truth'.[31] Yet, at the same time, Newman displayed inconsistency. For when Godfrey Faussett bitterly assailed the Tractarians on the basis of Froude's *Remains* from the pulpit of St Mary's in May 1838, Newman's reaction was fierce and indignant. Newman responded with a lengthy point by point rebuttal of Faussett's critique and produced a theological apologia for the Movement.[32] Newman deliberately helped fuel the controversy, and gave Faussett a handle, for in his own reply, Faussett was able to cite a series of reputable High Church authorities apparently supportive of part of his argument.[33] In short, the waters had been muddied, and those old High Churchmen most sympathetic to the Movement were given reasons for distancing themselves. Newman had forfeited the moral high ground.

The apparent bravado that Newman had first evinced on the publication of the *Remains* was no less in contrast with his complete over-reaction to the first very mild episcopal hints from his diocesan, Bishop Bagot, that all was not right with the Movement. In his charge delivered in 1838 Bagot was highly laudatory of the Tractarian endeavour. This commendation was only slightly offset by the Bishop's suggestion that there might have been language used in some of the tracts that could be misconstrued and points raised that could benefit by clarification or correction.[34] The Bishop was quite clear that he found no fault of substance. However, Newman appeared to be quite thrown off guard. He was inclined to exaggerate the very modest degree of criticism that had been made. The contradiction in Newman's conduct was well delineated by Abbott. For as Abbott observed, at this time Newman wished,

> to use extreme language, which will, he knows, make many people call him a Papist; yet he is angry with the people who call him so. He trades on the chance that the silence of the Bishops may imply a sanction of his principles; yet he is irritated when they refuse to give him this tacit sanction.[35]

There was the same, somewhat disingenuous double aspect to Newman's response to the first expressions of disquiet by the Oxford Heads of Houses. Newman appeared to cultivate a certain ambiguity over the status and relation of the Movement to the University, designed to capitalise on the link when circumstances favoured, but to disavow it when it might prove disadvantageous.

Of course, Oxford University *qua* university was not formally responsible for the Oxford Movement, either in its achievements or failures. I have explored the exact nature and degree of the relationship elsewhere.[36] The sense of Tractarian detachment has been noted above, but alongside this attitude went a close identification with what Tractarians considered historic ethos as well as privileges of the University. The leaders of the Movement not only aimed to preserve this historic, traditional Oxford, but contrary to what its liberal critics may have thought, had a clear, definite vision and ideal of the University. In Dean Church's words, the University was 'the fulcrum from which the theological revival hoped to move the Church'.[37] The Tractarian orchestration of the campaigns against the admission of Dissenters, in defence of the traditional mode of subscription to Articles by all undergraduates as well as MAs, and against Hampden's appointment, in the mid-1830s, was motivated and infused by devotion to this ideal.

Yet, try as they might, the Tractarians had no claim or mandate to speak for the University as a whole. By the late 1830s, the Tractarians could claim no monopoly of moral or religious earnestness in the University. The latitudinarian Dr Arnold arguably had done as much as Newman to leaven the University with a higher moral and religious tone than existed for generations. Moreover, Newman's stress on the 'monastic' character of the collegiate system and call for a restoration of the 'spirit of our founders',[38] was not only highly unpalatable to the liberal reforming party at Oxford but presented potentially destabilising implications in the eyes of many High Churchmen who were content with the mere *status quo*. The bulk of the Oxford Heads inclined to the latter position, somewhat reluctantly following the Tractarian lead in the stand against admission of Dissenters and the appointment of Hampden, but fearful of the radical direction and implications of the Movement. It was inevitable that they should come to resent Newman's tendency to appear to speak on behalf of the University in some sort of official capacity. The rising external hostility to Tractarianism began to run off on the University as a whole, and parents began to prefer the sister university, Cambridge, as a safer haven for their sons.[39]

When questions began to be asked in Parliament identifying the whole University with what was said and done by the leaders of the Movement,[40] the Heads not unnaturally felt it was time to make a stand. The spectre of a parliamentary visitation of the University was already on the horizon. Newman, who was always emphasising the University aspect of the Movement was in no real position to complain, but complain he did. As Abbott declared, Newman,

> makes much of the name of the University and of the deference paid to Oxford, and of the consequent authority reflected on the 'Oxford' Tracts and 'Oxford' principles: and yet we shall find him aggrieved at an attempt on the part of the University authorities to dissipate this popular delusion.[41]

The attempt here alluded to was the formal judgment of the Oxford Heads in March 1841 condemning the 'modes of interpretation' of the Thirty-Nine Articles suggested in Tract 90, which followed the initial letter of protest to the editor of the Tract by four Senior Tutors. It was a protest which brought the controversy surrounding the Movement to a climactic head and crisis. It brought Newman face to face with the raw reality of the undercurrent of hostility to the Movement that had been smouldering since 1838. Tract 90 touched a nerve, and Newman was to pay for it.

The official protest as well as popular reaction to Tract 90 can only be fully appreciated against a background of the growing theological divergence of Newman from even the Movement's avowed original starting-point. Up until 1839, as he later confessed, Newman remained secure and confident in his Anglicanism. Yet, even in the *via media* phase of Newman's religious history, one can sense that Newman's concept of Anglicanism was nebulous and somewhat theoretical. Much to his friend Rose's chagrin, Newman insisted on arguing in his classic treatise, the *Prophetical Office of the Church* published in 1837, that Anglicanism had never, even in the seventeenth century, been fully 'realised'.[42] At the same time, Newman did honestly throw himself into the spirit and writings of the great Anglican divines as well as the early Fathers.[43] In truth, it was not the case that his commitment to the ideal of Caroline Anglicanism, was always half-hearted, shallow or insincere, as some critics like Abbott maintained. Viewed in retrospect, Newman's *via media* phase seems but a temporary staging-post in his overall religious odyssey, but at the time it was held and propounded with a conviction, passion and 'fierceness' which could not have been excelled.

It is not then the genuineness of Newman's commitment to historic Anglicanism for a time that should be doubted, but the basis on which that commitment was erected and the manner in which it increasingly came to be expressed. Newman tried to erect a dogmatic edifice on a structure not designed to support it. The key perhaps to Newman's eventual loss of faith in High Anglicanism, lay in his misconceived desire to systematise and harmonise a body of divinity that was essentially unsystematic and varied, if not sometimes discordant. He conceived of the *via media* as but a 'paper theory', lacking in substance and only existing in outline. He sought to make it 'professed, acted on and maintained on a large sphere of action'. As Newman put it, 'we too have a vast inheritance, but no inventory of our treasures. All is given us in profusion; it remains for us to catalogue, sort, distribute, select, harmonise and complete'.[44] Yet, the dangers of such an approach were only too obvious to the Movement's critics and even erstwhile friends. As Abbott not unfairly deduced, in the *Prophetical Office*,

> substitute 'pick and choose' for 'discriminate and select', and we have Newman himself here gravely proposing that he and a group of Oxford friends of his should set up that which he regarded as an abomination of desolation, that portentous impiety called 'Private Judgment', by sitting in a Commission of Inquiry into the great Divines of the Anglican Church.[45]

In essence, Newman had an 'idea of catholicism', and was yet unsure whither it might lead. In contrast, the old High Churchmen were on no such voyage of discovery. As Rose cautioned Newman,

> We know exactly what the Truth is. We are going on no voyage

> of discovery. We know exactly the extent of the shore. There is a creek here, and a bay there, – all laid down in the charts; but not often entered or re-surveyed. We know all this beforehand, and therefore can lay down our plans, and not, (as I think), feel any uncertainty where we are going, or feel it necessary or advisable to spread our sails, and take our chance of finding a new Atlantis.[46]

Newman could never accept such limitations. He wanted the Church of England literally to represent the Church of antiquity in fullness of doctrine and devotion, ceremonial and ritual, if it were to compete with the Church of Rome on an equal basis. However, it can be said that Caroline divinity and the many different facets of the High Church tradition which Newman sought to blend, harmonise and complete, could never have fulfilled this expectation. Newman was seeking the impossible.

The somewhat tentative, albeit sincere, nature of Newman's advocacy of the *via media* arguably always rendered him vulnerable to external challenge. During the summer of 1839, eighteen months prior to Tract 90, Newman's faith in Anglican catholicity had been dealt its first blow and his first doubts were sown. Newman was unsettled by an article by Nicholas Wiseman in the Roman Catholic *Dublin Review* in which the Church of England's relation to the Church of Rome was likened to that of the Donatists with the early Catholic Church. As Newman put it in a well-known passage in the *Apologia*, with Wiseman's application of the words of St Augustine, 'securus judicat orbis terrarum', 'the theory of the *via media* was absolutely pulverised'.[47] Newman remained convinced of Anglicanism's conformity with antiquity, but the doubts raised about her catholicity were not easily shaken off. He continued to seek to prove the catholicity of Anglicanism, as in a famous article entitled 'The Catholicity of the English Church', in the *British Critic* in 1840, but he increasingly felt that the Thirty-Nine Articles were perceived at least by some of his younger followers as a major stumbling block. This question mark being raised over the Articles might seem ironic given the vigour of Newman's rebuttal of the liberal campaign to relax the terms of subscription at Oxford in the mid-1830s. However, it was the principle of subscription, and the apparent submission of intellect and reason to a test of doctrinal authority involved, on which the Tractarians had laid stress. As to the actual terms of the Articles themselves, Newman had confided as early as 1835, that he was 'no friend to them'.[48] Implicitly, he appeared to perceive the Articles as Protestant and a potential obstacle to the fuller development of Catholic views which he envisaged. Tract 90 was an attempt to come to terms with and overcome this apparent obstacle. Newman freely admitted that it represented an experiment, an 'experimentum crucis'.[49] The formulation of the Tract can be said to have been a consequence of the breakdown of his earlier confidence in Anglicanism. Without the doubts in 1839, it probably would never have been written.

In much of the historiography of the Movement, emphasis is laid upon the apparent unreasonableness and unfairness of the reaction to Tract 90, with the response of the Heads being particularly censured. Thus, according to Dean Church, the resolution of the Heads criticising the Tract, 'was an ungenerous and stupid blunder, such as men make, when they think or are told that "something must be done", and do not know what'.[50] Yet, the reality seems to show otherwise. The mood in Oxford was more favourable to the action of the Heads than the Tractarians assumed. As one Oxford resident put it, 'the general feeling is that some interference was absolutely required and that the Heads of Houses have done perfectly right in putting forth their protest'.[51] In fact, a policy of universal proscription against the Tractarians, as desired by zealots like C.P. Golightly, manifestly was eschewed by the University authorities. Indeed, there were some bitter complaints that the Heads had not acted sooner, and that their declaration of 15 March 1841 against Tract 90 had not been applied to the whole series of the *Tracts for the Times*.[52] Moreover, it can be argued that the action of the Heads in 1841 and the arguments by which they defended it, were precisely in accord with the type of exercise of the University authorities' religious function as enshrined in the statutes, which in any other circumstances, as when employed against Hampden in 1836, the Tractarians themselves would have welcomed. By the statutes, the authorities had a duty to ensure that the hitherto received meaning of subscription was adhered to, and to repudiate evasions or quibbles likely to unsettle, as Vice-Chancellor Philip Wynter put it, 'the minds of our younger members'.[53] Regardless of any theological errors, High Churchmen at Oxford who in the mid-1830s had defended the high religious theory of subscription alongside the Tractarians, now felt that the very ecclesiastical conception of the University which they both had upheld against liberals, was being undermined by Tract 90. It was on this ground that a High Churchman like Robert Scott, Fellow of Balliol, defended the course taken by the Heads. As Scott told his colleague A.C. Tait, one of the signatories of the Letter of the Four Tutors,

> There was undoubtedly a cause why the University, which exists on the condition of teaching – i.e. affixing a sense to – these Articles, should protest against their having a no-sense-at-all peremptorily fixed upon them. This publication struck a blow at the very mission of the University; and therefore the interference could never at another time have been so well timed.[54]

In short, if it really was the duty of tutors to instruct undergraduates in the Articles – and this all the pamphlets in defence of Oxford's system of subscription at matriculation in 1834-5, and not least those penned by Tractarians had taken for granted – then it could not be a matter for indifference to the Heads, in what sense those Articles were going to be subscribed and their meaning conveyed.

Much of the historiography of the Movement has also emphasised the apparent modesty of Newman's aim in Tract 90. This aim was explained as an attempt to show that while the *Prayer Book* was acknowledged as Catholic, the Articles though the 'offspring of an uncatholic age' were capable or 'patient' of a Catholic meaning.[55] At the same time, Newman's conduct is portrayed as meek and patient, and he is commended for the perfect simplicity and honesty with which he undertook his task.[56] Yet, the evidence suggests that Newman's task was rather more ambitious than is often assumed, while his approach and mode of treating opposition is somewhat less than open or simple. For in effect, in Tract 90, Newman was putting the Church of England on a trial of his own devising. Tract 90 may have been intended as a peace offering, but as Paul Avis has recently aptly put it, it was 'a peace offering to the Church of England – delivered with a slap in the face'.[57]

It was not so much the principle of Tract 90, the attempt to demonstrate the compatibility of the Thirty-Nine Articles with Catholic truths, however defined, that would most concern critics. After all, there were at least some historical precedents, albeit ill-fated, for such an exercise. One such precedent was that made by Christopher Davenport in 1634. Another was undertaken by a little known pre-Tractarian High Churchman, Samuel Wix in 1818.[58] What prompted the most disquiet was the execution of the Tract, and its reasoning. Newman's meaning was unclear. Ambiguity abounded. Newman claimed to be arguing that only what he called the 'dominant errors' or 'the actual popular beliefs and usages sanctioned by Rome in the countries in communion with it' rather than 'the Catholic teaching of early centuries' was condemned in the Articles.[59] However, Newman attempted to distinguish the so-called 'dominant errors' or popular abuses, from the formal dogmas of Rome as enshrined in the Council of Trent, and thus representing 'official' teaching. Newman insisted that some of these dogmas were condemned in the Articles, but that some were not. In general it was only the abuses and popular interpretations that were repudiated in the Articles. Here was rich ground for confusion and misunderstanding. The distinctions drawn between these categories, like the categories themselves, appeared to some to be as vague as they were arbitrary. Where was the clear principle for sifting the wheat of Catholic teaching from the chaff of 'dominant errors', critics asked? Such critics felt that there was an almost conscious and deliberate straining of hitherto accepted doctrinal limits, in the Tract. It is true that earlier in the century orthodox and evangelical Churchmen had disputed the meaning of certain Articles, notably Article 17 covering election and free will. Moreover, pleas for latitude in the interpretation of such disputed Articles had been made by High Churchmen since the days of Laud. What Newman was pleading for, was for something new, a latitude or elasticity in the interpretation of Articles that bore on the Church of Rome whose meaning and terms had hitherto been accepted as clearly and unequivocally Protestant by High Churchmen and Evangelicals alike.[60]

What did Newman mean by 'Catholic'? The term became overworked by the Tractarians but was rarely satisfactorily defined. Newman's admittedly biased and embittered brother, Francis, later argued that in Tract 90 his use of three epithets, 'Roman', 'Catholic' and 'Papal' enabled him 'to play his own game on simple minds'.[61] Even Liddon felt that Newman's use of the phrase 'doctrine of the Old Church'[62] with which he sought to render the Articles compatible, was an ambiguous expression, open to misunderstanding. Certainly, there was more than a suspicion that by 'Catholic', Newman meant not only the teaching of the early Church alone but also part of the official teaching of the Church of Rome as enshrined in the Tridentine decrees, which High Churchmen had always insisted that the Thirty-Nine Articles authoritatively condemned. In this context, Newman's assertion that the Articles were 'not uncatholic', though they were 'the offspring of an uncatholic age' could scarcely be welcomed as a concession by traditional High Churchmen. In what sense was the age of the Reformation 'uncatholic'? Was it because the authority of the papacy had been rejected? Many already feared that Newman was working, albeit perhaps unconsciously, towards this viewpoint. As one High Church critic complained,

> What does our author mean by an 'uncatholic age', or by what rule does he measure his catholicity? Surely he leaves his readers the option of measuring catholicity by simple subjection to the Papacy; for we cannot find any other proof of the uncatholicity of England in the day when her Articles were delivered, than a determination not to submit any longer to the usurped tyranny of the Pope.[63]

The difference between Newman's proposed *rapprochement* with Rome and that pursued by individual divines like Samuel Wix in an earlier period was clear. The latter took for granted that the creed of Pius IV which Anglicans accused Rome of having added to the Faith, would have to be abandoned as a precondition of any reconciliation between the two Churches. The Church of Rome thereby would be back in the state of the primitive Church in possessing the three creeds,

> and the Church of England, continuing to hold those three ancient Creeds, could then dispense with all her negative articles, which are the subject of inquiry in the Tract before us.

In complete contrast, Newman in Tract 90 regarded the Council of Trent as not only the real point of reference or contact, but almost as the actual basis around which the two Churches might be brought closer together. The Tract did envisage a softening down of the Articles, 'so as to no longer hinder any of us taking them in a Catholic, or – if the author of the Tract had spoken more correctly – a Popish sense'.[64]

The principle of selecting and harmonising which Newman had applied to the *Prophetical Office*, was taken a stage further in Tract 90. Many baulked at some of the logical distinctions which Newman attempted to draw between, for instance, Romish 'Masses' and 'the Mass'. Certainly, the use of the plural in the text of the Article enabled Newman 'to turn topsy-turvy a plain meaning'.[65] Moreover, some considered that the citations which Newman made of particular Anglican divines apparently holding particular tenets often condemned as 'Romish', bordered on the far-fetched, if not sophistical. As Abbott later complained, Newman,

> seemed to assume that every opinion, however extreme in the

> direction of Rome, that had been once expressed by any one High Church Bishop or Divine, and had not been authoritatively censured, at once became part of justifiable Anglican doctrine.[66]

An example of Newman's method, was in his treatment of Articles 20 and 21 on Church Authority and General Councils respectively. These Articles were hardly supportive of Tractarian claims. The definition of the Church seemed inadequate, while Article 21 in contradiction of Tractarian argument, stated that General Councils could err. Some nimble reasoning was needed to bridge this gap, and this Newman provided. Newman was able to offset the letter of these Articles by selective statements from Anglican divines apparently more in accord with a 'Catholic' position. Yet, while Newman cited Henry Hammond on the infallibility of General Councils, no authority was given. Moreover, statements of Hammond suggesting that General Councils were fallible were conveniently ignored.[67]

Other instances of Newman's selectivity and one-sidedness were noted by critics of Tract 90. For instance, while at one moment Newman would repudiate the teaching enshrined in the Book of Homilies as Protestant and a 'yoke of worse than Egyptian bondage', at another, in order to evade the literal meaning of the Articles, he would refer 'to the Homilies to show that more Catholic notions were held at the time'. It was a case of following the line of least resistance to finding official authority or precedent for the particular Catholic notion he happened to be advocating. To many, it appeared worse that disingenuous. In particular, by attempting, as it were, to 'correct' ambiguities in the Articles by reference to the Homilies for which on other occasions he had shown little respect, Newman seemed to be guilty of imposing 'on the construction of the Articles, documents [i.e. the Homilies] which he does not recognise himself'.[68] By such logical twists and turns, Newman might appear to adhere to the letter of a particular portion of the Anglican formularies, but in practice he was going against the overall spirit underpinning the whole. As a leading Oxford critic of Tract 90 tellingly remarked,

> I do think, (to borrow Mr. Newman's illustration), that the Articles are not a heap of stones but a building, and that he who induces himself by thirty-nine quibbles to assent to them piecemeal, and then denies them as a whole, is guilty of the most hateful verbal sophistry and mental reservation.[69]

The straightforwardness and fairness of Newman's interpretation of other particular Articles was called in to question by many who were otherwise sympathetic to the Movement. One such critic, cited above, especially complained of a false distinction drawn between 'Romish' and 'Tridentine'[70] that seemed to pervade the whole edifice of argument in the Tract. The essence of Newman's argument seemed to be that on such and such a particular doctrine, the Articles actually 'by anticipation' approved of the Tridentine position and merely condemned a corrupt, albeit popular, 'Romish' version of that sound doctrine. By such an argument, even a modified version of the worship of images could be supported. High Church critics of this reasoning felt that Newman was throwing dust in the eyes of his readers. To highlight what was deemed to be the sophistical nature of the argument, using an interesting analogy, the above critic witheringly maintained,

> By this fanciful mode of reasoning a sinner may justify any sin or species of vice, if only he comfort himself by merely saying, 'Not every view of this sin or this vice is condemned, but only the one as practised in such or such a place'; for vice has its changes and fashions as well as doctrines. In the New Testament epistles we find sins marked out by name, and mentioned as peculiar to the church to which the apostle wrote. Well, how easily any sinner of another church might have remained at ease in the indulgence of sin, by saying, 'Not every sin of this nature is condemned, but the Corinthian or the Galatian view'. And so they might all have gone on in their sins, if only they did not adopt the precise opinions or mode of indulgence in that sin as practised in other places. We never met more extraordinary reasoning; it is mere trifling; it is perversion of reason.[71]

This critic went on to complain about what he regarded as the no less specious reasoning and unsatisfactory language which Newman adopted apparently to escape the force of the grammatical sense of Article 38 – 'The Bishop of Rome hath no jurisdiction in this realm of England'. Certainly, the critic had reason to consider Newman's extrapolation of the Article rather lame. For Newman, it was sufficient to state that 'we find ourselves, as a church, under the king now, and we obey him; we were under the Pope formerly, and we obeyed him'. For one who frankly confessed to an admiration for the political doctrines of passive obedience and even sacral kingship enshrined in the Homilies, this did seem to be placing the basis of loyalty and allegiance on too low and utilitarian grounds.[72]

Was Newman aware that by his reasoning alone he gave ground for much offence in the Tract? It would appear so. Newman himself appeared to reveal an element of self-conscious cynicism in the method he adopted, when he admitted in the *Apologia* that,

> Every Creed has texts in its favour, and again texts which run counter to it: and this is generally confessed. And this is what I felt keenly; – how had I done worse in Tract 90 than Anglicans, Wesleyans, and Calvinists did daily in their sermons and publications?...why was I to be dishonest and they immaculate?[73]

This was hardly taking the moral high ground, and such admissions go some way to blunting the force of the complaints by himself, his friends and followers, that the hostile reaction to Tract 90 was entirely unfair and undeserved. As in the furore over Froude's *Remains*, there surfaced an element of provoking verbal sparring with opponents that did not seem designed to conciliate, disarm or win over. Pertinent here was Newman's admission in the *Apologia* about his conduct and frame of mind at this critical turning-point in the Movement's history;

> 'Two can play at that game', was often in my mouth, when men of Protestant sentiments, appealed to the articles, homilies, or Reformers; in the sense that if they had a right to speak loud, I had both the liberty and the means of giving them tit for tat.[74]

There was a widespread perception of an undutiful tone permeating the Introduction to the Tract, with its references to 'ambiguous formularies' and to 'stammering lips', and with the Church of England described as 'in bondage'.[75] Objections to tone and language far outweighed complaints over the substance of the Tract from this quarter. Gladstone expressed a common view when he later maintained that, 'there never was an uproar, and there never were censures, which were more attributable to the manner and language of a publication as contrasted with its substance'.[76]

Yet, for some of the older High Church school, the apparently disrespectful language and way of viewing the Church of England it implied, was but symptomatic of a deeper flaw and malaise in Newman's evolving theory of Catholicism. Joshua Watson, the acknowledged leader of the standard bearers of this older school, the so-called 'Hackney Phalanx' always retained a warm regard for Newman and Pusey, who in turn looked up to him as something of an oracle in his generation.[77] What he thought of Tract 90 could not lightly be dismissed. Characteristically, Watson avoided outward criticism, but privately, according to his biographer, Edward Churton, Watson 'felt very acutely the wrongfulness of the words in the Introduction to No. 90, and expressed his grief'.[78] What Watson, quite as much as Protestant High Churchmen like Godfrey Faussett who indulged in public rebuke, disliked was the apparent arraignment by Newman of the living, existing Catholicism enshrined in the Church of England's formularies, on the bar of a preconceived, theoretical and nebulous concept of what was 'primitive'.

Newman's friend and erstwhile ally, Palmer of Worcester, was no less convinced of an implicit animus against the Church as she was, running throughout the Tract. It is interesting to see how Palmer took account of this, when one compares the relevant section of the first and second editions of his *Treatise on the Church of Christ,* published in 1838 and 1842 respectively. In the 1838 edition of the *Treatise*, Palmer had simply stated as one of the rules of interpretation of the Thirty-Nine Articles, that they were to be understood in 'the sense most conformable to Scripture and to Catholic Tradition, which she [the Church] acknowledges to be her guides'.[79] Clearly, four years later, Palmer felt that he had to be more precise, in the light of Tractarian assumptions as to what constituted 'Catholic Tradition'. Thus, in the enlarged 1842 edition, in the wake of Tract 90, Palmer added a highly significant note of caution, explaining just what he meant by interpreting the Articles in the 'most catholic sense'. In an added passage clearly aimed at the principle of Tract 90, Palmer now made clear that,

> the rule of interpreting the Articles in the most catholic sense, is one which must not be vaguely and indiscriminately applied to all the Articles, as if we were at liberty to affix to them whatever meaning seems to us most consistent with Scripture or with Tradition. The principle thus applied would lead to a most dangerous tampering with the authorised formularies of the church; would open the way for evasions of their most evident meaning, and thus render them wholly useless as tests of belief or persuasion.

On the contrary, such a rule of interpretation could only apply to,

> particular cases where a legitimate doubt of the meaning of any Article exists, and where it cannot be solved either by the language of other parts of the Articles, or of other formularies of the church.[80]

Moreover, it was a similar objection that prompted the discriminating critique of Tract 90 undertaken by an Irish High Churchman, Charles Elrington. Elrington made quite clear that he did not disagree with Newman's basic premise that the Thirty-Nine Articles should be 'interpreted according to the teaching of the Church Catholic'. His complaint was simply that, in practice as expounded by Newman, this amounted to interpreting the Articles 'according to the view each has of the teaching of the Church Catholic'.[81]

Old High Churchmen tended to feel placed in an invidious and vulnerable position as a consequence of Tract 90. They feared that the broader cause in favour of 'Church principles' was endangered by the course that Newman was taking. They were alarmed, and not without reason, at the prospect of a Low Church backlash against such principles. Thus, the Movement of 1833 seemed as if it would now weaken rather than bolster the traditional High Churchmanship which they represented. Several in the group of younger, so-called 'Z's such as Palmer of Worcester felt most threatened, as they were bound by ties of personal allegiance and that network of 'spiritual amicitia' which Newman tended to foster. It is these personal ties which help to explain Palmer's extraordinarily favourable public reception of Tract 90, which contrasted not only with that of Watson and the older generation, but with his own private misgivings, given lucid theological expression in the subtle and judicious revisions to the relevant portion of the *Treatise* as described above. It is striking that a time when the Tract was attracting widespread public opprobium, Palmer stood by Newman, and wrote him a generous letter, full of comfort, sympathy and encouragement. In it, Palmer declared that he had 'no hesitation in expressing an opinion that' Tract 90 was 'the most valuable of the series of Tracts that has come under my observation'.[82] The evidence suggests that this letter was written to anchor Newman in his attachment to the Church of England. Certainly, the sentiments did not reflect Palmer's true attitude. According to James Mozley, 'Palmer sent this letter quite spontaneously, and it does him great credit, especially as he and Newman were rather on cool terms some time ago'.[83] However, it was Edward Churton who provides evidence as to Palmer's real alarm, albeit hidden from public view. Churton confided to Arthur Perceval in December 1841 that he had received,

> a painfully interesting letter from my friend William Palmer, a good true hearted Irishman, with whose opinions and yours on

the later proceedings of the Tracts, I have the happiness almost entirely to agree. He condemns No. 90, as Mr. Joshua Watson and all good churchmen of my acquaintance do.[84]

The same conflict between personal loyalty and private disapprobation was evident in the attitude of another 'Z', W.F. Hook. As Hook explained, 'I had intended to answer Tract 90 and had begun to do so, but I would not attack my friends when they had fallen'.[85] No little personal sacrifice was involved, evident in Hook's avowal to Gladstone, that 'I sacrificed my own character rather than give' up 'the good men at Oxford', 'on the publication of Tract 90'.[86] Clearly, Newman had no grounds for complaint of lack of support, understanding or loyalty from those who had perhaps the most to lose in any vigorous Low Church backlash against the Movement which Tract 90 seemed likely to provoke.

Newman showed little concern for the predicament in which Tract 90 placed erstwhile supporters like Palmer, Hook and Churton. He could only insist that he had never written Tract 90 with them in mind. Newman had avowedly composed Tract 90 in order to help settle the growing doubts about Anglicanism held by a substantial portion of his younger followers who seemed to be drifting in the direction of the Church of Rome. Newman became aware of this 'Romanising' undercurrent to the Movement from 1840 onwards. He was aware of the possibility of secessions in a way which Palmer of Worcester could not yet have comprehended. As Newman confided to his friend, John Bowden, at this time, 'the danger of a lapse into Romanism, I think gets greater daily. I expect to hear of victims. Again I fear I see more clearly that we are waking up to a schism in our Church'.[87] In short, it cannot be said that Newman did not have his eyes open. Moreover, if Newman's aim in writing Tract 90 partly was to check the 'Romanising' trend, from the Anglican viewpoint his aims could be commended as laudable. Yet, whatever his intentions, the result of Tract 90 was to be a strengthening rather than weakening of the Romeward trend among Newman's followers. Why was this so?

In the first instance, Tract 90 soon came to be perceived more as a concession to, or compromise with, an existing Romanising spirit than an effective braking operation. Roman Catholic controversialists encouraged the popular impression that Newman was playing into the hands of Rome by appearing to argue that the Thirty-Nine Articles were reconcilable with the decrees of Trent. The feeling was that Newman was aiding and abetting, albeit unintentionally, the work of

Roman Catholic priests in England.[88] Moreover, some of the specific argument in Tract 90 had flaws which were readily capitalised upon by Roman Catholic writers. In particular, a contradiction with Newman's earlier position in regard to the Council of Trent became apparent. Earlier, Newman had argued that the corruptions of Romanism only became formalised and made binding at Trent.[89] Even Hurrell Froude had described Roman Catholics as 'wretched Tridentines'.[90] Tract 90 involved something of a *volte-face* in Newman's attitude. The formal, 'official' Tridentine position was now deemed worthy of accommodation with the Articles, and contrasted favourably with a pre-Tridentine, corrupt, popular Romanism which was deemed to have been the real object of repudiation by the Articles. In his own response to Tract 90, the Roman Catholic, Wiseman, was able to taunt and tease Newman over this. Wiseman's jibe, which strongly paralleled a similar observation from the High Churchman, Faussett, was designed to hit home. With some justice, Wiseman complained that Newman had hitherto blamed Roman Catholics for adhering to the decrees of Trent, 'yet you now blame us for departure from them. Why not suspect your judgments, if you find that they vary?'[91]

Newman's professed aim of halting the drift towards Rome might have succeeded in the months after Tract 90's publication if Newman and the Tractarian leaders had sat quiet and bided their time. This was the earnest hope of the High Churchmen, and they did all they could to calm the situation and assuage popular fears. Thus, when John Keble set about publishing a robust defence of Tract 90 and proposed dedicating it to Joshua Watson himself, Watson 'exhorted him from heaping fuel on the fire', adding to his friend, Henry Handley Norris, another leader of the 'Hackney Phalanx', that 'indeed it has been a painful thing, more than I should choose to say to any but yourself, to decline any request from the author of the "Christian Year"'.[92] Watson and his Hackney friends clearly foresaw division and disaster if Newman refused in effect to take his medicine and patiently accept the implied rebuke and strictures on the Tract. Watson's niece, Mary, recorded in her diary at this time, her uncle's opinion expressed later in the same year, 'that all might have been safe, if "they" had been quiet after No. 90. His great fear was that the extreme into which the Oxford men had gone would produce a strong Protestant reaction, which again would drive many into Romanism'.[93] In the event, Watson's hopes were to be dashed, and his worst fears soon realised.

At first, all had seemed well. In response to the first wave of clamour, Newman, albeit after great prompting, did publish an apparently conciliatory letter to his diocesan, Bishop Bagot, and another, to Pusey's Oxford friend, Richard Jelf. Both these works had at least the appearance of clarifying ambiguous passages and explaining away objections. For instance, though not really borne out by the text of the first edition of the Tract, in his Letter to Jelf, Newman insisted that he believed the Articles did 'contain a condemnation of the authoritative teaching of the Church of Rome' and that Rome's present authoritative teaching went 'very far indeed to substitute another Gospel for the true one'.[94] Moreover, Newman sheltered behind the apparent precedent for his distinction between 'official' and 'popular' Roman teaching, provided by the pre-Tractarian High Churchman, Charles Lloyd, one-time Bishop of Oxford.[95] Furthermore, in a second edition of Tract 90, Newman excised and modified certain passages and phrases, especially in the introduction. Newman also appeared to agree to a request from Bishop Bagot that the series of the 'Tracts for the Times' be closed, and that Tract 90 be withdrawn from circulation. However, the direction of events was soon wrenched once more from Newman's control by the actions of some of his more impetuous younger followers, such as W.G. Ward and Frederick Oakeley.

Pusey had given a conservative interpretation of Newman's aim in Tract 90, insisting that by 'catholic', Newman did not include even elements of 'the later definite system in the Church of Rome'.[96] Yet, as even Liddon was forced to point out later, the two were by now quite at cross purposes. Pusey was mistaken about and unmindful of Newman's real position by 1841. For instance, Pusey still did not fully realise that Newman had long since abandoned the English Reformers.[97] In short, Pusey defended Newman on grounds which the latter eschewed. However, if Pusey, as it were, bent Newman's meaning one way, Ward and Oakeley bent his meaning the other way, professing to draw out the latent but legitimate pro-Roman inferences in the Tract to their logical conclusion.

Oakeley was less extreme than Ward, but he did not help Newman's case in the eyes of the High Churchmen, by his cynical justification of Newman's apparently one-sided citations of various Anglican divines in Tract 90. Oakeley perhaps over candidly admitted that such citations could be just as easily constructed to refute as well as uphold various propositions advanced about individual Articles in

Tract 90. Thus, Oakeley explained Newman's claim that it was tenable for members of the Church of England to hold such 'primitive' views as a 'comprecation of the saints with Bramhall', while at the same time discreetly ignoring other aspects of Bramhall's theology which militated against Newman's gloss on the Articles in the Tract. As Oakeley argued,

> the object, in these cases, is not to justify the Caroline divines, any more than to ground particular doctrines upon their authority, but merely to show what they felt themselves at liberty to say without protest. And this fact has its own weight, whatever these divines may chance to have said elsewhere.[98]

To many traditional High Churchmen this may have smacked of playing fast and loose with Anglican formularies, and could not have inspired confidence. Moreover, it was possible for the Evangelical, William Goode, to appeal to the testimony of the same Anglican divines cited by Newman, in order to refute the interpretation of the Articles advanced in Tract 90.[99] However, Ward's intervention in favour of Tract 90 was more seriously subversive of traditional Anglicanism. His glosses on Tract 90 compounded the original offence given by the Tract many times over.

Ward had been a disciple of Arnold's and influenced by Utilitarianism. He came under Newman's spell and became an enthusiastic follower of the Movement, but he gave it a new turn. He remained more interested in ethical theories and ideals than in the history of the early Church.[100] He had even less sympathy than Oakeley for the more traditional High Anglican phase of the early Oxford movement. While influenced by Newman, Ward in turn influenced Newman's own thought at this time. He seemed to be always one step ahead of his leader, extending and developing what was yet but latent in Newman's mind. Ward's 'defence' of Tract 90 well illustrated this. Newman had been notoriously unclear as to what he actually meant by the phrase, 'the authoritative teaching of the Church of Rome'. Pusey had sought to sidestep the question of the status of the Tridentine decrees, by lamely arguing that 'this part of the question relates rather to the hope of the future repentance and restoration of Rome than to any thing which concerns ourselves at this moment'.[101] However, Ward had no such reticence. He admitted that Newman's terminology had been ambiguous, but sought to draw out what he thought was Newman's real meaning. In two pamphlets, 'A Few Words' and 'A Few Words More in Defence of Tract 90', Ward took further Newman's argument that the Articles be subscribed in 'a literal and grammatical sense' without regard to the known opinions of their compilers or even of the 'imponens' or authority enjoining subscription. Ward insisted that the Articles had to be interpreted in a 'non-natural' sense if they were to be accommodated to Catholic truth.[102] Newman had avoided that phrase. In effect, as F.L. Cross has argued, what Ward was saying was that we,

> interpret the Articles rightly when we make them mean the very reverse of what they appear to say! Whereas Newman had expressed his readiness to withdraw the phrase which he had used of the Articles, viz. 'ambiguous formularies', Ward held that the only means of giving them a Catholic sense at all was to defend their ambiguity.[103]

Ward's line of argument paved the way for the startling contention which underpinned his notorious *Ideal of a Christian Church*, published in 1844, that it was possible to hold the whole cycle of Roman Catholic doctrine, and yet remain a member of the Church of England – a conclusion which he was to repudiate by his own secession to Rome in 1845.

Of course, it can be argued that Ward misrepresented Newman's views or at least put an unfairly 'Romanising' gloss on them. Certainly, Newman would have felt uneasy at Ward's unguarded language. He always professed to deny an individual's right to sign the Articles in a 'non-natural sense'. On the other hand, Newman made no effort to disown Ward's views. If he was a step behind, Newman did seem to be moving in Ward's direction. The Swedish scholar, Rune Imberg has recently demonstrated that later editions of the tracts tended to be modified somewhat in a 'Roman' direction, with Newman's clear approval.[104] There is also evidence that in Tract 90 itself, Newman came near to adopting a form of the 'non-natural' interpretation of the Articles, when he argued in the *Apologia*, as noted above, that 'every creed had texts in its favour and texts that ran counter to it', and that what he proposed in the tract was no worse than what Evangelicals did. The clearest and most striking evidence that Newman became increasingly more inclined to acquiesce in Ward's 'ultra' notions being propagated, comes from his private correspondence over Tract 90. For instance, as early as March 1841, less than two months after publication of the first edition of the Tract, Newman could confide to Pusey, in reference to Ward's pamphlets, 'clever men will not content themselves with defending theories which they feel in their hearts to be indefensible, e.g. Palmer's views'.[105]

Newman used the critical outcry against Tract 90, and especially the charges of the Bishops in the summer of 1841, as his reason for virtually withdrawing from taking any further active public part in Anglican affairs. There followed the retreat to Littlemore. Over three more years followed of waiting in the wings, before the final secession to Rome in October 1845. As Newman later recalled somewhat bitterly, 'I considered that after the Bishops' charges and the general disavowal of the Tract on the part of the clergy, it was not for me to represent or to attempt to champion, the Church to which I belonged'.[106]

Nevertheless, it must have been a puzzle at least to Newman's more conservative supporters that he should have allowed himself to become so stunned and paralysed by the official reaction to the Tract. Some have found it hard to accept Newman's surprise as quite genuine. As Brilioth put it, 'one must feel surprise that Newman does not seem to have foreseen at all the storm he was conjuring up'.[107] This was in complete contrast to Ward. Ward was convinced from the start, that the Tractarians would completely electrify the University and the Church.[108] Moreover, Newman's dismay at the reaction was the more surprising, given that he always regarded Tract 90 as an experiment. He felt he was straining the bounds of what was permissible as if to see how much he could get away with. Was it not disingenuous not to expect that it might attract condemnation? As Paul Avis has put it, for many of Newman's erstwhile supporters, the whole tenor of the Tract seemed to say 'turn me down'.[109] Furthermore, if, as he complained, the Tract was only designed to meet the needs of one set of his followers, 'by what contrivance did he hope to keep it out of the hands of those for whom it was inexpedient?'[110] Above all, why was Newman apparently so ready to give up his important public role and throw away the mantle of leadership once it became clear that what had always been a 'gamble', had not, after all, paid off?

It seems that Newman convinced himself that in condemning Tract 90 in their charges, the Bishops had committed some kind of betrayal of himself and thereby humiliated him. Newman was always liable to be sensitive to criticism from this quarter, since for him, his Bishop was, in effect, 'his pope'. Precisely because he regarded episcopal charges as a vital organ of doctrinal expression of the visible Church, the charges were bound to be regarded in a serious and solemn light. In this way, Newman came to regard some of the hostile charges to Tract 90 as 'virtually silencing a portion of the truth in particular dioceses'.[111] In taking this attitude, Newman was very different from both Keble and Pusey who consequently never felt the viability of their own positions threatened by the episcopal reaction. However, there was a more personal element in the sense of betrayal that Newman came to feel. This sense of betrayal partly stemmed from the apparent breach of some sort of 'understanding' which Newman felt he had reached with his sympathetic diocesan, the mild-mannered Bishop Bagot, whereby in response to Newman's closing the series of the tracts, the Bishop apparently was to refrain from criticising Tract 90. How justified was the claim of episcopal breach of trust, intolerance and even persecution?

With regard to Bishop Bagot, such claims would be especially misplaced. Many years later, Bagot's chaplain, Francis Paget, left a record that illustrated Bagot's kindly sympathies and extreme anxiety not to offend the leaders of the Movement, though his High Churchmanship could not but have made him uneasy about the Movement's later direction and development. In one such note about Newman, Paget recorded that, 'I have the strongest desire that it should be known how deeply Bishop Bagot admired, venerated and loved him'. Moreover, in 1879, in a letter to Bishop Eden, who succeeded Newman as Vicar of St Mary's in 1843, Paget related to Bishop Bagot that,

> nothing is so indelibly fixed in my mind as the earnestness of his desire to shield and shelter those whom he entirely believed to be bringing back sound doctrine and saintly life. He came of a race of most faithful 'old fashioned' churchmen, to whom nine-tenths of what was staggering the men of that day, presented nothing at all staggering, or novel, or Roman.[112]

This, of course, applied to Bagot's attitude to the early and even middle phase of the Movement. By 1841, he had cause for alarm, though he yet bent over backwards to avoid outright rebuke. Did Newman sufficiently appreciate all this?

In fact, Newman was on the whole fair and for the most part gracious and respectful in the view he took of his diocesan. In the *Apologia*, he made clear that 'I impute nothing whatever to him, he was ever most kind to me'.[113] Nevertheless, with Newman, insinuation could have more edge than open criticism. Certainly, Newman's account of a supposed bargain which he struck with his Bishop and its eventual breach by the rest of the bench, casts an unfair shadow over Bagot's good name. The evidence for Newman's 'understanding' with

Bagot needs to be reappraised to see exactly whose conduct was at fault.

According to Abbott,

> in no part of the 'Apologia' does its author show himself more inaccurate and unfair than in his account of a supposed 'understanding' between himself and the Bishops after the condemnation of Tract 90 by the Heads of the Oxford colleges.[114]

For Abbott, Newman's conduct towards Bishop Bagot amounted to 'sharp practice'. In so far as any verbal agreement was reached, it appears that Newman agreed to withdraw Tract 90 from sale, but in his own time, so as to avoid the suggestion that the Tract had been withdrawn at episcopal bidding because it was doctrinally unsound. Newman was to pronounce his 'own condemnation' by means of a submissive published letter to his Bishop. In turn, the Bishop apparently promised not to condemn the Tract himself publicly. Newman felt that he had gained what he wanted,[115] and that he had obtained a definite understanding not only that the Bishop of Oxford but 'they' – presumably meaning the bench of Bishops – 'would not condemn it', either jointly or synodically. Pusey repeated this claim in his *Historical Preface* to a republication of Tract 90 in 1866. Pusey then declared that it was he who had been the medium for conveying to Newman Bagot's opinion that the Bishops as a body would not censure the Tract or series as a whole, and that at most only perhaps two or three Bishops might 'mention it' in their charges.[116] However, in the *Apologia*, Newman had gone further. Newman argued that 'they' – an ambiguous word, as he never defined who 'they' were – had not only said that they would not condemn Tract 90, but also allowed Newman to let it continue to be sold.[117]

The Bishop of Oxford clearly was surprised that Tract 90 continued to be reprinted. In fact, the Tract was republished on the very day that Newman's published *Letter to the Bishop of Oxford* appeared. Newman was being disingenuous in making it appear that Bishop Bagot had, or could have, tied the hands of his fellow Bishops. It was simply not in the Bishop of Oxford's power to have done this. On the contrary, as Abbott argues,

> Newman was expressly warned that the individual action of the Bishops (not 'some' of the Bishops) would (not 'might perhaps') not be in any definite way influenced by his arrangement with his own Diocesan. Some, even though he quietly dropped Tract 90, would think it necessary to condemn it (not 'say something about it'). Some

> might not. There was no 'understanding' at all that could affect the individual right of the Bishops to speak or to keep silence.[118]

Moreover, Newman's later claims as to the existence of such an 'understanding' are not even borne out by his own correspondence which is, in fact, entirely silent on the matter. In his letters to his sister, Jemima, in April 1841, Newman never mentions any 'understanding', and he appeared to sense and accept that other Bishops might take a very different line from that of his own diocesan.[119] Moreover, even in the *Apologia* Newman subsequently contradicted his statement that 'they' 'said they would not condemn it'. For soon after that statement, Newman conceded that 'they said they could not answer for what individual Bishops might perhaps say about the Tract in their own charges. I agreed to their conditions'.[120] At the very least, it would seem that Newman was guilty of a certain obfuscation and blurring of the question.

In the event, a majority of the Bishops did exercise their right to censure the Tract in their charges. Yet, Newman still raised the complaint of breach of trust and unfair practice, rather bitterly observing in the *Apologia*, that 'a clever man had warned me against "understandings" some years before: I have hated them ever since'.[121] Had Bagot perhaps broken faith? Although he never said so, for his part, the Bishop must have felt that it was Newman who had not kept to the spirit of his part of the supposed bargain. Newman's published letter to him, which, he confided to Manning, he had composed 'how unwillingly you know',[122] had contained no real self-condemnation. As Abbott concluded, 'while disclaiming any desire to procure Episcopal sanction for what were called distinctive Tractarian doctrines', Newman 'practically circulated them under' Bagot's authority. Moreover, the Tract which the Bishop,

> had pronounced 'objectionable' was still circulated in his diocese, and the other Tracts had not been 'discontinued' in accordance with his 'advice' as he interpreted it. Lastly Tract 90 was being defended in Oxford by one of Newman's followers and, as was publicly avowed, with Newman's sanction, upon grounds which increased the scandal that it had already caused. A similar defence was being circulated on the continent.[123]

In this light, Newman's later sharp attack on Bagot – which belied his assertion of constant submissive reverence in the *Apologia* – for 'the incredible weakness of doing what he did, at the bidding of great people in London',[124] was less than fair. Yet, even Bagot's chaplain,

Paget, later explained the Bishop's increased tone of opposition to the Tractarians after 1841 on account of his succumbing to 'Lambeth atmosphere'.[125] In fact, if anything, Lambeth was a counsel for moderation.

Certainly, like other Bishops in 1841, Bagot was under intense pressure to condemn not only Tract 90 but the Movement as a whole. This pressure came not so much from Lambeth or London clerical dignitaries, but the evangelical laity. Alongside other Bishops such as Blomfield of London, Bagot was actually assailed by Evangelicals and Low Churchmen for taking a far too moderate, sympathetic line with the Tractarians. The evidence of this relentless pressure needs to be set alongside Tractarian complaints of episcopal interference. For instance, the Evangelical Vicar of Islington, Daniel Wilson, later complained that there was no combined movement against Tract 90 by the bench of Bishops. Significantly, Wilson contrasted the lack of a collective episcopal stand in 1841-2 against Tract 90, with the collective protest which they would make in 1850 against error in an opposite direction, namely the Privy Council's decision in the Gorham case which appeared to leave Baptismal Regeneration an open question for the Church of England. Referring to the muted response to Tractarianism, Wilson lamented that,

> many even of those bishops who in their public charges expressed their disapproval of those doctrines mingled their admonitions with so many expressions of respect for the motives of the movement party, as greatly to weaken the effect of their reproof.[126]

In particular, Bagot's own charge was attacked by Evangelicals for its conciliation of Tractarianism. The moderate and learned Evangelical divine, William Goode, complained to that arch anti-Tractarian, but by no means Low Churchman, C.P. Golightly, that he had read Bagot's charge,

> with very great pain...he is a weak and dishonest man, evidently completely taken in by the representations of the Tractarians... It is a great trial of one's patience and forebearance in not taking him to task for it.[127]

However, Bagot's refusal to take a stronger line was actually commended by Lambeth. Archbishop Howley, himself something of a High Churchman, rejoiced that the Bishop had shunned the more popular course.[128] In fact, it was the Bishop who was behind Palmer's *Narrative of Events Connected with the Publication of the 'Tracts for the Times',* first published in 1843, in which Palmer broadly distinguished the early phase of the Movement which he defended, from its later excesses. Bagot was responsible for the first 1843 edition, being as moderate and sympathetic to Pusey and Newman as it was. For in the 1883 edition, Palmer recalled that he had expunged from the first draft of the 1843 edition, letters from various Churchmen condemning the Romish tendencies. He made clear that this had been at the Bishop's suggestion, but given the subsequent course of events, Palmer wished that that material had been left in.[129]

Of course, not all the Bishops adopted the gentle, considerate tone of Richard Bagot. Some High Church critics of Tract 90 regretted any indiscriminate criticism, especially where it seemed to involve an apparent slighting or denial of truths which they felt integral to traditional Anglicanism. Even Samuel Wilberforce, quite out of sympathy with the Movement since at least 1838, could criticise the charge of Henry Pepys, Bishop of Worcester, as 'essentially unchurch', while he felt the charge of J.B. Sumner, Bishop of Chester, betrayed 'the thorough ingraining of Puritanism'.[130] Wilberforce also thought the charge of Charles Sumner, Bishop of Winchester, was 'too little Church in his conscientious opposition to Tract errors'. What Wilberforce feared was that such a line of criticism would 'form all into two sects: one "Anti-Church", the other "Tract", instead of Church-anti-Tract versus Newman'.[131]

Yet, the consensus of the episcopal response to Tract 90 was more akin to 'Church-anti-Tract' or High Church than 'Puritan' or 'ultra-Protestant'.[132] The critique of Tract 90 was largely a High Church alarm at apparent disloyalty to the Anglican formularies that for some seemed suspiciously akin to the latitudinarian evasiveness that seemed to characterise the old Low Churchmanship.[133] The Bishops simply took it for granted that Catholicism, properly understood, was already enshrined in the Articles. Moreover, it was precisely because many of the Bishops were of the old High Church stamp, and some connected with the 'Hackney Phalanx', that they had had such high hopes of the Movement in its early phase. This made them still tread carefully even after 1841.[134] When William Copeland, one of Newman's younger followers, complained that Newman was being treated like 'a criminal under sentence pronounced by the rulers of our own church', Edward Churton fairly retorted that 'there is scarcely a single bishop...who has not spoken as much in praise as censure'.[135]

High Churchmen indeed had cause to criticise 'the almost frantic desire for persecution manifested by some persons'. Edward Churton felt that the complaints about the charges were far-fetched, telling Pusey in December 1841, 'I can only say that the church of all times will know how to make a distinction between those who patiently abide under persecution, and those who do all they can to bring it upon themselves'.[136] It would seem that Newman was included in this. Even his friend, John Bowden, felt the need to caution him at this time: 'check your zeal for martyrdom'.[137]

Not all the Tractarians themselves believed that they were ill-treated by the Bishops. In contrast to Newman's view, even Frederick Oakeley in the 'Romanising' vanguard, could yet pay gracious tribute to the attitude of the Bishops. In his very defence of Tract 90, Oakeley candidly defended the Bishops, maintaining that, 'we are...under especial obligation to our Bishops, to aid them in the course of moderation and forebearance which they have hitherto maintained, amid many temptations to deviate from it, under the excitement of this anxious controversy'.[138] Moreover, even in the wake of the often critical episcopal charges, Oakeley did not alter his opinion. In an article in the then 'ultra' *British Critic*, in January 1843, Oakeley was no less generous. According to Oakeley,

> Even by the admissions and very complaints of those persons who are most opposed to us, the general tenor of the charges delivered during the past year have been in an unprecedented degree in favour of Catholic views, and in condemnation of the lax and rationalistic opinions and usages that have so long been stealing upon the English church.[139]

Pusey's *Letter to the Archbishop of Canterbury* in 1842, while criticised by some High Churchmen for a disrespectful tone towards the Church authorities, was drawn up with the avowed object of analysing the episcopal charges in such a way as, 'to show that some do not object to our main principles, but to matters of detail, that others...do not object to our principles at all, but to certain principles which they conceive to be ours'.[140] In short, as Pusey told James Hope, 'I wished also to show that we were not really so condemned as we seemed to be'. A significant difference with Newman indicated here, is that in the last portion of this private letter of Pusey's to Hope, marked 'private', referring to Pusey's *Letter to the Archbishop*, occurs the statement, 'Newman was against it from the first; he thought Harrison (the Archbishop's chaplain) wanted to commit me to say things which Newman thought I could not say; in a word to Harrison's own views'.[141]

In fact, Pusey's attitude was typically muddled. On the one hand, in his desire to defend Newman, he criticised the Bishops for speaking out. On the other hand, he takes comfort in the fact that they had spoken so guardedly and falteringly. In his *Historical Preface*, Pusey lamented that the Bishops had not kept silent as he felt Newman had been led to believe they would. However, Pusey did stress that only twelve English Bishops had not done so, and contradicted Newman's point about 'Lambeth atmosphere'. Pusey felt that Archbishop Howley 'more than any other, understood the objects of the Tracts and of the whole "movement"'.[142] This was praise indeed.

Newman's more devoted followers, including some who did not follow him into the Roman Catholic Church, continued to propagate and even embellish the legend of their leader's ill-treatment. They argued that the episcopal charges were the cause and not the consequence of the Romeward movement. This view was enshrined in Copeland's unpublished narrative of the Movement, completed in 1878; in Dean Church's influential and masterly history published in 1889; and in Liddon's four-volume biography of his great mentor, Pusey, in the early 1890s. On the other hand, the alternative interpretation of High Churchmen such as Churton, though finding less of a public expression, continued to be argued in private correspondence. In fact, for over a quarter of a century, Churton debated the matter in correspondence with Copeland. For instance, in 1860 after a letter from Copeland in which the latter complained as if it were yesterday that the Oxford Heads and Bishops had driven Newman out of the Church of England, Churton retorted indignantly, 'how any of their acts could be considered to enforce the secession of J.H. Newman, or to justify it, I do not see, nor shall I ever see. You love the man too much to see the question in its true light'.[143] Churton continued to insist that the bulk of the episcopate had acted fairly and judiciously. As he told Copeland in 1865,

> The bishops seem then to have thought it their duty to act the part of the Isthmus of Corinth, and were only afraid lest the encroaching tide on one side or the other would burst over them. We are all inclined to prefer a course which may leave us to take our ease. They little thought of the tragical consequences to a mind of such fine fibres as John Henry Newman's. They only wished to be left alone, safe on shore, 'high and dry' as before.[144]

It was a view, even in the very metaphor chosen, that accorded remarkably precisely with that of Thomas Arnold. It was Arnold who, in similar vein, likened the Bishops in the Tract 90 controversy, 'to ships caught in a tornado, whose wisdom is to cast all their anchors firmly and wait till the fierceness of the gale is spent'.[145] Moreover, Churton, who had once been close to establishment circles, was able to corroborate his viewpoint by recalling the testimony of a leading protagonist, Charles Blomfield, Bishop of London. Churton made much of Blomfield's comment to him about Tract 90, that it 'would tend to break the church asunder'.[146] Both Blomfield and Howley clearly felt let down by the Movement. This sense of disillusionment in the highest quarters had been conveyed by Thomas Henderson to Pusey back in 1842. Henderson confided to Pusey,

> A fortnight since, the Bishop of London said this to myself: 'I remarked yesterday to the Archbishop and he quite agreed with me, that we had been worse treated by the Oxford writers than we have ever been by the Evangelical party in the whole course of our government in the Church'...'They might have strengthened the Church, and I believe they intended to do so – they are now doing all they can undesignedly to weaken her. But she will survive the infatuation of friends as well as the hostility of foes'.[147]

Old High Churchmen honestly felt that they had the most cause to feel betrayed. In the reaction to the Movement, there was a real danger that 'Puritanism' might triumph and that the sober values of traditional High Churchmanship might become marginalised as in the mid-seventeenth century.[148] Certainly, by the 1850s representatives of the High Church party had lost pre-eminence in the counsels of Church and State which they had enjoyed in the pre-Tractarian era. It was such considerations that gave an edge to Churton's impatience with some of the assumptions of Tractarian hagiography. After all, it was High Churchmen like Churton who had shown themselves ready to bear obloquy on behalf of the Tractarians. Yet, what had been the thanks they had received, and what had been the consequences? As Churton, in reference to Newman, objected to Copeland in the 1860s,

> If all this evil comes from the loss of that one man, why do you lay all the blame on the Inquisitors, and none on the victim, who fled rather than endure[d] the torture? And fled, when he knew that, if he had stayed, there were hundreds, whom he was leaving behind,...who were ready to endure the torture with him.[149]

Churton's disillusionment was echoed by Palmer of Worcester. Palmer only slowly came to terms with Newman's abandonment of his earlier moorings. His chivalrous defence of Newman not only in 1841 but in the first edition of the *Narrative*, extended to as late as 1844. The extent of Palmer's misplaced confidence in Newman's loyalty was revealed in a letter to Pusey after Newman's final resignation as Vicar of St Mary's in late 1843. Palmer was even then able to assert that he 'never had, any the least doubt of his steadfastness in the church, and his wish to prevent Romish tendencies – and I am sure that this step, however it may be interpreted, is not to be understood as any symptom of defection'.[150]

Palmer still hoped that Newman might emerge from his Littlemore retirement, to repudiate Ward, Oakeley and the *British Critic*. It was only when Palmer came to review Newman's last volume of Anglican sermons in the *English Review*, that such illusions were finally laid to rest. Palmer had come to find, in G.S. Faber's prescient words, that Newman was too much of 'a burden to any determined excuser'.[151] Palmer was now provoked by a caustic note in Newman's *Sermons on subjects of the day*, in which Newman gave space to criticising the episcopal censures of Tract 90. Palmer felt the unfairness of this, given Newman's own admission that he had always thought that his principles 'without a strong safeguard' would tend towards 'the theology of Rome', especially when Newman manifestly had failed to provide such a safeguard. Palmer was led to conclude that,

> it seems as if there were in this, some want of humility – some reluctance to take blame, unless it were shared with others... We are of the opinion that, considering all this, Mr. Newman ought to have abstained from such very severe condemnation of the church, and of her prelates.[152]

Of course, Newman was quite entitled to have changed his position and to lose faith in the Church of England. Opponents of the Movement deemed secession to Rome to be a much more open, manly course than that adopted by those Tractarians who would remain as 'Puseyite' or 'Anglo-Catholic' members of the Church of England. It was just that in Palmer's view there had to be a price. There were inevitable consequences to Newman's shift, and Anglican authorities could not be blamed for a certain criticism and censure of him. In the final 1883 edition of his *Narrative*, Palmer took a broad, measured view which yet summed up the essence of the High Church complaint at Newman's course very clearly. As Palmer now wrote of Newman,

> If this great man had been really faithful to the Church of England, his own condemnation (however unjust in his own opinion) should not have prevented him from interfering to check the excesses of young writers, which were doing such harm to the church... But he was detached from the church. He was like the shepherd 'that seeth the wolf coming, and leaveth the sheep, and fleeth', whose 'own the sheep are not'.[153]

Churton and Palmer's later attitude was shared by William Ewart Gladstone, who was always as much a committed Churchman as politician. Gladstone was another of that large group who were supporters of the Movement up to a certain point, but were not classifiable as 'Tractarian'. As late as 1840, Gladstone was confident, in the same way as Churton and Palmer were, that certain extravagances of Tractarianism eventually could be brought into harmony with the older High Churchmanship. After Tract 90, the process of gradual disillusionment set in. Complaints about episcopal persecution came to irritate him. As he told his friend Manning, in relation to Pusey's *Letter to the Archbishop*, 'Pusey's note is still one sided. What made the charges of the Bishops as unfavourable as they are? Was there no cause but their own ignorance?...they were themselves caused by error or excess'.[154]

Given revelations of Newman's wavering allegiance, Gladstone felt that Newman was disqualifying himself from a right to pass judgment on the state of Catholic principles in the Church of England. By 1843, it was clear to Gladstone that enormous advances in the progress of Catholic principles had been made in a decade and that Newman had done much to foster this. However, what was extraordinary was the despondent way in which Newman now seemed to disregard it all. As Gladstone remarked in dismay,

> that he does not see the English Church in her members to be growing more Catholic from year to year, I am astonished. Yet can he be not aware how much more plain and undeniable the sway of Catholic principles has become in the Church of England, since the time when he entertained no doubt about it? Can he have measured the drifting movement of his own mind, seen what the most vulgar observer, the most cursory reader, cannot fail to see? Is he under the delusion that he is fixed, and that others are moving away from truth, when in fact all have been running

> in the same direction but he faster than others, and I fear somewhat past his peak.[155]

In truth, it cannot fairly be maintained that Newman was driven out of the Church of England. The condemnation of the Tract by the Bishops may well have opened his eyes to the incompatibility of contemporary Anglicanism with Catholicism or Antiquity – and to this extent, as a Roman Catholic he could owe them an albeit back-handed complimentary debt of gratitude – but the emergence of this conviction in the early 1840s was always latent within himself. Arguably, Newman's relationship to the Church of England was always *ab extra*, an external one.[156] His aim was to see how great an 'infusion of Catholic truth' the Church of England could bear without damage. There was always the real possibility for Newman, 'that the metal will burst in the operation', and so it proved. It would not be difficult for Anglican critics, in consequence, to argue that Newman's own religious odyssey was a personal, individual matter, for all the discipleship that he built up, and quite a distinct phenomenon from the 'Catholic movement' that had 'sprung up out of the genuine English Church soil'. As one such Anglican critic explained, Newman took up the Oxford Movement,

> as distinct from originating, and joined, as distinct from creating it. He saw a rising movement as a fact, and he saw it at its rise. He saw around him a genuine ground of Church temper, hope, aspiration, beginning to work; he was in the midst of a circle of such Church of England minds. The movement had a pre-existence in them; he took it from them. He was their convert originally, and not their teacher; and a convert of a particular kind: that is to say, never to the absolute acceptance of their ground, but only to the trial of it. In this way Mr. Newman adopted a movement, threw himself into it, and lent the whole form, fertility and richness of his mind to it. It advanced and spread rapidly with such a powerful aid; perhaps more rapidly even than was exactly healthy for it... But the use which this movement thus had of Mr. Newman's mind, was a loan, alas! and not a gift: the support was had, and not the supporter.[157]

In truth, Newman never adequately realised the objective existence of the Church of England. He was never able, even in his 'fiercest' High Anglican phase, to appreciate 'that his church membership was something far above his citizenship'.[158] From such a viewpoint, the converts to Roman Catholicism in the mid-1840s would be dismissed as having never really been in unison with static, traditional Anglicanism, anyway. Certainly, the Evangelical background of many of those who did convert, in contrast to the commonly High Church background of those Tractarians who remained, gives probably more than circumstantial credibility to the argument.[159] At any rate, there was basis enough for the above Anglican critic to conclude, in regard to Newman's own secession,

> that our Church has been left upon an original objection to her, and upon no other ground really. We have in the theological movement before us, an instance of a body of opinion rising in the Church, passing through her, and going out of her, without ever having really belonged to her.[160]

From this angle, Tract 90 could have seemed like an expedient to meet this 'original objection', and as such, was doomed and deserved to fail.

CONCLUSIONS: LOSS AND GAIN

It has become clear that Tract 90 was the pivotal episode in Newman's Oxford and Anglican career, and the one on which his final journey into the Church of Rome partly hinged. Much more could have been said about the theological merits both in favour and against the arguments and content of the Tract itself. However, this is ground that has been well covered in innumerable theological studies. Certainly, the impression should not be given that in the long-term, Newman necessarily 'lost' the theological argument. Not only is that issue not central to our study, but the answer ultimately depends on one's particular theological or denominational standpoint. Nonetheless, viewed strictly historically, Newman ultimately 'won' the argument in the limited sense that his principle of 'catholic' interpretation of the Articles gradually came to win widespread acceptance within the Church of England.

This wider acceptance was already evident by the mid-1860s when Pusey published his *Historical Preface.* It became axiomatic for Anglican Churchmen to maintain that Newman's method of interpretation was no more 'forced' or any less 'natural' than that preferred by Evangelicals on the one hand or by Broad Churchmen on the other.[161] In fact, the growing theological polarisation characteristic of the post-Tractarian Church of England and emergence of more rigid

Church party divisions, helped Newman's view to triumph as a tenable option. Catholic 'latitude' became acceptable, as the so-called 'liberal Catholicism' emerged. Distinct as it was from the rising liberal Protestantism, 'liberal Catholicism' flourished in the climate of greater theological pluralism in the Church, once the initial 'Oxford controversy' had died down.

Ironically it was to be the long-term success of Newman's view that the Articles were compatible with 'catholic' teaching that enabled subsequent generations of Anglo-Catholics to rest at greater ease than they otherwise might in the Church of England, and to refrain from following Newman's example in seceding to Rome. In short, Newman's Tract 90 was more successful in the very long term than Newman had the patience to foresee at the time. The sense of resentment felt by Tractarians like Copeland who remained Anglicans, at the authorities' treatment of Newman, was sharpened by this very consciousness of later success and fulfilment.

Yet, while later Anglo-Catholics benefited from the gradual growth in tolerance of different shades of theological opinion in the Church of England, including the principle of Tract 90 itself, it cannot be said that Newman the Roman Catholic could have welcomed this belated trend. It came twenty years too late, and probably succeeded then in putting the brake on potential conversions to Rome which Newman had evidently envisaged in the early 1840s. Moreover, while his view of the Articles had benefited from support from the younger generation of liberals at Oxford such as A.P. Stanley, with Stanley and Jowett defending Tract 90 on latitudinarian principles in the mid-1840s, this was always in part a source of embarrassment for Newman. Tactical support from Oxford liberals might be one thing, but Newman and above all, Pusey, remained adamant that rationalism was the great evil of the day. Newman, and Pusey in his *Historical Preface*, stressed that the claim to 'catholic latitude' as proposed in Tract 90 could not be applied to the fundamental Catholic doctrinal verities of the 'faith once delivered to the saints'.[162] Therefore, they were adamant that the principles of Tract 90 could in no way support a general latitudinarianism in regard to creeds and tests, and did not discountenance the principle of subscription which the Tractarians had stoutly defended against the Oxford liberals in the mid-1830s.

However, this did not prevent a much later generation of Anglo-Catholic commentators from anachronistically appealing to a doctrinal liberalism and relativism in ridiculing the Protestant High

Church opponents of Newman's arguments for 'elasticity' in interpreting the Articles in the 1840s, which in other circumstances they would have been the first to disavow. Moreover, the Tractarian reluctance to submit to or obey the dictates of episcopal authority in the early 1840s, was to leave an unhappy legacy to later Anglo-Catholicism which was to carry resistance to such authority to ever greater lengths. In fact, many contemporary opponents of the Movement had cause to note the apparent contradiction between the theoretical exaltation of episcopal authority by the Tractarians, and at the same time, a practical evasion, if not repudiation of that authority if exercised in what leaders of the Movement deemed to be defiance of true Catholic principles.[163] Ultimately Newman was perhaps more sensitive to this apparent contradiction than many of his followers, especially those who remained in the Church of England. It was probably a factor in his decision to retire once and for all from the public Anglican arena in 1843. Certainly, the cynical view that developed among many of those who did not take Newman's honest step was less creditable – this was the argument that 'some among us may... have been unfaithful both to our duties and to our knowledge of Scripture and Antiquity, by aggrandizing the Episcopate in the tacit depression of the Presbyterate'.[164] It seemed too coincidental that it was only when he was at the receiving end of episcopal authority that these first doubts should have been raised.

At the heart of our discussion, though, has not been the respective theological 'pros' and 'cons' of Tract 90, or the issue of who 'won' or who 'lost' ultimately. The central question, and one of perennial fascination, has been what the Tract 90 episode reveals about the Anglican Newman's personality and human leadership, and above all, his place in the history of the Oxford Movement. Our study has brought to light some slight flaws in Newman's personality and psyche. These flaws need to be set alongside Newman's undoubted literary genius and his moral and spiritual heroism. Nothing that has been argued here could or should detract from Newman's holiness of life, the quality of his preaching and ability to inspire and enthuse a whole generation of young men with religious fervour and a sense of mission. The positive, dynamic aspect of Newman's religious odyssey, the drama and poetry as well as negative features should never be forgotten. In this context, while the reaction to Tract 90 was a trial for Newman and helped to undermine his confidence in Anglicanism, it should not be argued that Newman became a Roman Catholic simply in recoil from this defeat, or from any mere display of wounded pride. Of course, his grounds for conversion were much deeper and more positive than this. In short, Newman's later jocular refrain, 'Oxford made us Catholics' does not represent the whole truth. One must not overlook the deeply spiritual motivation at the heart of Newman's religious quest. The search for holiness and the mark of sanctity as a formal note of the true Church became an abiding concern after 1842.[165] Ultimately, Newman became a Roman Catholic because he could no longer be sure of his own salvation outside her communion.

Newman was a great religious teacher and moral exemplar in his generation. At the same time, it is unfortunate that many have been almost blind in overlooking, ignoring or denying some of the weaknesses and flaws that the Tract 90 episode revealed in the Anglican Newman. At the time, and not only to avowed enemies, these flaws were more apparent than later hagiography has allowed. Sometimes, it is true, there were personal reasons for some of the animus against him. There were those such as Richard Whately who had befriended the young Newman at Oxford and to whom Newman owed much, but between whom misunderstanding arose and a parting of the ways. It may seem harsh to suggest that Newman had a martyr-complex, but he could exaggerate the extent to which people were against him, as the way he reacted to the Bishops' charges proved. Newman was conscious that many thought him devious. He later recalled that for a time, nearly the whole world thought that at Oxford he had deliberately pursued a policy characterised by deep design and conscious duplicity.[166] Yet, was there not some basis to such criticism? Certainly, there were those even in sympathy with him who could accuse him of over-subtlety, and of literary or verbal sleights of hand. Typical of an instinctive reaction to Tract 90 aroused even among natural allies, was that of a Yorkshire High Churchman, Miller of Scarborough. Commenting on Miller's tract against No. 90, Edward Churton, himself resident in Yorkshire, concluded that Tract 90,

> has certainly given some, who were well disposed to us, an impression that Newman is not an honest man...I do think, with all respect for him, and great admiration of all that he has written, that his mind, which is a mind of great subtlety, played him a trick, and made him write what our Yorkshire common sense...cannot digest.[167]

Examples of such an impression being inspired are very numerous, and it is nearly always Tract 90 that was cited as the most glaring instance of the manifestation of this apparent trait in the Anglican Newman. As Gladstone put it, shortly after Newman's death in 1890, 'Tract 90 opened a joint in Newman's armour, it showed that in his wonderful genius there was a distinct flaw – a strong sophistical element'.[168] Moreover, liberals such as Jowett, Huxley, Henry Sidgwick and Lord Acton, all alluded to an element of sophistry and even habitual untruthfulness in Newman's writings and argument.[169] Many felt there was an often unconscious sceptical tendency in his remorseless logical applications. As the historian, G.M. Young has remarked of him,

> He is always skimming along the verge of a logical catastrophe, and always relying on his dialectic agility to save himself from falling: always exposing what seems to be an unguarded spot and always revealing a new line of defence when the unwary assailant has reached it.[170]

Yet, Newman knew what he was doing. One can say that his method of argument was not to everybody's taste, and that it could repel as many as it might attract. Less subtle minds could all too easily misunderstand him and mistake his drift. Nonetheless, the grosser charge of deliberate dishonesty which Newman's harshest and least fair critics such as Abbott and his own embittered brother, Francis, freely raised, deserves to be discounted. The *Apologia* itself, for many, laid such a charge conclusively to rest. For even a hostile reviewer of the *Apologia* admitted that Newman had indeed,

> convincingly established his own personal truthfulness. Whatever in his cause or in his teaching may have seemed inconsistent with personal sincerity, we now see must be attributed to the very difficult circumstances in which he was placed, which at a certain period rendered a policy of reserve the only one possible for him.[171]

Nevertheless, even the *Apologia*, while settling some of the question marks over Newman's mental integrity in his favour, at the same time threw up some new doubts as to Newman's selectivity and interpretation of events surrounding the Oxford Movement which have become all too apparent in this essay. We have remarked upon his unfair dealing with opponents, to which he himself admitted in the *Apologia*. A glaring instance, for which he did not apologise, was his apparent misrepresentation of Hampden's position in his polemical *Elucidations* published in 1836. There was also a one-sided selectivity about many of the 'catenae patrum' which Newman constructed for various numbers of the *Tracts for the Times*. Certainly, there is ample room for faulting what has been called Newman's 'subjectivism', and the *Apologia* itself abounded in fresh instances of this. It was Julius Hare who accused the Anglican Newman, in the context of the latter's hostile view of Martin Luther, 'of a practice which has been gaining upon him, that of substituting the creations of his own mind for the realities of history'.[172] If this was true of Newman's portrayal of Luther and Lutheranism, the same can be applied to Newman's own, inevitably very personal, view of the history of the Oxford Movement and Tract 90.

Factual errors and mistatements can readily be detected in Newman's version of the Oxford events. We have seen that Newman could be unfair and perhaps mistaken in his estimate of the real principles and motives of the Anglican Bishops in the early 1840s. However, a specific, glaring instance of unfairness in the *Apologia* was Newman's somewhat ungracious as well as mistaken notice of Bishop Blomfield. In a travesty of Blomfield's real position, Newman accused Blomfield of having, 'for years engaged in diluting the high orthodoxy of the church by the introduction of the Evangelical body into places of influence and trust'.[173] Yet, this was the same Bishop who was linked to the 'Hackney Phalanx', had well demonstrated his High Church credentials at Chester,[174] and who as Bishop of London had himself been often accused of Tractarianism, not least on account of his influential episcopal charge in 1842. That charge was itself denounced for being Tractarian in inspiration,[175] and was reputed to have been instrumental in drawing more than one Low Churchman over into the Tractarian camp.[176]

Other instances of Newman's inaccuracies could be multiplied. Yet, there was probably far more of self-deception than deliberate distortion in them.[177] Given the nature, background, and real purpose of Newman's *Apologia* perhaps this should not surprise us. As Newman once candidly explained, he had a much better memory for what he called 'anxieties and deliverances' than actual outer facts and circumstances.[178] Thus, the latter perhaps could sometimes unconsciously be sacrificed or subordinated for an overall effect conveyed in the unfolding of the human and moral drama involved in the delineation of the 'anxieties and deliverances'. In a sense perhaps both elements – factual blemishes alongside the dramatic, heroic account – were inseparable in Newman's portrayal of events in which he had been so intimately involved. Thus, the *Apologia* deserves to be considered much more as autobiography than a full or authoritative history and elucidation of the *Tracts for the Times*.[179]

Newman was always at his strongest and most winningly persuasive when he was able to utilise the true religious passion which was always the great moral strength of the Oxford Movement and which gave it such a dynamic edge over the older, more prosaic High Churchmanship. It was a moral strength infused with Romanticism, and it was the combination of the two that explains the almost secret power which enabled the Movement to capture the hearts as well as the minds of the younger Oxford generation. This authentic voice of the Movement was much more evident in works such as the reply to Faussett and in the *Letter to Jelf* than in Tract 90 itself, with its logical nit-pickings.

The greatness of the *Apologia* lay in its recapturing of the religious passion integral to Newman's leadership of the Movement. It would be churlish to allow quibbles, albeit important, over its accuracy to overshadow our appreciation of this. In the last analysis, it is fitting that it should be through the medium of such a great literary work of art and chronicle of such a religious odyssey, that the full drama of the Movement and especially Tract 90 should be conveyed to us, even if that very medium can be shown to have been an often one-sided and distorting lens. For the revelation of Newman's flaws of intellect and even to an extent of character, cannot detract from his towering moral strength or status in the religious annals of nineteenth-century England. The Oxford Anglican Newman was a flawed genius, but a genius, nevertheless.

NOTES

1. The term 'Tractarian', defined as applicable to those who were 'the authors, editors and approvers of the *Tracts for the Times*', appears to have been first coined by the Master of the Temple, Christopher Benson. See C. Benson, *Discourses upon Tradition and Episcopacy* (London, 1839), p. 101; cf. *British Critic* XXVI (October, 1839), p. 508.

2. J.B. Marsden, *History of Christian Churches and Sects* (London, 1865), p. 40; M.C. Church (ed.), *Life and Letters of Dean Church*, R.W. Church to F. Rogers, 14 March 1841 (London, 1895), p. 33. For

full publishing data on Tract 90, see R. Imberg, *Tracts for the Times: a complete survey of all the editions* (Lund University, 1987), p. 133.

3. J.H. Newman, *Apologia pro Vita Sua; being a reply to a pamphlet entitled 'what then, does Dr. Newman mean?'* (London, 1864), p. 100. For the argument against accepting Newman's view, see F.L. Cross *John Henry Newman* (London, 1933), Appendix IV, 'The myth of July 14, 1833' pp. 162-3. The so-called old High Churchmen resented the later tendency to make too much of 1833 and thus impute too much specifically to the Oxford Movement in the wider Church revival. This was the view of the acknowledged leader of a dominant grouping among the pre-Tractarian High Churchmen, the 'Hackney Phalanx', Joshua Watson. See A. Webster, *Joshua Watson: the story of a layman* (London, 1954), p. 29. Cf. B. Harrison to W.E. Gladstone, 16 November 1843, Gladstone MSS, British Library, MS Add. 44204ff. pp. 114-15.

4. According to his former friend and one-time Fellow of Oriel, the renegade Spanish priest, Blanco White, Newman's sudden shift into union with the anti-Catholic Emancipation party against Robert Peel in 1829, represented, 'the first manifestation of the mental revolution...from which we have those very strange productions, entitled, Tracts for the Times'. J.H. Thom (ed.), *The life of the Rev. Joseph Blanco White, written by himself, with portions of his correspondence* (London, 1845) III, p. 131.

5. R.W. Church, *The Oxford Movement: twelve years* (London, 1892), p. 251.

6. T. Gornall, 'Newman's lapses into subjectivity', *Heythrop Journal* XXIII (1982), pp. 46-7.

7. See J.H. Newman, *Certain difficulties felt by Anglicans in Catholic teaching considered: in twelve lectures addressed in 1850 to the party of the religious movement of 1833* (London, 1850).

8. C. Dawson, *The Spirit of the Oxford Movement*, Fourth impression (London, 1945), chap. 2.

9. See P. Nockles, 'The Oxford Movement: historical background, 1780-1833', in G. Rowell (ed.), *Tradition renewed: the Oxford Movement conference papers* (London, 1986), pp. 24-50.

10. P. Nockles, 'Continuity and change in Anglican High Churchmanship in Britain, 1790-1850', Oxford D.Phil thesis, 1982 (to be published in revised form by CUP, *c*.1991).

11. P. Avis, *Anglicanism and the Christian Church: theological resources in historical perspective* (Edinburgh, 1989), p. 158.

12. J. Garbett, *Dr. Pusey and the University of Oxford* (Oxford, 1843), p. 8. cf. *Christian Remembrancer* I (April, 1841), pp. 425-6. Cf. G.V. Cox, *Recollections of Oxford* (London, 1870), p. 289. The comment on the Tractarians by the then Vice-Chancellor of the University, the High Churchman, A.T. Gilbert, Principal of Brasenose, is pertinent here; – 'At first rise, and for some succeeding years, they were looked upon not unfavourably by many of all ranks in the church', A.T. Gilbert to Duke of Wellington, 26 December 1839, Wellington MSS, 2/250/64, Southampton University Library.

13. *Remains of the late Richard Hurrell Froude M.A*. [Part I] Vol. I (London, 1838), p. 429. For convenience, the so-called 'old High Churchmen' or 'Z's' will be simply referred to in our text as High Churchmen, only the epithet 'traditional' being added where deemed appropriate. Such 'High Churchmen' are to be distinguished from unreserved and active adherents of the Oxford Movement, who will be described as 'Tractarian', though it is recognised that, as with all such labels, the distinctions were often less than clear-cut.

14. W.J. Copeland to the Warden of Keble (Talbot), 22 September 1879, Keble MSS, Keble College Library, Oxford.

15. W. Palmer to J.H. Newman, August 1843, Newman MSS, No. 50, Birmingham Oratory Library.

16. A. Mozley, *Letters and correspondence of John Henry Newman during his life in the English Church* (London, 1891), I, p. 484. R.H. Froude to J.H. Newman, 17 November 1833, cf. *Letters and Diaries of John Henry Newman* IV (London, 1981), pp. 98-9, J.H. Newman to J.W. Bowden, 13 November 1833.

17. J.H. Newman, *Apologia*, p. 108.

18. *Apologia*, p. 109.

19. *Apologia*, pp. 107-8.

20. A. Dwight Culler, *The imperial intellect: a study of Newman's educational ideal* (New Haven, 1955), p. 67, cf. H. Tristram (ed.), *John Henry Newman: autobiographical writings* (London, 1956), p. 90, also cf. F. Oakeley, *Historical notes on the Tractarian Movement* (London, 1865), p. 180.

21. *Apologia*, p. 132.

22. *Apologia*, pp. 133-4.

23. Testimonies to Newman's influence over undergraduates are numerous. The complaint of the Whig and anti-Tractarian Warden of New College, Philip Shuttleworth in 1836, can be taken as representative; – 'Our undergraduates I fear are much bitten by the

self-mortifying spirit of Newman and Pusey', P. Shuttleworth, 19 June 1841 (copy) Bodleian Library, Oxford, MS Eng. Hist. *c*.1033, f. 230. However, a contemporary American observer insisted that it was the MAs who were the most susceptible to Tractarian influence. See C.A. Bristed, *Five years in an English University* (New York, 1873), p. 82. By 1845, it was estimated that among the resident members of Convocation in Oxford, the Tractarians had a majority of nearly four to one J. Bateman, *Tractarianism as described in prophecy. A word to the wise on the Oxford crisis* (London, 1845), p. 43; cf. M. Ward, *The young Mr. Newman* (London, 1948), p. 321; cf. D. Newsome, *The parting of friends: a study of the Wilberforces and Henry Manning* (London, 1966), pp. 63-9.

24. J.C. Shairp, *Studies in poetry and philosophy* (London, 1868), p. 273, cf. J.C. Shairp, *John Keble* (London, 1866), p. 17. Cf. K. Lake, *Memorials of W.C. Lake* (London, 1901), pp. 49-50. Cf. A.I. Dasent, *John Thadeus Delane: editor of* The Times, *in his life and correspondence* (London, 1908) I, 20. Cf. W. Lockhart, *Cardinal Newman: reminiscences of fifty years since* (London, 1891), pp. 5-6. Cf. C.E. Mallet, *A History of the University of Oxford* (London, 1927) III, pp. 241-3.

25. *Apologia*, pp. 114-15.

26. Faussett was to be the victim of a satirical, if not scurrilous Tractarian caricature, painted by Thomas Mozley. See *British Critic* XXX [T. Mozley], 'The Oxford Margaret Professor' (July 1841), pp. 241-3. Cf. T. Mozley, *Reminiscences chiefly of Oriel College and the Oxford Movement* (London, 1882) II, p. 245. Faussett had long been honoured by Tractarians with the facetious nickname, 'Il Dottore Falsetto'. G. Tracey (ed.), *The Letters and Diaries of John Henry Newman* VI (London, 1984), p. 324.

27. *London Quarterly Review* XXIII, 'Mr. Kingsley and Dr. Newman' No. XLV (October, 1864), p. 147.

28. *Apologia*, p. 116.

29. *Apologia*, p. 117.

30. Samuel Wilberforce wrote of 'the mischievous delirium of publishing Froude's unguarded thoughts to a morbidly sensitive and unsympathetic age as this...that work has put back Church principles for fifty years'. Bodleian Library MS Wilberforce d.38, f. 130. Cf. A.R. Ashwell, *Life of the Rt. Rev. Samuel Wilberforce* I (London, 1880), p. 112, H.J. Rose to J. Watson, January 1838. Cf. W.F. Hook to W.E. Gladstone, 22 January 1839 Gladstone MSS B.L. MS Add. 44213f.19.

31. P. Brendon, 'Newman, Keble, and Froude's "Remains"', *Eng-*

lish Historical Review LXXXVII No. CCCXLV (October, 1972), p. 706. Newman's justification to Churton, of the decision to publish the 'Remains', is characteristically revealing; – 'I have never repented publishing them one single moment...I do dislike uncommonly to keep things in, and seem to be playing a double part'. G. Tracey (ed.), *Letters and Diaries* VI, p. 325, J.H. Newman to E. Churton, 3 October 1838. Cf. G. Tracey (ed.), *Letters and Diaries* VI, pp. 118-19, J.H. Newman to J. Keble, 21 August 1837.

32. J.H. Newman, *A letter to the Rev. Godfrey Faussett D.D. Margaret Professor of Divinity, on certain points of faith and practice* (Oxford, 1838).

33. G. Faussett, *The revival of popery: a sermon preached before the University of Oxford at St. Mary's... May 1838* third edition (Oxford, 1838), pp. vii-viii.

34. R. Bagot, *A charge delivered to the clergy of the diocese of Oxford* (Oxford, 1838), pp. 20-1. In private correspondence with Newman and Pusey, Bagot relentlessly stressed his continued sympathy with the apparent aims of the Movement at that date, and urged them not to be disheartened by his charge. See Pusey MSS Pusey House Library (P.H.L.) Oxford, R. Bagot to E.B. Pusey, 12 September 1838, cf. Pusey MSS P.H.L. Oxford, R. Bagot to J.H. Newman, 20 August 1838.

35. E.A. Abbott, *The Anglican career of Cardinal Newman* (London, 1892) II, p. 95.

36. P.B. Nockles, 'The great disruption: the University and the Oxford Movement' in M. Brock (ed.), *History of the University of Oxford* Vol. VI (to be published, 1991/2). Cf. W.R. Ward, *Victorian Oxford* (London, 1965) chap. 6.

37. R.W. Church, *Oxford Movement*, p. 154.

38. For further discussion of Newman's Oxford 'idea of a university', see A. Dwight Culler, *The imperial intellect*, chap. 3, pp. 96-120. For an example of Newman's romanticised, medievalist conception of a revived 'monastic' Oxford, see [J.H. Newman], 'Memorials of Oxford', *British Critic* XXIV (July 1838), pp. 133-44. Cf. [J.R. Hope-Scott], 'The statutes of Magdalen College', *British Critic* XXVI (January 1840), pp. 367-96 and R. Ormsby, *Memoirs of James Robert Hope-Scott of Abbotsford* (London, 1884) I, chap. 10.

39. *A letter of remonstrance, addressed to an undergraduate of the University of Oxford, concerning the tenets of Dr. Pusey and Mr. Newman* (Oxford, 1840), p. 20. Cf. [E. Fry] *The listener in Oxford* (London,

1839), p. 22.

40. M.C. Church (ed.), *The life and letters of Dean Church,* R.W. Church to F. Rogers, 14 March 1841 (London, 1895), p. 28.

41. Abbott, pp. 95-6.

42. J.H. Newman, *Lectures on the prophetical office of the Church viewed relatively to Romanism and popular Protestantism* (London, 1837), p. 20. In the second edition, the sentence, 'the Via Media has never existed' to which Rose so strongly objected, was altered to, 'the Via Media viewed as an integral system has scarcely had existence'.

43. T. Parker, 'The rediscovery of the Fathers in the seventeenth century Anglican tradition', J. Coulson and A.M. Allchin (eds), *The rediscovery of Newman: an Oxford symposium* (London, 1967), p. 41.

44. J.H. Newman, *Lectures on the prophetical office*, p. 30.

45. Abbott, p. 81. It must be said that Newman was never an uncritical admirer of Caroline divinity, so that to 'pick' and 'choose' would become a necessity for him. For instance, see Newman's comment to Churton as early as 1837; – 'How come [Jeremy] Taylor to be so liberal in his Liberty of Prophesying? And how far is Hammond tinctured as regards the Sacraments with Grotianism?' G. Tracey (ed.), *Letters and Diaries* VI, p. 41. J.H. Newman to E. Churton, 14 March 1837. See Note 98, for evidence of the application of this selective method in Tract 90.

46. J.W. Burgon, *Lives of twelve good men* I (London, 1889), p. 219, H.J. Rose to J.H. Newman, 13 May 1836.

47. *Apologia*, p. 212.

48. Newman had gone so far as to refer to the Articles in private, as countenancing 'a vile Protestantism'. T. Gornall (ed.), *Letters and Diaries of John Henry Newman* V (Oxford, 1981), p. 70, J.H. Newman to R.H. Froude, 13 May 1835.

49. *Apologia*, p. 232.

50. R.W. Church, p. 292.

51. Lambeth Palace Library Longley Papers I, f. 205, J.R. Hall to C.T. Longley, 23 March 1841.

52. (R. Whately), *The controversy between Tract No. XC and the Oxford tutors* (London, 1841), pp. 10-11.

53. P.H.L., Oxford. Pusey MSS, MS 'Memoir of Dr. Wynter' (1845). Joshua Watson's guarded support for the action of the Oxford Heads in 1841, and later, in 1845, is significant; – 'The cards were dealt to them; and if they had refused to play, they had surely failed in their duty to the University as "custodes judiciae academicae". Nothing

could release the body from their obligation to protect those entrusted to their charge from looking upon the bonds of subscription as a mere rope of sand.' E. Churton, *Memoir of Joshua Watson* (London, 1861) II, p. 152.

54. Lambeth Palace Library Tait Papers 77, f. 34. R. Scott to A.C. Tait, April 1841. Cf. J. Jordan, *A second appeal to the Rt. Rev. the Lord Bishop of Oxford* (Oxford, 1841).

55. [J.H. Newman], 'Remarks on certain passages in the Thirty-Nine Articles', *Tracts for the Times* No. 90, second edition (London, 1841), p. 4.

56. R.W. Church, p. 281.

57. P. Avis, *Anglicanism*, p. 226.

58. See S. Wix, *Reflections concerning the expediency of a Council of the Church of England and the Church of Rome* (London, 1818), p. 13. Cf. G. Tavard, *The quest for Catholicity: a study in Anglicanism* (London, 1963), pp. 149-50.

59. *Apologia*, pp. 159-60.

60. As Godfrey Faussett inconveniently pointed out, 'unfortunately for his object, the very questions he feels interested in leaving open, are for the most part precisely those which our Reformers were especially careful to close'. G. Faussett, *The Thirty-Nine Articles considered* (Oxford, 1841), p. 17.

61. F.W. Newman, *Contributions chiefly to the early history of the late Cardinal Newman*, second edition (London, 1891), p. 97.

62. H.P. Liddon, *The life of Edward Bouverie Pusey* II, fourth edition (London, 1894), pp. 162-3. As Brilioth tellingly puts it, 'here already occurs a shadow, which falls ever thicker over the path of progressive Anglo-Catholicism right down to the present day, the absence of any clear content in the idolised formula of catholicity'. Y. Brilioth, *The Anglican revival: studies in the Oxford Movement* (London, 1925), p. 155. Cf. G. Tavard, chap. 7.

63. J.R. Page, *The position of the Church of England in the catholic world suggested by a perusal of No. XC of the 'Tracts for the Times'* (London, 1844), p. 47.

64. Page, p. 10, nonetheless for all the ambiguity of his language, it cannot be maintained that Newman was formally advocating reunion at this stage. O. Chadwick, *The mind of the Oxford Movement* (London, 1960), p. 55.

65. Brilioth, p. 154. Newman himself later was dissatisfied with his own reasoning on the subject of Article 31, the 'sacrifice of

Masses'. This is significant in that it was to be the only portion of Tract 90 over which he ever came to express the slightest regret. See *Correspondence of John Henry Newman with John Keble and others ... 1839-1845. Edited at the Birmingham Oratory* (London, 1917), p. 76.

66. Abbott, p. 247. Bishop Knox later argued that Newman's assumption that the Articles supported a 'Catholic' as opposed to 'Protestant' position, 'finds no support in the Articles except by insisting on what the Articles do not say. Tract XC is a supreme example of the argument "ex silentio", the most unsafe of all historical or theological arguments'. E.A. Knox, *The Tractarian Movement, 1833-1845* (London, 1933) p. 260.

67. Abbott, p. 250.

68. R. Lowe, *Observations suggested by 'A few more words in support of No. 90'* (Oxford, 1841), pp. 20-1.

69. Lowe, p. 18.

70. Page, p. 198.

71. Page, p. 199.

72. Page, pp. 226-7, cf. W. Sewell, *A letter to the Rev. E.B. Pusey on the publication of No. 90 of the Tracts for the Times* (Oxford, 1841).

73. *Apologia*, p. 171.

74. *Apologia*, p. 182.

75. [J.H. Newman], 'Remarks' Tract 90 first edition (London, 1841), p. 4. In the second edition, 'stammering lips' was altered to, 'through the medium of indeterminate statements'. [J.H. Newman], 'Remarks' Tract 90 second edition (London, 1841), p. 4. See R. Imberg *Tracts for the Times: a complete survey*, pp. 163-4.

76. W.E. Gladstone, *Correspondence on Church and Religion* D.C. Lathbury (ed.) I (London, 1910), p. 281.

77. P.H.L., Pusey MSS, E.B. Pusey to J. Watson, 30 October 1839. Cf. P.H.L., Pusey MSS, E.B. Pusey to J.H. Newman, 11 September 1839.

78. Churton MSS, Sutton Coldfield, E. Churton to W.J. Copeland, 28 February 1860.

79. W. Palmer, *A treatise on the Church of Christ* first edition (London, 1838) I, p. 204.

80. Palmer, *Treatise* third edition (London, 1842), II, p. 214.

81. C.R. Elrington, *Subscription to the XXXIX Articles* (Dublin, 1842), p. 15, cf. H. Phillpotts, *A Charge to the clergy of the diocese of Exeter* (London, 1842) p. 28.

82. P.H.L., Pusey MSS, W. Palmer to J.H. Newman, 9 August 1841.

83. A. Mozley (ed.), *Letters of the Rev. J.B. Mozley* (London, 1885), p. 113, J.B. Mozley to A. Mozley, 13 March 1841. Cf. L.P.L. Williams Deposit 9/36; I. Williams to J. Keble, 22 March 1841. Cf. National Library of Scotland, Edinburgh, Hope-Scott MSS, MS 3668 pp. 173f. F. Rogers to J.R. Hope, 28 April 1841. However, Owen Chadwick has suggested another explanation. See O. Chadwick, *Mind of the Oxford Movement*, p. 54.

84. P.H.L., Pusey MSS, E. Churton to A.P. Perceval, 20 December 1841.

85. Birmingham Oratory Library, 'Tract 90 Correspondence', W.F. Hook to W.G. Ward, 20 March 1841.

86. W.R. Stephens, *The life and letters of Walter Farquhar Hook* (London, 1878) II, p. 136. W.F. Hook to W.E. Gladstone, 11 December 1841. Gladstone likewise initially accepted the Tract 'with surprising equanimity'. P. Butler, *Gladstone, Church, State and Tractarianism: a study of his religious ideas and attitudes, 1809-1859* (Oxford, 1982), p. 174.

87. Mozley, *Letters* II, p. 297. J.H. Newman to J.W. Bowden, January 1840. Cf. Birmingham Oratory Library Newman MSS, J.H. Newman to H.A. Woodgate, 3 March 1839.

88. E. Thompson, *A triumph of Christianity* (London, 1841), p. 20.

89. *Tracts for the Times*, No. XV (Oxford, 1834), p. 10. Cf. R. Imberg, *In Quest of Authority* (Lund, 1987), p. 96 and Imberg, *Complete Survey*, pp. 149-50.

90. Quoted in N. Wiseman, *A letter respectfully addressed to the Rev. J.H. Newman, upon some passages in his letter to the Rev. Dr. Jelf* (London, 1841), pp. 29-30.

91. Wiseman, p. 30; cf. Imberg, *In Quest*, p. 131.

92. Bodleian Library Oxford, Norris MSS MS Eng. Lett. *c*.790 fols. 82-3. J. Watson to H.H. Norris, 5 April 1841.

93. Watson MSS, St Mary's, Torquay (in private possession) M. Watson, MS, 'Reminiscences', pp. 46f. Cf. Bodleian MS. Eng. Lett. *c*.790, pp. 82-3ff. J. Watson to H.H. Norris, 5 April 1841.

94. J.H. Newman, *A letter addressed to the Rev. R.W. Jelf in explanation of No. 90 in a series called the Tracts for the Times* (Oxford, 1841), p. 7.

95. Newman, ibid., p. 11. However, some of Newman's critics complained that he garbled and twisted Lloyd's testimony to suit his own argument. See [Dr Bandini], 'Brief remarks on Mr. Newman's Letter to Dr. Jelf', Oxford, 23 March 1841 (printed sheet). Cf. W.J.

Baker, *Beyond port and prejudice: Charles Lloyd of Oxford* (Orono, Maine, 1981), pp. 211-12.

96. E.B. Pusey, *The Articles treated on in Tract 90 reconsidered and their interpretation vindicated* (Oxford, 1841), p. 5.

97. Liddon, *Life of E.B. Pusey* II, pp. 225-9.

98. F. Oakeley, *The subject of Tract XC examined* (London, 1841), p. 3.

99. W. Goode, *Tract XC historically refuted* (London, 1845), pp. 151-90, cf. W. Goode, *The case as it is* (London, 1842), pp. 1-80.

100. W. Ward, *William George Ward and the Oxford Movement* second edition (London, 1890), chap. 4.

101. Pusey, *The Articles treated on in Tract 90 reconsidered*, p. 5.

102. Ward, *William George Ward*, p. 173.

103. Cross, p. 125, cf. [W.K. Firminger], *What then did Dr. Newman do?* (Oxford, 1892) p. 16.

104. Imberg, *A Complete Survey*; and Imberg, *In Quest of Authority*.

105. Birmingham Oratory Library, 'Tract 90 Correspondence' No. 115, J.H. Newman, 7 April 1863.

106. Ibid.

107. Brilioth, p. 105.

108. Quoted in Cross, p. 115.

109. Avis, p. 226.

110. [Dr Bandini], 'Brief remarks on Mr. Newman's Letter', p. 3.

111. Newman complained of 'the growing consensus of the episcopal bench against the Catholic truth'. Bodleian Library MS Eng. Lett. d.102, pp. 103f. J.H. Newman to H.A. Woodgate, 8 November 1841, cf. Mozley, *Letters and correspondence of John Henry Newman* II, p. 352. J.H. Newman to J. Keble, 5 October 1841.

112. P.H.L., Bagot MSS, F. Paget to R. Eden, 24 January 1879.

113. *Apologia*, p. 174. Yet, elsewhere, Newman contradicts himself. For evidence of Newman's bitter comment on Bagot's 'incredible weakness', see note 124.

114. Abbott, p. 257. Fr Gornall has recently argued most persuasively along the same lines, shedding revealing light on the double-edged nature of Newman's relations with the Bishops. As Gornall puts it, 'Newman was cornered by the Bishops in the sense that he had failed to win any of them...the objective situation was that he had been given a very fair run for his money and had failed'. Faced with this failure, Newman rationalises after the event, and comes up

with a purely subjective and thoroughly confused explanation – a supposed 'understanding' the terms and basis of which Newman appeared to shift as circumstances appeared to dictate. See T. Gornall, 'Newman's lapses into subjectivity', *Heythrop Journal* XXIII (1982), pp. 46-7.

115. Mozley, *Letters and correspondence of John Henry Newman* II, p. 341, J.H. Newman to J. Mozley 30 March 1841. Cf. *Apologia*, pp. 241, 243. Cf. I. Ker, *John Henry Newman: a biography* (Oxford, 1988), pp. 225, 233.

116. *Tract XC on certain passages in the XXXIX Articles by the Rev. J.H. Newman. B.D. 1841. With a historical preface by the Rev. E.B. Pusey* (Oxford, 1866), p. xxvii.

117. *Apologia*, pp. 174, 244, cf. Ker, *John Henry Newman*, p. 222.

118. Abbott, p. 266. Fr Ker appears to accept somewhat uncritically Newman's very misleading and unfair assertion that 'authorities in London have increased their demands according to my submissions'. Yet, from the very evidence which Fr Ker presents, it can be seen that it was Newman who first promised to comply, and then demurred at the apparent 'terms' set by his Bishop. See Ker, p. 221.

119. In particular, see Mozley, *Letters and correspondence of John Henry Newman* II, p. 343, J.H. Newman to J. Mozley, 5 April 1841.

120. *Apologia*, pp. 174-5.

121. *Apologia*, p. 175, cf. Ker, 233.

122. Abbott, p. 269.

123. Abbott, p. 285.

124. Ibid.

125. P.H.L., Bagot MSS, F. Paget to R. Eden, 22 January 1879.

126. D. Wilson, *Our Protestant faith in danger* (London, 1850), p. 9. For Evangelicals complaints as to 'Puseyite bias' among the Bishops, see S. Kay, *Puseyism in power* (London, 1844), p. 4, cf. Lambeth Palace Library, Golightly MSS, MS 1804, f. 106. J.H. Browne to C.P. Golightly, 28 February 1843. See note 132.

127. Lambeth Palace Library Golightly MSS, MS 1804, fols. 102-3. W. Goode to C.P. Golightly, 9 June 1842; cf. W. Goode, *Some difficulties in the late Charge of the Lord Bishop of Oxford* (London, 1842), p. 30 and E. Thompson, *The triumph of Christianity*, pp. 9-10.

128. H.P. Liddon, *Life of E.B. Pusey* II, p. 199, W. Howley to R. Bagot, 26 March 1841, cf. P.H.L. Pusey MSS, W. Howley to R. Bagot, 27 March 1841.

129. W. Palmer, *A narrative of events connected with the*

publication of the 'Tracts for the Times', revised and enlarged edition (London, 1883) pp. 80-1.

130. Bodleian Library, MS Eng. Lett. d. 367, fols. 69-70. S. Wilberforce to J.W. Croker, 19 April 1843.

131. Ashwell I, p. 202.

132. One Evangelical complained, 'I have met with no Charge which appears even to suspect that the quarrel of the new lights is with Evangelical religion, or the preaching of the Gospel', J. Poynder, *A word to the English laity* (London, 1843), p. 17. For evidence of the traditional High Church or orthodox character of the episcopal charges of 1841-3, see *Testimonies to Church Principles, selected from Episcopal Charges and sermons* (London, 1843).

133. A comparison was drawn between Newman's theory of interpretation of the Articles, those of advocates of 'Arian' subscription such as Samuel Clarke in the eighteenth century. See C.A. Ogilvie, *Considerations on Subscription to the Thirty-Nine Articles* (Oxford, 1845), pp. 11-12, cf. Faussett, *Thirty-Nine Articles*, p. 8.

134. For instance, James Monk, Bishop of Gloucester and Bristol, and during the 1810s and 1820s an associate of the 'Hackney Phalanx', explained in his anti-Tractarian Charge of 1841, that 'there are reasons of no small importance that would rather dispose me to regard the authors of the Movement with favour and approbation'. J.H. Monk, *A Charge to the clergy of the diocese of Gloucester and Bristol* (London, 1841), p. 31.

135. Churton MSS Sutton Coldfield (priv.) E. Churton to W.J. Copeland, 18 September 1843.

136. P.H.L., Pusey MSS, E. Churton to E.B. Pusey, 9 December 1841. According to his niece, Mary, Joshua Watson much lamented, 'the almost frenetic desire for persecution manifested by some person of whom my uncle said scornfully, "verily they have their reward". Any appearance of courting persecution always roused his indignation'. Watson MSS M. Watson, MS, 'Reminiscences', pp. 116f., 7 August 1843.

137. Birmingham Oratory Library, 'Tract 90 Correspondence' No. 21, J.W. Bowden to J.H. Newman, 15 March 1841.

138. F. Oakeley, *The subject of Tract XC examined*, p. 26.

139. *British Critic* XXXIII [F. Oakeley], 'Episcopal Charges of the past year' (January 1843), p. 274.

140. N.L.S. Edinburgh, Hope-Scott MSS, MS 3692, f. 217, E.B. Pusey to J.R. Hope, September 1842. Cf. E.B. Pusey, *A letter to his*

Grace the Archbishop of Canterbury (Oxford, 1842), pp. 96-7.

141. N.L.S. Edinburgh, Hope-Scott MSS, MS 3692, f. 210. E.B. Pusey to J.R. Hope, 21 January 1842. This letter is quoted in R. Ormsby, *Memoirs of James Robert Hope-Scott of Abbotsford, with selections from his correspondence* (London, 1884) II, pp. 8-9.

142. *Tract XC... With a historical preface by the Rev. E.B. Pusey,* p. xxvii.

143. Pusey's apparent attempts to evade the criticisms of the charges, explaining them away as only condemning what the Tractarians themselves condemned, while at the same time misapprehending the real meaning of the tracts, provoked some scorn. One critic commented pertinently, 'whether their Lordships will feel gratified at this compliment to their innocence, at the expense of their understanding, I know not'. J. Davies, *The present crisis of the Church* (London, 1842), p. 31.

144. Churton MSS, Sutton Coldfield (priv.), E. Churton to W.J. Copeland, 7 February 1865.

145. F.W. Newman, *Contributions*, pp. 98-9.

146. Churton MSS, Sutton Coldfield (priv.), E. Churton to W.J. Copeland, 7 February 1865, cf. P.H.L. Pusey MSS. C.J. Blomfield to C.P. Golightly, 14 April 1841.

147. H.P. Liddon, *Life of E.B. Pusey* II, p. 275, T. Henderson to E.B. Pusey, Ash Wednesday 1842.

148. Exeter Cathedral Library, Spenser Gift, Phillpotts MSS, ED/11/3 H. Phillpotts to T. Baker, 10 January 1842, cf. P.H.L. Pusey MSS H.H. Norris to A.P. Perceval, 28 July 1843.

149. Churton MSS, Sutton Coldfield (priv.), E. Churton to W.J. Copeland, 22 January 1861.

150. P.H.L., Pusey MSS, W. Palmer to E.B. Pusey, 12 September 1843.

151. Lambeth Palace Library, Golightly MSS, MS 1805 f. 255. G.S. Faber to C.P. Golightly, 14 November 1843.

152. *English Review* I, 'Sermons on Subjects of the Day' (July, 1844), p. 309.

153. Palmer, *Narrative* revised edition (London, 1883), p. 237.

154. British Library, Gladstone MSS, MS Add. 44247, f. 196. W.E. Gladstone to H.E. Manning, 2 December 1843.

155. B.L., Gladstone MSS, MS Add. 44247, fols. 173-4. W.E. Gladstone to H.E. Manning, 24 October 1843.

156. W.K. Firminger, *Some thoughts on the recent criticism of the*

life and works of John Henry Cardinal Newman, printed for private circulation (Oxford, 1892), p. 41. The Tractarian, Isaac Williams, was adamant that it was not the condemnation of Tract 90 that 'gave his sensitive mind the decided turn to the Church of Rome'. On the contrary, Williams insisted, 'his decided leaning to Rome came out to me in private, before that Tract [90] was written'. G. Prevost (ed.), *The Autobiography of Isaac Williams B.D.* (London, 1892), pp. 108-9. Recent scholarship supports this view. In particular, Rune Imberg persuasively argues that Newman's perception of the Anglican *via media* was always slanted in a Romanist direction. See R. Imberg, *In Quest of Authority*.

157. *Christian Remembrancer* IX, 'The recent schism' (January 1846), pp. 214-15.

158. Firminger, *Some thoughts*, p. iv.

159. R.I. Wilberforce, *The Evangelical and Tractarian Movements* (London, 1851), p. 11 cf. *Advance of Tractarianism* (Birmingham, 1853), p. 7; also Firminger, *Some thoughts*, p. iii and C. Dawson, pp. 29-30. Even some Evangelicals themselves conceded this argument. See D. Wilson, *Our Protestant faith in danger*, pp. 15-16.

160. *Christian Remembrancer* IX, 'The recent schism', p. 209, cf. Imberg, *In Quest of Authority*, pp. 136-43.

161. Cross, pp. 127-8.

162. *Tract XC With a historical preface by Pusey*, p. xliii, cf. F.L. Cross, p. 113.

163. William Goode pointed out to Bishop Bagot that by the way in which they had conducted themselves, the Tractarians had not put into practice their professed principle 'of doing nothing without the Bishop'. 'For did they consult your Lordship when they originated the Tracts for the Times, and commenced that "mighty movement", which they now tell the Bishops is too late to check, however much they may wish to do so?' W. Goode, *Some difficulties*, p. 17, cf. W.S. Bricknell, *The judgment of the Bishops upon Tractarian theology* (Oxford, 1845). Appendix G 'Tractarian reverence for Episcopacy', pp. 695-7. For further discussion of Tractarian/Anglo-Catholic practical defiance of episcopal authority, see J.R. Griffin, *The Oxford Movement: a revision* (Edinburgh, 1989), pp. 270-4. Newman's own explanation of the apparent contradiction, is interesting: 'the more implicit the reverence one pays to a Bishop, the more keen will be one's perception of heresy in him', *Apologia*, p. 275, cf. Imberg, *In Quest of Authority*, pp. 181-7.

164. *English Churchman* I, No. 56 (1843), pp. 56-7.

165. J.H. Newman, *A letter to the Rt. Rev. Father in God, Richard, Lord Bishop of Oxford* (Oxford, 1841), p. 45.

166. *Apologia*, pp. 30-1, 41-2. In fact, such a charge was confined to Newman's more extreme Protestant opponents. For instance, see S. Minton, *An exposure of the inconsistencies, fictions and fallacies of Dr. Newman's lectures at Birmingham* (London, 1851), p. 8.

167. Churton MSS, Sutton Coldfield, (priv.), E. Churton to W.J. Copeland, 11 February 1842.

168. Quoted in Cross, p. 127.

169. Avis, p. 233.

170. T. Vargish, *Newman: the contemplation of mind* (Oxford, 1970), p. 19.

171. *London Quarterly Review* XXIII, No. XLV, 'Mr. Kingsley and Dr. Newman' (October, 1864), p. 116.

172. Quoted in Avis, *Anglicanism*, p. 256.

173. *Apologia*, p. 94.

174. Bodleian Library, Norris MSS, MS Eng. Lett. cf. 789. C.J. Blomfield to H.H. Norris, 2 September 1824, cf. E. Churton, *Memoirs of Joshua Watson* I, pp. 249-50.

175. *The Bishop's Charge, not as it was,but as it should have been. By a Protestant* (London, 1843), cf. J.T. Holloway, *The reply, Baptismal Regeneration and Sacramental Justification not the doctrine of the English Church* (London, 1842).

176. F. Bennett, *The story of W.J.E. Bennett* (London, 1909), pp. 38-9, cf. W.J.E. Bennett, *A farewell address to his parishioners* (London, 1861), pp. 4-23.

177. Even one of the most bigoted and intemperate of Newman's later critics conceded, 'it is evident, on every page, that Dr. Newman has deceived himself before deceiving his readers'. Pastor Chiniquy, *The Perversion of Dr. Newman to the Church of Rome* (London, 1883), p. 21.

178. W.E. Houghton, *The art of Newman's Apologia* (London, 1945), p. 22.

179. *London Quarterly Review* XXIII, 'Mr. Kingsley and Dr. Newman', p. 129.

3

NEWMAN AND KINGSLEY

P.J. FitzPatrick

'The embedded fly in the clear amber of his antagonist's Apology': the judgment passed on Kingsley in the *Quarterly Review* for October 1864 by Bishop Wilberforce exhibits the general verdict ever since upon the controversy between Newman and Charles Kingsley. But there have been dissenting voices about Newman. For Jowett, he was 'in speculation habitually untruthful and not much better in practice' (Asquith, Vol. I, p. 123). For one Archbishop of Canterbury, Newman in matters of belief was in 'a condition in which he is practically unable to distinguish between truth and falsity' (Davidson and Benham, Vol. I, p. 89). And T.H. Huxley was even more vehement: 'That man is the slipperiest sophist I have ever met with. Kingsley was entirely right about him' (Huxley, Vol. I, p. 226). What is it about Newman that has aroused such admiration and such adverse judgments?

I have contended elsewhere that the debate with Kingsley was by no means wholly in Newman's favour.[1] I have also investigated elsewhere the positions taken up by Newman in the work he published half a dozen years after the *Apologia*, his *Grammar of Assent* (FitzPatrick 1969, 1978). In the two essays I contribute to this volume, I mean to move beyond what I wrote then in order to bring together the observations I made. The first of my essays examines the *Apologia*, and concentrates upon Newman's relationship to evidence and his relationship to his adopted Church. The second examines the *Grammar of Assent*, and takes up topics which will emerge in this examination of the *Apologia*. All references are to the Bibliography on p. 132 (following my second essay), where methods of citation are explained.

The controversy with Kingsley arose from a passage in a review by Kingsley of volumes in Froude's *History of England*. Denouncing mediaeval religious frauds and the papal dispensing power, he wrote:

> Truth, for its own sake, had never been a virtue with the Roman clergy. Father Newman informs us that it need not, and on the whole ought not to be; that cunning is the weapon which Heaven

has given to the saints wherewith to withstand the brute male force of the wicked world which marries and is given in marriage. Whether his notion be doctrinally correct or not, it is at least historically so (*N* p. 6).

Newman protested to the proprietors of *Macmillan's Magazine*, received a discourteous and unsatisfactory withdrawal from Kingsley, and published the whole correspondence, with mordant comments by himself, in February 1864. Kingsley retaliated the next month with another pamphlet, which – among other accusations – suggested that Newman was already a papist while still in the Church of England. Newman saw that this charge of insincerity could count on popular prejudice in its favour, and fastened on the charge as the starting-point for his *Apologia pro Vita Sua:* 'I will draw out, as far as may be, the history of my mind' (*A* p. 99). That Newman definitively and movingly vindicated his own honesty on his journey to Rome is a plain truth I have no wish to question. My concern, both in my book and in this essay, is with the specific charges made by Kingsley in his pamphlet; because I think that – for all the intemperance of his style – he raised genuine objections that Newman did not and could not answer.

It is among these objections, and Newman's replies to them, that I fasten upon the relationship of Newman to evidence. The relationship of Newman to the Church of Rome I shall then consider, by examining the final part of the *Apologia*, the 'General Answer to Mr Kingsley'. And I shall, as far as possible, exhibit the points I make by a process of juxtaposition, setting side by side different texts from different writings of Newman. It will be my contention throughout that Newman exhibits an uneasiness over evidence; the causes of the uneasiness will be one of the topics in the next essay.

I first find uneasiness over evidence in Newman's reply to the most elaborated of Kingsley's charges. This touched the *Lives of the English Saints*, which began to appear in 1843. Kingsley blames Newman in general for allowing his disciples to write with such superstitious credulity, and in particular for formally connecting himself – by means of a contributed 'Advertisement' or Preface – to a 'Life of St. Walburga'. Newman is able to show the very limited responsibility he had for what the *Lives* contained, and is also able to pass to wider considerations about belief in the miraculous, and about myths and legends. But juxtaposition points to a disconcerting gap between past and present in what Newman writes of the 'Life of St. Walburga'.

***Newman in 1864, replying to Kingsley in Section 4 of the Appendix to the* Apologia**

It is hard on me to have this dull, profitless work, but I have pledged myself; – so now for St. Walburga.

Now will it be believed that this Writer suppresses the fact that the miracles of St. Walburga are treated by the author of her Life as mythical? Yet that is the tone of the whole composition...

Now, first, that the miraculous stories *are* treated, in the Life of St. Walburga, as legends and myths. Throughout, the miracles and extraordinary occurrences are spoken of as 'said' or 'reported'...[2]

And so in like manner the Author of the Life says, as this writer actually has quoted him, 'a story *was told and believed*,' p. 94. 'One evening, *says her history*,' p. 87. 'Another incident *is thus related*,' p. 88. 'Immediately, *says* Wulfhard,' p. 91. 'A vast number of other cases are *recorded*,' p. 92. And there is a distinct intimation that they may be myths, in a passage which this Assailant himself quotes, 'All these have the *character* of a gentle mother correcting the idleness and faults of careless and thoughtless children with tenderness.' – p. 95. I think the criticism he makes upon this Life is one of the most wanton passages in his Pamphlet. The Life is beautifully written, full of poetry, and, as I have said, bears on its very surface the profession of a legendary and mythical character...

In saying all this, I have no intention whatever of implying that miracles did not illustrate the Life of St. Walburga; but neither the Author nor I have bound ourselves to the belief of certain instances in particular (*A* pp. 404-6).

Newman in 1844, in the 'Advertisement' preceding the Volume in which 'The Life of St. Walburga' appeared

The question will naturally suggest itself to the reader, whether the miracles recorded in these narratives, especially those contained in the Life of St. Walburga, are to be received as matters of fact; and in this day and under our present circumstances we can only reply, that there is no reason why they should not be. They are the kind of facts proper to ecclesiastical history, just as instances of sagacity and daring, personal prowess or crime, are the facts proper to secular history. And if the tendency of credulity or superstition to exaggerate and invent creates a difficulty in the reception of facts ecclesiastical, so does the existence of party spirit, private interests, personal attachments, malevolence, and the like, call for caution and criticism in the reception of facts secular and civil. There is little or nothing, then, *primâ facie*, in the miraculous accounts in question to repel a properly taught and religiously disposed mind; which will, accordingly, give them a prompt and hearty acquiescence, or a passive admission, or receive them in part, or hold them in suspense, or absolutely reject them, according as the evidence makes for or against them, or is not of a trustworthy character.

As to the miracles ascribed to St. Walburga, it must be remembered that she is one of the principal Saints of her age and country. 'Scarcely any of the illustrious females of Old or New Testament can be named,' says J. Basnage, 'who has had so many heralds of her praises as Walburga; for, not to speak of her own brother Willibald, who is reported, without foundation, to have been his sister's panegyrist, six writers are extant, who have employed themselves in relating the deeds or miracles of Walburga; – Wolfhart, Adelbold, Medibard, Adelbert, Philip, and the nuns of St. Walburga's monastery. – Ap. Canis. Lect. Ant. t.ii., part iii., p. 265.

Nor was this renown the mere natural growth of ages. It begins within the very century of the Saint's death. At the end of that time Wolfhard, a monk of the diocese of Aichstadt, where her relics lay, drew up an account of her life, and of certain miracles which had been wrought in the course of three years, about the time he wrote, by a portion of her relics bestowed upon the monastery of Monheim in Bavaria; his information, at least in part, coming from the monk who had the placing of the sacred treasure in its new abode. The two mentioned below, p. 88, seem the only miracles which were distinctly reported of her as occurring in her lifetime, and they were handed down apparently by tradition: 'haec duo tantum praeclara miracula,' says Wolfhard, 'quae Virgo beata peregit in vita, huic inserere dignum putavi opusculo, quae nostram ad memoriam pervenere.'

J.H.N.

LITTLEMORE
Feb. 21, 1844

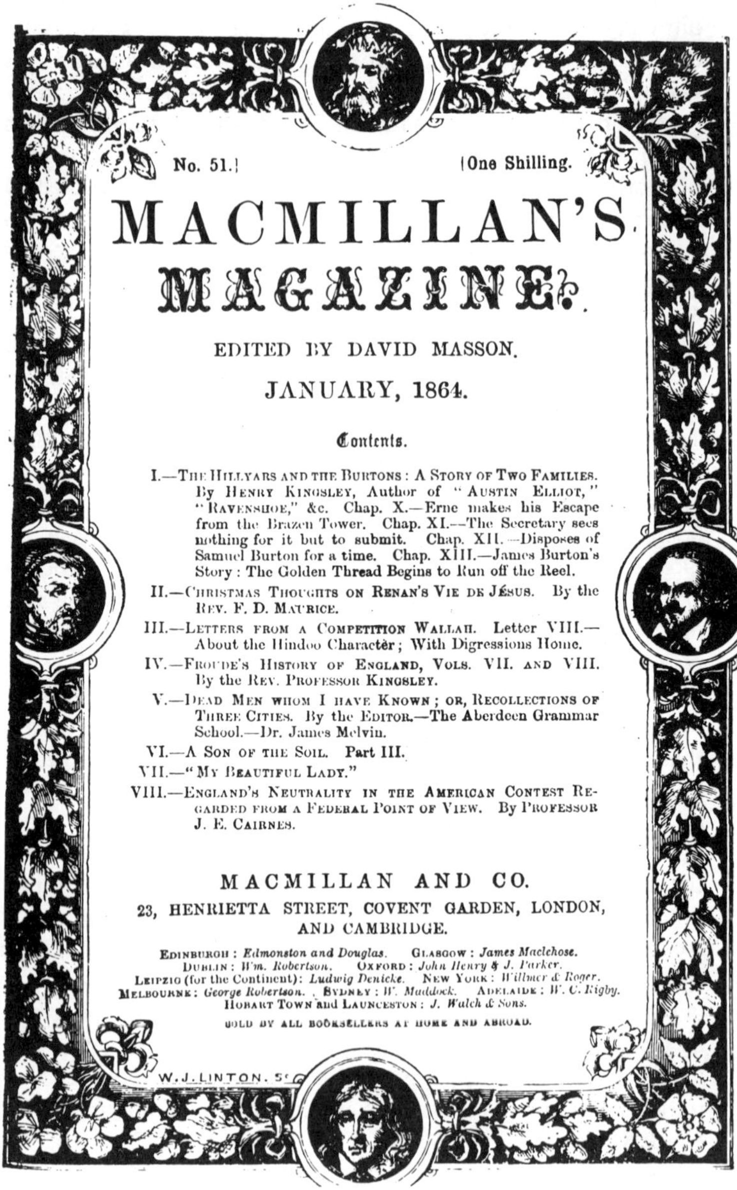

No. 51.] [One Shilling.

MACMILLAN'S

MAGAZINE.

EDITED BY DAVID MASSON.

JANUARY, 1864.

Contents.

I.—The Hillyars and the Burtons: A Story of Two Families. By Henry Kingsley, Author of "Austin Elliot," "Ravenshoe," &c. Chap. X.—Erne makes his Escape from the Brazen Tower. Chap. XI.—The Secretary sees nothing for it but to submit. Chap. XII.—Disposes of Samuel Burton for a time. Chap. XIII.—James Burton's Story: The Golden Thread Begins to Run off the Reel.

II.—Christmas Thoughts on Renan's Vie de Jésus. By the Rev. F. D. Maurice.

III.—Letters from a Competition Wallah. Letter VIII.—About the Hindoo Character; With Digressions Home.

IV.—Froude's History of England, Vols. VII. and VIII. By the Rev. Professor Kingsley.

V.—Dead Men whom I have Known; or, Recollections of Three Cities. By the Editor.—The Aberdeen Grammar School.—Dr. James Melvin.

VI.—A Son of the Soil. Part III.

VII.—"My Beautiful Lady."

VIII.—England's Neutrality in the American Contest Regarded from a Federal Point of View. By Professor J. E. Cairnes.

MACMILLAN AND CO.

23, HENRIETTA STREET, COVENT GARDEN, LONDON, AND CAMBRIDGE.

Edinburgh: *Edmonston and Douglas.* Glasgow: *James Maclehose.*
Dublin: *Wm. Robertson.* Oxford: *John Henry & J. Parker.*
Leipzig (for the Continent): *Ludwig Denicke.* New York: *Willmer & Roger.*
Melbourne: *George Robertson.* Sydney: *W. Maddock.* Adelaide: *W. C. Rigby.*
Hobart Town and Launceston: *J. Walch & Sons.*

SOLD BY ALL BOOKSELLERS AT HOME AND ABROAD.

W. J. LINTON. Sc

The cover of *Macmillan's Magazine*, January 1864.

The evident inconsistency between these two texts may prompt the question whether Newman ever does quote the 'Advertisement' he had written twenty years before. He does indeed quote it – but only in the next section of the Appendix (*A* p. 417), where he moves to those wider questions of the credibility of miracle-stories. Here and now, his task was to reply to Kingsley's specific charges of credulity and superstition found in the 'Life of St. Walburga'. And his reply treats the narrative in the 'Life' as mythical, while in the 'Advertisement' he had treated the narrative as – whether true or false – calling for the assessment of evidence. The two attitudes are simply different.

From uneasiness over evidence here, I pass to three specimens of uneasiness in the conduct of the controversy itself. The first two can be dealt with briefly enough, the third will call for a longer treatment – and for the juxtaposing once more of Newman's texts. The first of the three touches Kingsley's authorship of the review in *Macmillan's Magazine*. When he acknowledged it, Newman replied to him:

> When I received your letter, taking upon yourself the authorship, I was amazed (*N* p. 9).

And the next day Newman wrote to the proprietor of *Macmillan's Magazine*:

> I have heard from Mr. Kingsley, avowing himself, to my extreme astonishment, the author of the passage... had anyone said it was Mr. Kingsley, I should have laughed in his face. Certainly, I saw the initials at the end; but, you must recollect, I live out of the world... And so of the Editor: when I saw his name on the cover, it conveyed to me absolutely no idea whatever (*N* p. 9).

But on the cover, which Newman admits having seen, Kingsley's authorship is to be found, as the reproduction of the cover given opposite will show. A footnote in *Letters and Diaries* explains this by saying that the editor's name figured prominently on the cover, while the attribution of the review to Kingsley was in small print (*LD* XXI,12). Readers can now look at the cover for themselves and will, I think, share my dissatisfaction.[3]

The second uneasiness touches the nature of Kingsley's accusation. His first offending sentence ran in the review:

> Truth, for its own sake, had never been a virtue with the Roman clergy (*N* p. 6).

But the title-page of Newman's first pamphlet described the controversy as 'Whether Dr. Newman teaches that truth is no virtue', while in the satirical reflections at the end of the pamphlet Kingsley is represented as attributing to Newman the view 'that lying is never any harm' (*N* p. 20). Kingsley complains in his opening paragraph at what was on the title-page and in the reflections (*K* p. 25). He writes later:

> He has economised the very four words of my accusation, which make it at least a reasonable one; namely – 'For its own sake' (*K* p. 57).

Newman offers two answers concerning the title-page; he did print the words 'for its own sake' five times over in the course of his pamphlet; and the omission is immaterial – 'what kind of virtue is that, which is *not* done for its own sake?' (*A* p. 431). I find neither reply satisfactory, because a substantial difference goes with the missing words. 'Truth is no virtue' removes veracity from moral considerations altogether, and Kingsley rightly complains that he never ascribed so preposterous an opinion to Newman. But 'truth, for its own sake, is no virtue' is more subtle; it would make the virtue in truth come from its concomitants, so that truth can be sacrificed in the cause of edification or policy. I do not think that Newman taught this either, but he had no right, whether on the title-page or in the admittedly amusing 'Reflections', to suggest that Kingsley ascribed the other, preposterous opinion to him. Nor is it enough to say that he printed the words 'for its own sake' five times over. He did so print them, but on each occasion when quoting Kingsley – in modern terms, he *mentioned* the qualification, but did not thereby *use* it himself. Kingsley's comment is harsh but understandable:

> I never said what he makes me say, or anything like it. I never was inclined to say it. Had I ever been, I should be still more inclined to say it now (*K* p. 58).

The third and last uneasiness will, as I warned, take longer to elucidate. Kingsley took some words from Newman as the motto of his pamphlet:

> It is not more than a hyperbole to say, that, in certain cases, a lie is the nearest approach to truth.

These words come from a footnote at p. 343 of 'Sermon on the Theory of Developments in Religious Doctrine' (hereafter, 'Sermon on Developments'). It was preached by Newman in 1843 and the volume containing it was published the same year. The context of the words is the problem of communicating religious knowledge in a necessarily imperfect form to unbelievers or beginners. The teacher must sometimes state his message in a way which, though inaccurate by mature standards of discourse, will less mislead. The whole process, known as 'the Economy', had preoccupied Newman and his friends in their Oxford days, as they made themselves acquainted with the writings of the Fathers of the Church, where they found much to do with it. I observe at once that the problem is very real, and that I hope the topics of my next essay will throw some light on it. What I want to investigate here is the fortunes of the text where Kingsley found the words he cited; and for this I shall once more resort to juxtaposition of Newman's texts:

Newman's footnote at p. 343 of his 'Sermon on Developments', edition of 1843

> Hence it is not more than an hyperbole to say that, in certain cases, a lie is the nearest approach to truth. This seems the meaning, for instance, of St. Clement, when he says, "He [the Christian] both thinks and speaks the truth, unless when at any time, in the way of treatment, as a physician towards his patients, so for the welfare of the sick he will be false, or will tell a falsehood, as the Sophists speak. For instance, the noble Apostle circumcised Timothy, yet cried out and wrote, "Circumcision availed not," &c. – Strom. vii. 9. We are told that "God is not the son of man, that He should repent"; yet "it repented the Lord that He had made man."

Newman's footnote at p. 341 of his 'Sermon on Developments', edition of 1872

> Hence it is not more than an hyperbole to say that, in certain cases, a lie is the nearest approach to the truth. [Vide *Hist. of Arians*, p. 67, &c. Edit. 3] We are told that 'God is not the son of man, that He should repent'; yet 'it repented the Lord that He had made man.'

My comments on this change in the footnote begin with another juxtaposition. I compare what Kingsley says about the footnote in its original form with what Newman has to say about Kingsley's comment here:

Kingsley's comment upon this footnote in its original form

> The whole sermon [i.e. on Developments] is written in so tentative a style, that it would be rash and wrong to say that Dr. Newman intends to convey any lesson by it, save that the discovery of truth is an impossibility. Only once, and in a note, he speaks out. P. 342. [*sic*; Kingsley then prints the footnote of p. 343, down to and including 'as the sophists speak'].
>
> If St. Clement said that so much the worse for him. He was a great and good man. But he might have learned from his Bible that no lie was of the truth, and that it is ill stealing the devil's tools to do God's work withal (*K* p. 55).

From Newman's remarks in the* Apologia *on Kingsley and the 'Sermon on Developments'

> He puts into his Title-page these words from a Sermon of mine: "It is not more than an hyperbole to say, that, in certain cases, a lie is the nearest approach to truth." This Sermon he attacks; but I do not think it necessary to defend it here, because anyone who reads it, will see that he is simply incapable of forming a notion of what it is about. It treats of subjects which are entirely out of his depth; and, as I have already shown in other instances, and observed at the beginning of this Volume, he illustrates in his own person the very thing that shocks him, viz. that the nearest approach to truth, in given cases, is a lie (*A* p. 430).

Newman is entitled to claim that the 'Sermon on Developments' contains themes that go beyond what Kingsley raised in his pamphlet. None the less, the passage from St Clement which Kingsley blamed has gone from the revised footnote. Why it has gone, a passage earlier in the *Apologia* will show. In his 'General Answer to Mr. Kingsley', Newman says something of the Economy and of its various forms, and something of St Clement. He writes:

> Of late years I have come to think, as I believe most writers do, that Clement meant more than I have said. I used to think that he used the word "lie" as an hyperbole, but I now believe that he, as other early Fathers, thought that, under circumstances, it was lawful to tell a lie (*A* pp. 360-1).

But since it is precisely the view Newman now ascribes to Clement that Kingsley attacked, it was not fair to dismiss him as incapable of understanding what the Sermon was about. He understood enough to grasp Clement's meaning and to condemn it; a meaning which Newman admits he had not grasped himself when he preached the Sermon.

But there is yet more uneasiness to come. We encounter it if we follow up the reference Newman gives in the revised form of the footnote to the Sermon. It is 'Hist. of Arians, p. 67, &c. edit. 3'. This sends us to Newman's *History of the Arians of the Fourth Century*, first published by Newman in 1833, given a second edition in 1854, and a third and revised edition in 1871. The page reference to the third edition sends us to the point where the nature and limits of the Economy are being discussed. (Newman had already in the *Apologia* referred his readers to the *History* for more about the Economy, *A* p. 430.) The discussion naturally leads Newman to consider the opinions of St Clement. As we know, it was to these that Kingsley originally objected, so it is interesting to notice once more, if we compare earlier and later editions of the *History*, a gap between present and past. I have italicised in the earlier form whatever was changed or omitted in the later:

History of the Arians, ***first edition (1833), p. 81***

> The Alexandrian Father who has already been *referred to*, accurately describes the rules which should guide the Christian in speaking and acting economically. 'Being *ever* persuaded of the omnipresence of God,' *he says*, 'and ashamed to come short of the truth, he is satisfied with the approval of God, and of his own conscience. Whatever is in his mind is also on his tongue; towards those who are fit recipients, both in speaking and living, he harmonizes his profession with his *opinions*. He both thinks and speaks the truth; except when *consideration* is necessary, and then, as a physician for the good of his patients, he will *be false*, or *utter a falsehood*, as the Sophists say. For instance, the *great* Apostle circumcised Timothy, while he cried out and wrote down, "Circumcision availeth not;" *and yet, lest he should so suddenly tear his Hebrew disciples from the Law, as to unsettle them, accommodating himself to the Jews, he became a Jew, that he might make his gain of all*... Nothing, however, but his neighbour's good will lead him to do this... He gives himself up for the Church, for the friends whom he *has* begotten in the faith, for an ensample to those who have the ability to undertake the

> high office (οἰκονομίαν) of a *teacher, full of love to God and man; and so, while he preserves the sincerity of his words, he at the same time displays the work of zeal for the Lord.*[1]'

[The dots in this passage are Newman's. At the end of the citation, 'Lord' has a superscript '1', referring to a footnote, which I now give.]

> [1] Clem. Strom. vii. 8, 9.

History of the Arians, ***third edition, (1871), pp. 75-6***[4]

> The Alexandrian Father who has already been quoted, accurately describes the rules which should guide the Christian in speaking and acting economically. 'Being fully persuaded of the omnipresence of God,' says Clement, 'and ashamed to come short of the truth, he is satisfied with the approval of God, and of his own conscience. Whatever is in his mind is also on his tongue; towards those who are fit recipients, both in speaking and living, he harmonizes his profession with his thoughts. He both thinks and speaks the truth; except when careful treatment is necessary, and then, as a physician for the good of his patients, he will lie, or rather utter a lie, as the Sophists say. For instance, the noble Apostle circumcised Timothy, while he cried out and wrote down, 'Circumcision availeth not'...
>
> Nothing, however, but his neighbour's good will lead him to do this... He gives himself up for the Church, for the friends whom he hath begotten in the faith for an ensample to those who have the ability to undertake the high office (*economy*) of a religious and charitable teacher, for an exhibition of truth in his words, and for the exercise of love towards the Lord.[6]'

[Again, the dots in this passage are Newman's. At the end of the citation, 'Lord' has a superscript '6', referring to a footnote, which reads as follows.]

> [6] Clem. Strom. vii. 8, 9 (abridged). (Vide Plat. Leg. ii. 8 οὔποτε ψεύδεται κἄν ψεύδος λεγῃ. Sext. Empir. adv. Log. p. 378, with Notes T and U. On this whole subject, vide the Author's *History of my Religious Opinions*, notes F and G, pp. 343-63.)

The whole procedure in the latter passage is curiously indirect. Newman has changed the vocabulary in which he describes Clement's opinion, and for reasons we have seen: he now thinks Clement allowed lying under circumstances, which is what Kingsley claimed. But the only apparent link with Kingsley comes at the end of the new material in brackets[5] and this is a reference to the *second* edition of the *Apologia*, where Kingsley's name is not mentioned, and he appears only as 'a popular writer'. Curiously indirect, and surely ungenerous. But also curiously misleading, as two more juxtaposed texts will show. The first touches this revision of Newman's work on the Arians; the second touches his edition in 1872 of the volume containing the 'Sermon on Developments':

***From Newman's Preface (dated 1871) to revised edition of* History of the Arians**

> A very few words will suffice for the purpose of explaining in what respects the Third Edition of this Volume differs from those which preceded it.
>
> Its text has been relieved of some portion of the literary imperfections necessarily incident to a historical sketch, its author's first work, and written against time.
>
> Also some additions have been made to the foot-notes. These are enclosed in brackets...
>
> No change has been made anywhere affecting the opinions, sentiments or speculations contained in the original edition...

From Newman's Preface to the volume (1872) in which the revised footnote to the 'Sermon on Developments' appeared

> These discourses were originally published, except as regards some verbal corrections, just as they were preached. The author would gladly at that time have made considerable alterations in them, both in the way of addition and omission; but, professing, as they did, to be 'preached before the University,' he did not feel himself at liberty to do so. Much less does he alter them now; all that he has thought it right to do has been, by notes in brackets at the foot of the page, to draw attention to certain faults which are to be found in them, either of thought or of language, and, as far as possible, to set these right.

Let us first look at what is in the first passage. The changes made in Newman's translation of what St Clement wrote can, I think, be counted at a pinch as coming under the relieving of 'literary imperfections' – although the changes, by reflecting Newman's changed belief that Clement did sanction lying, do seem to touch 'opinions or sentiments or speculations contained in the original edition'. More disturbing is what is in the second text. A first reaction might be to claim that Newman is here simply contravening the truth; that he has indeed 'altered them now', by omitting from the revised foot-note everything to do with St Clement. But that would be over-hasty. All that Newman's Preface guarantees is that the sermons *as preached* have not been altered – and presumably the footnote was never delivered from the pulpit. But the tactic does strike me as a little near the wind. The anxious precision of the Preface might well lead a reader to believe that all changes are confined to what is added in brackets, whereas the omission of all to do with St Clement is not so confined – once more, what Kingsley complained of has silently sunk without trace.

From these uneasinesses in the relationship with evidence, I pass to a deeper uneasiness. This touches the relationship of Newman with the Church of Rome, and touches the whole relationship of that Church with truth and honesty. A man of the intelligence of Sir John Acton saw that any adequate reply to Kingsley must confront this. He wrote to him on 10 April 1864, while Newman was preparing the *Apologia*: the general opinion, he said, was that Newman's original pamphlet had vindicated his own honour, but had left untouched the difficulty felt by many – the practice in the Church of proscribing truth and positively encouraging falsehood. Replying on 15 April, Newman wrote: 'As to the points you mention, you may be sure that I shall go as far as ever I can' (both letters are at *LD* XXI p. 94). It was to this topic that Newman devoted the 'General Answer to Mr Kingsley' with which the *Apologia* concludes. My account of it must start from an event that both Acton and Newman then had in mind.

On 15 March 1864, Acton had informed Newman that he was closing the *Home and Foreign Review*, the successor of the *Rambler*, a journal whose editorship Newman had briefly held and then been compelled to relinquish (details are in Trevor, Vol. II). Acton said that his decision was prompted by a Papal Brief sent by Pius IX on 21 December 1863 to a theological congress held at Munich (referred to hereafter as the Munich Letter). The Munich Letter reprobated freedom of discussion in the sense of that Congress, and stated at considerable length the need for submission to dogmatic definitions – 'a guiding star' to all intellectual disciplines; to the ordinary teaching of the Church; and to the decrees of Roman Congregations (text in Denzinger-Schönmetzer, par. 2875-80). Rather than risk a censure,

Acton wrote, he would close the *Review* (*LD* XXI pp. 82-3). Newman replied on 18 March 1864: he had been shown the Munich Letter, and was studying it; its principles he could accept without difficulty, but he dreaded their application – 'I suppose they mean far more than they say' (*LD* XXI pp. 83-4). Let us keep in mind the Munich Letter, and these comments by Newman, as we examine the 'General Answer'. Summaries are poor things, but I shall begin by offering one myself. Or rather, I shall begin by offering a summary of the first dozen-and-a-half pages, where Newman sets the scene and lays out general principles. The rest, where he is concerned with practice, will need different treatment.

Newman states his aim: to show that those who accept the claims of the Church of Rome are not accepting a system which is dishonest (*A* pp. 331-3). Belief in God, he begins, is confronted with the spectacle in the world of sinfulness, anguish, uncertainty and irreligion. The vision appals – the human race must be involved in some terrible aboriginal calamity (*A* pp. 333-5). Were God, then, to interfere in this tragedy of evil, it is not surprising that he would choose a power with the prerogative of infallibility in religious matters, proof against the energy of human scepticism. The Catholic Church's claim appears then not difficult of belief but fitting. But does not the claim put the believer in bondage to the caprice of the Church? Newman will, then, state his own attitude towards the prerogative of infallibility (*A* pp. 335-8).

The infallible teaching will be characterised by a protest against the existing sinful state of mankind; and by the holding out of a hope of redemption for human nature, through an inward conversion and rebirth, in will and in intellect (*A* pp. 338-41). The infallible power will claim the ability to expound the very meaning of our Lord's words; it will claim the right to fix its own boundaries of exercise, to decide whether matters not directly religious pertain to religion, to determine controversies and to impose silence; and it will claim an outward submission from Catholics to these acts, whether or not the acts be judged by them expedient or harsh. And to this power Newman professes his own absolute submission (*A* pp. 341-2).

But he then denies what might seem to follow – that the human intellect is thereby repressed. The energy of the human intellect 'does from opposition grow', and the course of the Church's history displays infallibility and reason in an undying conflict which is necessary for the very life of religion. The Church's infallibility has for its object the control of human thought in religious speculation, not its enfeebling (*A* pp. 342-4). The infallibility is bounded and founded by the moral law, by natural religion, by the apostolical faith; whatever is promulgated in later times must be homogeneous with what was previously believed; examples show as much – as does the great rarity of such promulgations (*A* pp. 345-8).

So much for the general picture Newman gives, and the force it acquires in his own words will hardly be denied, whether or not we accept it or the conclusions he claims it implies. But now he turns to what is more concrete, and here it is that I claim to detect a deep unease – an unresolved tension and ambiguity. I summarise briefly, before juxtaposing texts once more. He acknowledges the right of the Church to 'animadvert upon opinions in secular matters', to censure books, to silence authors, and to forbid discussions. But these are no more than disciplinary; they must be obeyed without a word, but they demand no more than silence, they set no bounds to the exercise of the reason (*A* pp. 348-50). He acknowledges that this is a trial to the reason, but submits that, for all their severities, high ecclesiastics have been mainly in the right; speculations, even when warranted, may be unseasonable – and still unseasonable, even if the manner of their repression be inconsiderate (*A* pp. 350-1). Such repression may irritate those who would seek to face questions of the kind raised by the advance of modern science; but it is still unclear what those questions are, and the recent intervention of 'the highest Catholic Authority' (Newman means the Munich Letter) he has a cause to welcome as a clear directive (*A* pp. 352-4). History shows that this system does not destroy mental independence, for Rome has been slow to intervene, and those who put forward speculations know that the matter will be thoroughly ventilated before a decision is reached. (*A* pp. 353-4). It would be different if the interventions were made directly upon whatever was said. But the general run of things has not been so (*A* pp. 357-8).

That this too exhibits great power, I do not question. Nor do I question the fact that, in pointing to what 'the general run' of things has been in the Church, Newman was implicitly criticising the pattern of authority professed by Manning and W.G. Ward. Indeed neither of them liked the book, and Ward's refusal to do it justice in the *Dublin Review* led to resignations from among his staff (*LD* XXI pp. 323, 340). But for me things are not so simple, and once more I use juxtaposition. I use it first upon the passage in the 'General Answer' where

Newman claims that the exercise of power in the Church does not affect the exercise of the intellect. This I juxtapose with a passage from the very text to which Kingsley appealed as grounds for his charge (*N* p. 8; cf. *K* pp. 28f.) – Newman's 'Sermon on Wisdom and Innocence':

Newman in the 'General Answer to Mr Kingsley'

> I think history supplies us with instances in the Church, where legitimate power has been harshly used...But...what is there in this want of prudence...more than what can be urged...against Protestant...institutions?...We are called upon, not to profess anything, but to submit & be silent...Such injunctions, as I have supposed, are laid merely upon our actions, not upon our thoughts...authoritative prohibitions may tease and irritate, but they have no bearing whatsoever upon the exercise of the reason (*A* pp. 349-50).

Newman in his 'Sermon on Wisdom and Innocence'

> Those Nations which are destitute of material force, have recourse to the arts of the unwarlike; they are fraudulent and crafty; they dissemble, negotiate, procrastinate, evading what they cannot resist, and wearing out what they cannot crush...So it is with slaves; so it is with ill-used and oppressed children; who learn to be cowardly and deceitful towards their tyrants. So it is with the subjects of a despot...They exercise the unalienable right of self-defence by such methods as they best may; only, since human nature is unscrupulous, guilt or innocence is all the same to them if it works their purpose (*Subjects* p. 295).

Kingsley was foolish to offer this sermon to support his claim about 'the Roman Clergy' – Newman at the time of its preaching was still a member of the Church of England. But the passage I have cited does make clear what the text from the 'General Answer' does not: repression breeds habits that are unpleasingly indirect; it does not leave the mind's freedom intact and 'insulated', so to speak, from the effects of repressive interventions. Minds are simply not like that, life might be simpler if they were.

The effects upon Newman's own mind can be seen if we move on to what comes next in the 'General Answer' – his remarks about the facing of questions raised by secular disciplines, and about the

Munich Letter. And this time I juxtapose passages from the General Answer with passages from Newman's Private Journal for the preceding year; with parts of a letter to his friend Emily Bowles, also of 1863; and with the conclusion of the analysis he wrote in 1864 of the Munich Letter:

Newman in the 'General Answer to Mr Kingsley'

> Such a state of things may be the provoking and discouraging to... such as keenly perceived existing evil... We live in a wonderful age; the enlargement of...secular knowledge just now is simply a bewilderment... [T]he question arises how are the respective claims of revelation and of natural science to be adjusted (*A* p. 351)
>
> [The Catholic] does most deeply enter into the feelings of...[those] who are simply perplexed by the utter confusion into which late discoveries...have thrown their...ideas of religion...how often has the wish risen in [the heart of other Catholics] that someone from among themselves should come forward as the champion of revealed truth...Various persons... have asked me to do so; but...at the moment it is so difficult to say...what it is that is to be encountered and overthrown;...hypotheses rise and fall;...it has seemed to me very undignified for a Catholic to commit himself to the work of chasing what might turn out to be phantoms...It seemed to be a time of all others in which Christians...had no other way...than of exhorting [those who are alarmed] to have a little faith...And I interpret recent acts of [the highest Catholic authority]...as tying the hands of a controversialist such as I should be... And so far from finding a difficulty in obeying in this case, I have cause...to rejoice to have so clear a direction in a matter of difficulty (*A* pp. 353-4)

From Newman's Private Journal, 1863

> What am I living for?...Alas, it is my habitual thought, now for years...since I became a Catholic, I seem to have had nothing but failure personally...my powers go in a different direction and one not understood...at Rome...I should wish to attempt to meet the great infidel &c questions of the day, but both Propaganda and the Episcopate, doing nothing themselves, look with extreme jealousy upon anyone who attempts it...(Trevor II, pp. 290f).

Private Memorandum by Newman on the Munich Letter, 1864

> The language of the Brief [the Munich Letter]...is as if even men of science must keep theological conclusions before them in treating of science. Well...I could not write a word upon the...difficulties of the day...without allowing [free-thinking physicists] freedom...in their own science; so that...this Brief...is...a providential intimation...that, at this moment...we are simply to be silent while scientific investigation proceeds – and not say a word on...interpretations of Scripture &c &c when perplexed persons ask us – and I am not sure that it will not prove to be the best course (Ward I, p. 642).

Letter to Miss Bowles 19 May 1863

> Sometimes I seem to myself inconsistent in professing to love retirement, yet seeming impatient at doing so little...people say to me 'why are you not doing more? how much you could do!' and then, since I think I could do a great deal if I was let to do it, I become uneasy (Trevor II, p. 299).

That there are unresolved tensions here is scarcely at issue. It is, I hope, already clear that Newman cannot be charged with simulating an acceptance which he inwardly rejected – such a supposition is contradicted here by private texts where he had no occasion for writing anything except what he thought. This much is evident, that he was torn two ways: by a belief that, left to himself, he could do something; and by a belief that, given the rapid progress of secular disciplines, the silence prescribed by the Munich Letter was perhaps the best course. This second belief would be strengthened by his own love of retirement. But the tearing was real for all that, the discord unresolved.

Still later in the 'General Answer', as we have seen, Newman claims that the power in the Church does not destroy independence of mind. And here the juxtaposition of texts reveals the tearing and discord at their most painful:

Newman's 'General Answer to Mr Kingsley'

> ...Our question...simply is, whether the belief in an Infallible authority destroys the independence of the mind; and I consider that the whole history of the Church...gives a negative to the accusation.

...through all Church history from the beginning, how slow is authority in interfering!...a controversy ensues; Rome simply lets it alone...it comes before a Bishop...before a University...Rome is still silent... After a long while it comes before the supreme power. Meanwhile, the question has been ventilated... again and again...before it is ultimately determined.

It is manifest how a mode of proceeding such as this, tends not only to the liberty, but to the courage, of the individual theologian... Many a man has ideas, which he hopes are true... but he wishes to have them discussed...and by means of controversy he obtains his end. He is answered, and he yields; or he finds that he is considered safe.

He would not dare to do this, if he knew an authority, which was supreme and final, was watching every word he said, and made signs of assent or dissent to each sentence, as he uttered it. Then indeed he would be fighting, as the Persian soldiers, under the lash, and the freedom of his intellect might truly be said to be beaten out of him. But this has not been so: – I do not mean to say that...an interposition may not rightly take place...but, if we look into the history of controversy, we shall find, I think, the general run of things to be such as I have represented it (*A* pp. 357-8).

Letter of Newman, 20 January 1864, to Mrs T.W. Allies

I have never got over the *Rambler* being taken out of my hands...it has been the same shock to my nerves that a pat from a lion would have been (*LD* XXI, p. 23).

Letter of Newman to Miss Bowles, 19 May 1863

This age of the Church is peculiar – in former times, primitive or medieval, there was not the extreme centralisation which is now in use. If a private theologian said anything free, another answered him. If the controversy grew, then it went to a Bishop, a theological faculty, or to some foreign University. The Holy See was but the Court of ultimate appeal.

Letter of Newman, 12 February 1864, to T.W. Allies

...as well might a bird *fly* without wings as I write a book without the *chance*, the *certainty* of saying something or other (not, God

> forbid! against the Faith) but against the view of a particular school in the Church which is dominant... I cannot fight under the lash, as the Persian slaves (*LD* XXI, p. 48).

Continuation of Newman's letter to Miss Bowles

> *Now* if I as a private priest, put anything into print, Propaganda answers me at once. How can I fight with such a chain on my arm? It is like the Persians being driven to fight under the lash. There was true private judgment in the primitive and medieval schools – there are no schools now, no private judgment (in the religious sense of the phrase), no freedom, that is, of opinion. That is, no exercise of the intellect (Ward I, p. 588).

Comment is hardly necessary. We can notice the coincidence of phrases and sequences between public and private texts, and readers who are interested in such things can find the 'Persians under the lash' in the story of how Xerxes crossed the Hellespont (Herodotus VII, chapter 56). But that the discords were unresolved is beyond debate. We do not have – to make the point again – an insincere profession from Newman, who meanwhile writes to his friends in the opposite sense; the damage would be less real if we had. I think I am entitled to submit that the 'General Answer' cannot be taken as a prescription for authority in the Church. It is rather a symptom of the malady which that authority produces. The two sets of text yield no synthesis, they do but exhibit one man's maiming.

I hope that the next essay will throw further light on what I have claimed so far. But here and now I can state a conclusion, and it is not a happy one. Kingsley made specific charges against Newman, and I have tried to show, both here and in my book, that they were more substantial than has been generally believed. But Kingsley's charges were inspired by the wider belief that the Roman Church itself had an uneasy relationship with truth and with the quest for truth; and Newman's 'General Answer' was intended as a response to that belief. By a melancholy paradox, confirmation of Kingsley's belief can be found in the very fabric of this, the culminating section in his antagonist's most famous work.

NOTES

1. I first examined this controversy in *Apologia pro Charles Kingsley*, which touches more points than can be considered here. Since the book was published in 1969, more evidence has become available in Volume XXI of Newman's *Letters and Diaries*, which covers the period of the *Apologia*, and I give references to it.

2. At this point Newman refers to a story told of St Sturme, which is narrated in the 'Life of St. Walburga' at pp. 77-8. I omit the reference here; my dissatisfaction with what Newman writes I have explained in my book (FitzPatrick 1969), pp. 17-19.

3. In the book, I suggested that – predicament dear to logicians nowadays! – Newman did not know that Charles Kingsley was Professor Kingsley. I now suggest another explanation – his eye instinctively darted away when it alighted on the announcement of the contribution of F.D. Maurice. (See illustration of cover on p. 92 – did the mind of man ever devise a more ludicrously inapposite title?)

4. Newman's *History of the Arians*, in its revised form is usually found in later editions than the third. One of them, the fifth, differs in pagination. The only subsequent change I can find in the footnote is that Newman went back to the title *Apologia* after keeping for some years to *History of my Religious Opinions*, by which he had named the second edition of his book.

5. The references at the beginning of the brackets are to Plato and to Sextus Empiricus. I shall return to them in the next essay, as to Clement.

4

NEWMAN'S *GRAMMAR* AND THE CHURCH TODAY

P.J. FitzPatrick

In 1870, six years after the *Apologia*, Newman published his *Grammar of Assent* (the full title is more tentative). Its terminology can easily deter – which is a pity, because there are all manner of things in it that repay reflection. Of them, I consider what Newman writes about assent and inference as such; which means that I have to omit much that would be required for an adequate account of the book. But what Newman writes of them is interesting for its own sake, and proves at times strikingly like later accounts. In my opinion there are defects in it, defects that go with some things we have seen of his views in the preceding essay. From that essay I take up themes; and I consider in the light of both essays the position now held by Newman in the estimation of many Christians.

Assent and inference are sharply distinguished by Newman. In an inference, our affirmation rests upon arguments and is conditional ('such and such; therefore so-and-so'). But in an assertion – the expression of our assent – we assert without such dependence, and so unconditionally. Previous inferences may have been indispensable for our assent, just as antecedents of one sort or another may have been necessary preliminaries for a command. For all that, commands and assertions are independent of their antecedents (pp. 3-4; I.1). Newman shows what the independence means for him when he differs from Locke, for whom a love of truth shows itself by 'the not entertaining of any proposition with greater assurance than the proofs it is built on will warrant' (p. 162; VI.1. The reference is to Locke's *Essay*, IV.19). Newman offers counter-examples:

> We are sure beyond all hazard of a mistake, that our own self is not the only being existing, that there is an external world;...that the earth...is a globe;...that there are...cities...which go by the names of London, Paris...We laugh to scorn the idea that we had

> no parents though we have no memory of our birth;...that a world of men did not live before our time, or that the world has had no history... (p. 177; VI.1).

And he comments on them: 'On all these truths we have an unhesitating hold...Assent upon reasonings not demonstrative is too widely recognized an act to be irrational, unless man's nature is irrational' (p. 179; VI.1). For Newman, 'demonstrative reasonings' are the abstract and absolute proofs of mathematics and logic. In concrete matter, such proofs are not to be had; so, were we to follow Locke, we could never give an absolute assent in this matter. But the counter-examples show that we do: 'there are many truths in concrete matter, which no one can demonstrate, yet every one unconditionally accepts' (pp. 159-60; VI.1).

Newman's insight in offering these counter-examples will be better understood today if we set beside what he writes some very similar views to be found in Wittgenstein's *On Certainty*.[1] Newman's claims about his counter-examples find a similarity in Wittgenstein's denial that we can *know* that, say, the earth has existed for many years. The setting for knowledge demands that we be able to give extra grounds that are compelling – but what grounds here could be more compelling than the proposition they are expected to support? Rather, the whole complexity of our life is bound up with such propositions. Newman thinks so too. He takes 'Great Britain is an island' and comments: '...our whole natural history...imply it in one way or another...there is a manifest *reductio ad absurdum* attached to the notion that we can be deceived on a point like this' (pp. 294-5; VIII.2). Wittgenstein writes in a similar way: 'If I wanted to doubt the existence of the earth long before I was born, I should have to doubt all sorts of things that stand fast for me' (§234). For both, processes of inference and proof come to an end. Newman writes: 'if we insist on proofs for every thing, we shall never come to action: to act you must assume, and that assumption is faith' (p. 95; IV.3) Just so, giving grounds comes to an end for Wittgenstein, and the end is 'not a kind of *seeing* but our acting' (§204); and 'my *life* consists in my being content to accept many things' (§344).

There are yet more resemblances, but for the present I turn to a difficulty that I think will have occurred to readers. Are not the examples given by Newman and Wittgenstein *privileged*? Are not assents of that sort special? 'Central assents' we might call them – but what of assents that are not central? Newman claims an absoluteness for assent *as such*: does he not owe us a wider range of examples?

I think so; and he does indeed offer more examples. What they are, and my judgment on them, I will state when giving my evaluation of what Newman has to say about the two main types of inference he distinguishes. One, as we have seen, is abstract and absolute demonstrations, of which logic is the supreme example; the other is reasoning in concrete, individual cases. I begin by giving an account of what Newman has to say of them both; my criticisms will then follow. And I turn first to demonstration.

For Newman, demonstration is limited both in its conclusions and in its starting-point. It is limited in its conclusions because it proceeds in generalities, treating the words it uses as symbols. That is, its cogency is acquired at the cost of an inability to do justice to what is concrete, for demonstration cannot reach the particular. And Newman offers an example of the inability, which I shall use later:

> There is a multitude of matters, to which mathematical science is applied, which...require that reasoning by rule should be completed by the living mind. Who would be satisfied with a navigator or engineer, who had no practice...to carry...his scientific conclusions out of their native abstract into the concrete...? (p. 278; VIII.1).

But demonstration is also limited in its starting-point, for it reaches its cogent conclusions by taking premises for granted. If *they* are in turn to be demonstrated, we shall be driven back to the assumptions we make, and so on to what are called 'first principles' but are in fact not universally shared. Logic can arrange proofs, and decide where differences of opinion are hopeless. But for proof in concrete matter 'we require an *organon* more delicate, versatile, and elastic than verbal argumentation' (p. 271; VIII.1).

And so I pass from demonstration to what Newman has to say of concrete reasoning, and of this *organon* of it. I first give some texts, and I begin with one which describes the whole pattern of concrete reasoning:

> It is the cumulation of probabilities, independent of each other, arising out of...the particular case...probabilities too fine to avail separately,...too numerous and varied for...conversion [into syllogisms], even if they were convertible (p. 288; VIII.2).

This reasoning does not proceed by 'any possible verbal enumeration of all the considerations', but rather by 'a mental comprehension of the whole case, and a discernment of its upshot...' (p. 291; VIII.2). The mind is swayed by a body of proof, of which it cannot give a complete analysis; and so it is that what is proof for one will not be proof for another (p. 293; VIII.2). Newman introduces a term to describe our capacity for drawing such conclusions. 'Judgment then in all concrete matter is the architectonic faculty; and what may be called the Illative Sense, or right judgment in ratiocination, is one branch of it' (p. 342; VIII.3). In reasoning concretely, 'every one who reasons, is his own centre', whatever means we may take for securing a common measure. And he admits that the 'sole and final judgment' on inference in concrete matter 'is committed to the personal action of the ratiocinative faculty, the perfection or virtue of which I have called the Illative Sense...and I own that I do not see any way to go farther ...' (p. 345; IX, before §1).

So much for Newman's account of reasoning in concrete matter. I now state four characteristics of its *organon*, the 'Illative Sense', which I discern in the texts I have just given.

First, it is described in terms of *achievement*, or success. We saw it called '*right* judgment in ratiocination', and the *perfection* or *virtue* of their faculty'. Consequently, if our judgment be not right, we can no longer ascribe it to the illative sense. Next, the illative sense is described in terms of *supplementation* and *simplicity*. It supplements – it is an organon *more delicate* than verbal argumentation, and the probabilities on which it works are *too numerous for conversion* into syllogisms. The supplementation it provides is *simple*, for we reach concrete conclusions by *discerning the upshot* of the whole case, and are swayed by a body of proofs we *cannot completely analyse*. And, as we have also seen, it is described in terms of *autonomy*, for men differ over first principles, each in reasoning concretely is *his own centre*, and verdicts there are passed by the *personal* action of the reasoning faculty.

We can notice at once how well these four characteristics go with 'central assents', as I have called them. Achievement is there, for what sense is there in talking of error over things like 'Great Britain is an island'? So are supplementation and simplicity, for we do indeed seem to proceed by a simple perception of what is the case, a perception with a force that goes beyond and supplements any one argument we might put into words. Autonomy too, for what further appeal could we make beyond this 'discernment of the upshot' to use Newman's phrase? But the presence there of the four characteristics brings us back to the earlier difficulty: the characteristics fit central assents, but do they fit any others? Should not Newman give further examples? As I said, he does; and one of them will provide the starting-point for my criticism of what we have seen him claiming.

He takes his example from an article in *Blackwood's* for 1853[2]. (Note that I here follow Newman's account of what is in the article.) An annotated copy of the First Folio had been produced, and one of the emendations touched the description of Falstaff's death (*Henry V*, II.3). The Folio text has 'his nose was as sharp as a pen and a table of green fields'. The received text – by an emendation which in its present form we owe to Theobald – is 'his nose was as sharp as a pen and a' babbled of green fields'. The newly-produced copy, however, reads 'his nose was as sharp as a pen on a table of green frieze'. The author of the article, Newman goes on, claims that neither the First Folio nor the annotated copy should be followed – the former makes no sense, and the latter is anonymous. Theobald's reading should be retained because it has a prescriptive *right*, and has sunk into the hearts of generations (pp. 271-2; VIII.1).

Newman then comments on all this. Logical demonstration cannot solve conflicts here. Should we emend Shakespeare at all, or simply leave the text as (Newman says) the text of Greek tragedies is now left by their best editors? If we decide to emend, how can we verbally enumerate all arguments for and against what is in the discovered copy? If we hold to Theobald's emendation on the ground of prescriptive right, will not Shakespeare disintegrate? Must we not decide what place is had by myths? Newman comments that 'though controversy is possible and useful at times, yet it is not adequate to this occasion'. Instead of any delineation in language, the 'sum-total of argument...requires rather to be photographed on the individual mind as by one impression...' (p. 274; VIII.1).

He draws the general moral that, while many words are needed for a valid argument, 'how short and easy a way to conclusion is the logic of good sense'. Syllogisms – the demonstrative abstract arguments of logic – have little to do with the formation of opinion. Rather it is 'those pre-existing beliefs...in which men either already agree... or hopelessly differ, before they begin to dispute' (p. 277; VIII.1).

So much for the example. Newman has said that logical demonstration can do little in the case, so my criticism begins by noticing the *vocabulary* in which he describes the work of logic, a few pages before giving this example. When logic substitutes words for the symbols it uses (he means, when the letters in its patterns are replaced by words like 'men' and 'mortal'), it proceeds by *stinting* them of their connatural senses, *draining* them of their associations, and *starving* each term down to a *ghost* of itself, so that the word stands for just one *unreal* aspect of the concrete thing to which it properly belongs, stands for a notion *tame and subdued* because it exists only in definition. For the logician, dog is not a thing he sees but a *name suggesting ideas*. His task is not to ascertain facts in the concrete, but to find and *dress up* middle terms and to enable his pupils to *show well* orally or in writing or in a *popular harangue* (pp. 267-8; VIII.1).

The next step in my critique must be to deal with these curiosities because they touch, not only Newman's opinions of logic, but also what he has to say of reasoning in concrete matter. The structures of our language can be investigated in various ways. One way touches the preservation, independently of subject-matter, of relations of truth and of consequence. Such investigation is the scope of logic. How far its investigations lead to results that are of immediate concern to our ordinary use of language is a question to which a dull but inescapable answer must be given – 'it is a matter of degree'. Some logical investigations are remote from ordinary use. But others are not, and those who teach logic have learned that their pupils do benefit from training in analysing the structures of argument; and that links in the structure like 'and', 'not', 'some' and 'must' can prove surprisingly difficult to handle. Those who investigate the patterns of argument in fields like law, science, or history know that an ability to assess reasoning in a general way can be indispensable to their own specific investigations. But none of this proves, or could prove, that logic's assessments should include the possession or lack by a given individual of a given property. Newman's description of the incapacity of abstract reasoning to deal with what is concrete (p. 110) is of a piece with the vocabulary of dilution and exhaustion we have seen him use to describe the processes of that reasoning. Both are misleading pieces of rhetoric designed to enforce what is in part a platitude.

In part. The scope of logic – the study of patterns of inference – does not include the appraisal of an individual's qualities: that much is platitude. What is not platitude is that Newman's description of logic leads to a distorted account of concrete inference as well. To show this, I go to the next stage of my critique, and look again at those four characteristics we have found associated by Newman with concrete inference.

Achievement lay in defining the illative sense in terms of its success. Such a definition muddles things from the start. There is obviously no harm in describing successful exercises of a capacity – 'winning at Bridge', for instance. But it is not legitimate to treat winning there as the product of a capacity distinct from the capacity of playing. Success at a process is not a further process – we do not have two capacities, and (when we lose at Bridge) pick the wrong one. The characteristic of achievement amounts to thinking that there are two – which is why it leads naturally to the mistake in the next characteristic, supplementation. Let us see how.

We do indeed often draw conclusions in concrete matter far more quickly than we could verbally enumerate our considerations for so concluding. Indeed we should not last long if we did not so draw them – think of the skills involved in motoring. Drawing such conclusions is part of human life, and if we wish to say that the greater swiftness is due to the supplementation provided by our illative sense, we are free to do so. But we are only putting a new name to the processes of estimation and reaction we have acquired by conditioning and practice while on the road, and the new name can mislead if we think it labels a special faculty. Unfortunately, to think about a special faculty is particularly tempting if we have defined the faculty in terms of its successful exercise – obviously so, because we then seem to be awarding ourselves an infallible means of drawing conclusions, do we but employ it. Consequently, if we take the move seriously, we must be prepared to say things like 'I skidded because I did not use my illative sense'.

So much for the characteristics of achievement and supplementation. I turn to the others – simplicity and autonomy. And in so turning I recall the example given by Newman of the need in matters like engineering for 'reasoning by rule' to be completed by 'the living mind' (see p. 111). I go to the example, first of all because it disposes at once of what I called autonomy – that in concrete reasoning each is his own centre, and that the sole and final judgment lies in something personal. We may be as personal and self-centred as we please; if the ship sinks, we were wrong. But I go to the example for another reason, which touches the characteristic of simplicity, and indeed the whole idea of the illative sense. I set beside Newman's claim about engineering-practice a real example of it.[3] Towards the end of the last century, calculations of stress-concentrations by naval architects were proving dangerously inaccurate. Earlier, engineers had calculated with a large safety-margin, for fear that they might not do justice to the particular structure. But when speed and lightness became ever more important for ships, the safety-margins proved tragically inadequate. Experiments were carried out to test stress, but they were inconclusive. A new theoretical treatment pointed to the part played by *openings* and *cracks* in surfaces; and this theoretical treatment was complemented by studies of the materials to which it was to be applied.

Notice first what is right in Newman's account. Some engineers undoubtedly possess a 'feel' for their tasks that they cannot adequately put into words. There was also undoubtedly a gap between predictions of stress calculated from the principles of mechanics and the stresses produced in particular vessels, and the 'living mind' was undoubtedly needed for the gap to be bridged. But now notice what is wrong with his account. The closing of the gap was not affected by some activity of the reason which 'discerned the upshot' of all the evidence, and was 'swayed by a body of proofs we could not completely analyse' – as the characteristic of simplicity would have us believe. That some conclusions are reached in that fashion is certainly true, and I gave examples from motoring. But not all conclusions are like that. In our example of naval architecture, the gap was not closed by some act of 'the living mind' distinct from what else engineers had been doing. There was a whole interplay of theory, calculation, guesswork, experiment, modifications to theory, survey of results in practice, and all the rest. Not only was the interplay complex, it took much time and many took part in it. It is this *shared and protracted complexity* in the example that we should bear in mind, as we see more of what Newman has to say of concrete inference. And we can begin by casting a colder eye at another text to do with the concrete application of general principles:

> In its [science's] very perfection lies its incompetency to settle particulars and details...thought is too keen..., its sources too remote...its path too personal...to admit of the trammels of any language... (p. 284; VIII.1).

The Jumblies and the Wise Men of Gotham might be content to have their vessels designed like that, but I should not care to sail in them myself!

I have set a real example of engineering beside Newman's claim concerning it. I now go back to another example of his – the proposed emendation to Shakespeare (p. 113) – and I set a real example beside that too. The example is narrated by A.E. Housman; it concerns Greek, but no knowledge of the language is required to see the point it conveys. The claim had been made that a future infinitive might in certain uses be replaced by an aorist infinitive, and the claim was supported by many examples of the replacement in manuscripts. The great Danish scholar Madvig rejected the claim. The replacements occur; but when they do occur the two forms are always very similar (*dexesthai – dexasthai, poiesein – poiesai*); forms that are sharply unlike (*lepsesthai – labein*) never exhibit the replacement. So there is nothing more than scribal mistranscription: examples work by their character, not by their number (Housman 1972, III pp. 1067-8). See once more how far Newman is right. There is indeed no syllogizing your way to emending a text, and, if I may quote Housman's paper again, 'A textual critic engaged upon his business is not at all like Newton investigating the motions of the planets: he is much more like a dog hunting for fleas' (p. 1059).

But if there is no syllogizing, neither is there some wordless intuition of the sum-total of evidence – except in the harmless sense that Madvig's sagacity exceeded those of his contemporaries. And we need go no further than Housman's *Collected Classical Papers* to see just how much the critic's art involves: a seizing of the thought of a passage; a knowledge of the author's style, metre and vocabulary; an assessment of the manuscripts' relations; an acquaintance with transcriptional errors; an evaluation of what earlier critics have suggested. No one of these is enough, and not even the whole assembly of them will bestow the art of felicitous emendation. But we have, as we had in the example of ship-building, a process that is shared, protracted, multiform, and concerned with language or signs of one sort or another. Newman's picture of inference in concrete matter does not do justice to what actually takes place.

I used earlier the phrase 'it is a matter of degree', and I use it again here, by way of summary of my criticisms. The four characteristics do fit the examples of central assents, but fit them because of the special character of the assents – assents where the whole apparatus of argument and debate is not to the point. Elsewhere, the characteristics will fit to a greater or lesser degree, and examples like skills in motoring (see p. 115) will provide the contrast between the brisk effectiveness of what we do and the laboured inadequacy of any verbal account we might give. Newman himself goes to such examples when describing the processes of concrete inference – weather-wise peasants, physicians' skill in diagnoses, insights of attorneys and detectives, Newton's mathematical intuition, calculating prodigies, and the military sagacity of Napoleon (pp. 331-4; VIII.3). It is a very mixed bag, and Newman's own preferences have clearly gone into the selection. The reasons for his preferences lie partly in his conceiving verbally articulate thought in terms of mental dilution, and partly in the personal and individual cast to his own thought and interests, and of this I shall have a few words to say later. But they also lie in the topics to which all his book is directed – inference and assent in religious matters.

These can be accommodated very easily – all too easily – to the pattern of the four characteristics, because of the special nature of religious belief. The 'all-embracing' character of what is believed; the absoluteness of the assent compared with whatever might be achieved through a verbal formulation of reasons for it; the notorious differences that exist here between proof for one and proof for another – all those things can make religious assent seem to possess the four characteristics that we saw go with central assents. What Newman writes amounts to forcing all concrete inference into the pattern associated with central assents; and the forcing amounts to making assent in religious matters seem very like central assents, and also seem a paradigm for the other assents we give and inferences we make.

It is, I repeat, a matter of degree. Newman's taking central assents as his pattern explains the role he assigns in concrete argument to antecedent presuppositions, 'those pre-existing beliefs...in which men either agree...or hopelessly differ, before they begin to dispute' (p. 277; VIII.1). That antecedent presuppositions matter a good deal is true, and Newman's stress upon them is yet another point where he is close to philosophical positions of our own time. But Newman gave that text when discussing the proposed emendation to Shakespeare, and I have tried to show that the practice of textual criticism is simply different. In central assents, difference over principles might well seem hopeless – what kind of considerations would our opponent accept? Again, differences occur in some debates that reveal dissents of a deep and pervasive character – we might well feel that, if they are to be resolved, time and experience are needed rather than verbal argument. All that is true, but it is not the whole truth; the pattern of central assents is not the only one. Just so, Newman's picture of an endless series of successive attempts to demonstrate what our arguments assume is misleadingly *linear*. A *network* of propositions would be a better picture, with various constraints from experience and theory to be satisfied. And the picture is also misleading in its depiction of the weary would-be-demonstrator eventually arriving at what he deems first principles, only to find that others do not so deem them. We are misled by the picture of a solitary quest. The network is a *shared* network; it represents, as I put it, a complex interplay of activities, distributed among many, who all have in some degree to respect the constraints of the network or give reasons for not respecting them. And the examples I have taken from engineering and from textual criticism show something of the forms which the complexity of activities can take.

Once more – I am obliged to come back to the point – it is a matter of degree, and of acknowledging the range of inferences. Newman's presentation in terms of idiosyncratic first principles and a wordless discernment of the upshot of the whole case is oversimplified. The practice of argument is more varied than he admits: principles are not as irrevocable, incommunicability not as widespread, verdicts not as irretrievably personal, as he would have us believe. 'Too quick despairer' – Arnold's apostrophe to Clough may be fairly addressed to Newman, when he gives us his account of concrete inference.

I hope it is clear by now that I think a good deal more needs saying than that, and that Newman's book contains many insights which deserve respect, even from those who remain unconvinced by his proposals. I have considered only some of its themes; all are worth examination. But I do have more to say about what we have seen Newman write, whether in the *Grammar of Assent* or in the passages of the *Apologia* examined in the preceding essay. And what I have to say can be stated as a reflection on the place he now occupies, a century after his death, both inside and outside the Church of his adoption. His memory is widely revered, his name associated with the Second Vatican Council, his works regarded as having yet more to teach us. Indeed, by way of a symbolic summary of it all, there are moves afoot to have him declared a saint. If I understand aright what I have read, Newman's canonisation is seen as having a special significance for three reasons. He is seen as a model for intelligent Christians who want to combine religious belief with the exercise of their understanding. He is seen as pointing to a better way of faith within the Church of Rome than what was noisily proclaimed there by contemporaries of his. And he is seen as having patiently endured frustrations imposed upon him in that Church, so that now, when the passage of a century has seen the vindication of his better way, the vindication would be solemnly proclaimed by his being raised to the altars.

All these claims I reject. I do not think that Newman can provide, in any substantial sense, a model for intelligent Christians. I do not think that his way of faith within the Church of Rome was substantially different from the way of those who opposed him. And I think that, frustrated though he was within that Church, the real damage it did him lay in confirming defects he already possessed on entering it. As for the canonisation, it would indeed have a significance, but the significance would be deplorable. I spell out in turn my three rejections and I then turn to the project of canonisation itself.

'Too quick despairer': I borrowed Matthew Arnold's words to express my dissatisfaction with Newman's account of concrete inference in the *Grammar of Assent.* But what Newman wrote there was of a piece with what he had been writing for years: the range of reason and its communicability are restricted, and the easing or accommodation of the restrictions is reserved for religion. The *Grammar of Assent* sums up the position; '...we need the interposition of a Power, greater than human teaching and human argument, to make our beliefs true and our minds one.' (p. 375; IX.3).

But similar claims are made in much earlier writings. Kingsley, we saw in the preceding essay, objected to the footnote about St Clement in the 'Sermon on Developments' (p. 96), but in the very text I quoted there he also objects to the intellectual pessimism of the sermon. Its lesson is 'that the discovery of truth is an impossibility'; and he also writes that it exhibits a 'seemingly sceptical method, pursued through page after page' (*K* p. 54).[4] Other sermons in the same volume have similar passages – for one, controversy 'is either superfluous or hopeless' once meanings have been clarified (*Oxford Sermons* X §45). The 'Sermon on Developments' itself admits the appearance of scepticism, but solves the difficulty by appealing to divine providence – and expresses a solution in a way that is disconcertingly like Hume's[5]. The depreciation of reason in order to make faith more acceptable is nothing new. There will always be those who find the move attractive even though it brings them into incongruous company, and engenders a credulity just as undiscriminating as their original scepticism. But the move can hardly be recommended as a model for those who want to combine their understanding with their belief.

Scepticism and credulity both fail by being too generic. I have offered specific examples of the shared and protracted arguments that can be involved in concrete inference, because I think that the *Grammar of Assent* does not do justice to them. But, after what we have seen of the book, we need not now be surprised at the uneasiness over specific pieces of verbal evidence we encountered when examining the *Apologia* in the preceding essay. There was the failure to examine adequately the title-page of *Macmillan's Magazine,* and to state adequately what Kingsley's original accusation was. And juxtaposition showed a refashioning of past claims in the light of present opinions, both in what Newman wrote of St Walburga's life and in his treatment of the footnote about St Clement (pp. 90f.). The uneasinesses go with the account of concrete inference in terms of antecedent presuppositions and a wordless grasp of the upshot of a case. Those terms are part of the story, but only part; we need attention to details as well.[6]

But our study of *Grammar of Assent* can tell us yet more about what is in the *Apologia*. I return to Newman's 'Advertisement' to the volume containing the 'Life of St. Walburga', already cited in the preceding essay (p. 90). Here, I direct the reader's attention to one sentence in it: 'They [i.e. miracles] are the kind of facts proper to ecclesiastical history, just as instances of sagacity and daring, personal prowess or crime, are the facts proper to secular history.' I am not concerned with miracles here, but with the disconcerting naiveness of what Newman writes about *secular* history – after all, he wrote the words in 1844, when the work of ancient historians like Niebuhr, Thirlwall and Grote was known in England, as well as the work of modern historians like von Ranke and Lingard. Just as curious is the sentence he wrote in a lecture delivered as a Roman Catholic in 1851: 'Did I read of any great feat of valour, I should believe it, if imputed to Alexander or Coeur de Lion' (reprinted in the *Apologia*, *A* p. 421). No one writes sillinesses like that all of a sudden: what had happened to Newman? As I said, the *Grammar of Assent* can help us to arrive at an answer.

It provides the answer in the passage about the proposed emendation to Shakespeare (p. 113). I gave there an example of what textual criticism is really like, but I now have to point out that Newman himself spent more than twenty years of his life as a Fellow of Oriel, a College that had been distinguished by its pursuit of learning; that the foundations of modern textual criticism were being laid in those years by Lachmann in Germany; and that Elmsley, Newman's immediate predecessor in Oriel as Principal of St Alban Hall, had made eminent contributions to criticism in his editions of Greek drama. That Newman could have written as he did on textual criticism in the *Grammar of Assent* bears its own witness to how those twenty years had been spent by him. It is customary to blame Oxford dons of those days for devotion to port at the expense of their duties. Let us also blame those who neglected their studies in the interests of theological bickerings and superstitious credulity.[7]

Newman, then, cannot be taken as a model for intelligent Christians who want to use their intelligence. Can he be taken as pointing to a better way in the Church of Rome than those who successfully opposed him in his life-time? In an innocuous sense he obviously can, just as – equally innocuously – he can be taken as an intellectual mentor. He was a man of vivid and penetrating insight, able to find significance in all manner of life's chances (the *examples* in the *Grammar of Assent* bear witness to this); and, with his sensitive intelligence, he was able to write of matters ecclesiastical in a way beyond the dreams of his contemporaries. But innocuousness is not enough; press the point, and we shall find that Newman's relationship to the Church of Rome in his day is persistently ambiguous.

We saw that in the *Apologia* he argued, from the darkness of the human condition and the apparent absence of God from the world around us, for the need for an infallible organ, proof against scepticism, to determine the revelation God might bestow (pp. 101-2). We can now recognise in this – let us call it the 'argument to infallibility' – the intellectual pessimism we have been noticing in the *Grammar of Assent*. In fact, the final chapter of that book, devoted to inference and assent in religious matters, follows a similar line. Our conscience testifies to our state of sin and to the need to appease God's anger; the divine 'absence' prepares us to accept revelation; the place of Christianity as the heir to Judaism, and the nature of its propagation against so many odds, can lead us to accept it. I am not concerned here with the merits of this argument, to which my summary can do but scant justice. Rather, I notice how difficult such an argument is to *stop*. It deal with matters that go so very deep into the emotions and feelings; it moves from a sense of darkness, doubt and incompetence to what promises light, certitude and a mending of mind and heart. It is an argument whose pattern can be detected in writings of Newman like the Sermons, composed years before he joined the Church of

Rome. It was part and parcel of his make-up, and that it carried him to Rome is not surprising. We know what happened then: Newman found in the church of his adoption an all too efficient machinery for translating his argument into ecclesiastical practice. He found too that other Oxford men like Manning and W.G. Ward rapidly acquired competence at working the machinery (Ward is said to have expressed the wish that there might be a fresh Papal Bull every morning). They, and others who thought as they did, had gone over to Rome because of what Newman had said, written and done. He must have felt like the Sorcerer's Apprentice.

But, for all his sincere distress, he found the force of his own argument to infallibility hard to resist. We saw in the preceding essay that his comments on the preposterous Munich Letter of Pius IX were ambiguous (pp. 104-5), and that, as he wrote to Acton, he could accept its principles without difficulty (p. 101). Which makes his complaint in the same letter about 'the dull tyranny of Manning and Ward' (*LD* XXI p. 84) open to the obvious riposte that Manning and Ward were but applying those principles. They were certainly nearer to how Rome applied them. December 1864 saw the publication of something even more preposterous by Pius IX (just six months after the *Apologia* had tried to make sense of Roman interventions). This was the 'Syllabus of Errors', a kind of wine-list of theological and social heterodoxies, catalogued for convenience. Newman's correspondence at the time shows that he regretted its publication, but from a letter to a friend we can see the limits of his regret and the nature of the limits: '...we are bound to receive what the Pope says, and not to speak about it. Secondly, there is little that he says but would have been said by all high churchmen thirty years ago...' (*LD* XXI p. 378). Newman's intellectual pessimism had gone with social views of extreme reaction in his early writings, and the principles in those writings had found expression in what he wrote after going over to Rome.[8] The pattern is what we have found already: Newman changed far less on his journey than we might think, and the force that impelled him did not die out, even amid his dislike of things he found at his destination. His destination had been implicit in his views of the Christian Church in his Oxford days, although he took years to work out the implication. It is worth remembering that what he disliked at Rome was implied by those views as well.

In consequence – to move on to the third rejection I have to make – talk of Newman's frustration in the Church of Rome has to be qualified. In one, lamentable sense the frustration was real, the juxtaposed texts near the end of the preceding essay show how real it was, and the story of Newman's days in the Church of his adoption is well summed up by the title of Trevor's second volume: 'Light in Winter'. But I think it will be clear now why I claimed that the greatest damage done to him was the confirmation of defects he already possessed on arriving. His defence in the *Apologia* of oppressive Roman interventions on the grounds that they have 'no bearing whatsoever on the exercise of the reason' (see p. 103) did not tally with the effect we there saw them to have on his own reason. But the defence itself is of a piece with what we have now seen of his account of concrete inference. His picture in the *Apologia* of an essentially private freedom in ratiocination goes with his failure in the *Grammar of Assent* to do justice to what I have called the possibilities of shared and protracted argument. And, as we have seen, what he wrote in the book was a development of themes that go back to much earlier writings. Frustration there was, disfavour and sheer injustice; and there was patience and persistence on Newman's part. But the damage went deeper. Newman changed little on the way to Rome: that was the real trouble.[9]

What then of the proposal to declare him a saint? It is undeniable that his canonisation would give much joy to many who admire his story, sing his hymns, and will never read a word of what he wrote. I have expressed in these two essays much disagreement with what I have found in his writings, but I have also expressed my belief that the two works I have examined contain many good things. I also think that memorable and wise things can be found throughout his works. Moreover, although I have claimed that he changed less on the way to Rome than is commonly believed, I readily admit that he suffered a great deal on the way, and that within the Church of Rome he persevered through evil report and good report, working hard and not sparing himself at a variety of demanding activities.[10] He has left words that will be read, and will be worth reading, for years to come. Why then do I describe as lamentable the significance of canonising him?

I so describe it because I think Newman matters, and that what is done concerning him is bound to have a significance for Christians, and in particular for Roman Catholics. My objection, in a few words, is that Newman's canonisation, given what we have seen of his views in these two essays, would be all too *appropriate*. I have in particular two things in mind that we have seen, and a brief reflection on the

Church of Rome as it is today will show what they are.

The break at the Reformation concerned a text: the Bible, its use and its availability, and the challenge its words contained to things being taught in the Church. Small wonder that Rome's reaction was to keep strict control of the sacred scriptures. The advent of biblical criticism concerned a text: it exhibited the cultural and historical limitations of the Bible, applying to it the secular disciplines that were being applied to secular texts. Small wonder that Rome's reaction was to stifle and to contain the growth of criticism by scholars subject to its sanctions. But over the years there have been changes. The Bible is now part of worship and preaching in a way it previously was not; and biblical criticism is and has been practised within the Roman Church with a freedom that a generation back would have seemed out of the question. Of all this, one thing concerns me here – the apparent *advantage* which the Roman Church has gained from a critical approach to the Bible. The sacred text has been shown to be limited and of its own age; the challenge it once made to present belief has thereby lost its force; the Church itself is left without a rival in the claims it makes upon believers.

All this is, of course, mere nonsense. As Matthew Arnold put it, you might as well argue that, because there are no fairies, therefore there must be gnomes. Declaring a total fundamentalism about the Bible may be possible and can at least make a claim to consistency. But there is no consistency in allowing historical awareness in one place and not in another. Biblical criticism is but one example of how we have become aware of the limitations in every part of our inheritance from the past, and aware of what is involved in the processes of trying to understand and to evaluate it – processes undertaken by us inside our own limitations. The explicit articulation of all this has been understandably of late growth, and it calls for a variety of skills – I have had occasion to mention textual criticism, there are many others. Biblical criticism has been with the Roman Church for a while now, but the consequences of it are being felt only gradually. They are very real consequences; those who are perturbed by them have every right to be, and those who accept them must not disguise the gravity of what is happening. But there is neither sense nor honesty in accepting the application of criticism here, and then regarding it as a means of securing the absence of its application to the Church. In one case as in the other, we must face the consequences of time and of the changes it brings, and we must articulate as clearly as we can what it is we have inherited and what we are going to make of it. If coming to terms with a critical reading of the Scriptures is painful, more painful yet will be coming to terms with a critical reading of the Church.

Unfortunately, there is something about the Roman Church in our own day that makes this application of criticism ever less likely. That Church, to a degree that it is both difficult and uncomfortable to appreciate, is adapting itself to the pattern of modern media of communication, and in particular to the pattern of television. There it is displayed as a centralised body with a powerful and powerfully visual figure-head, whose picturesque travellings – travellings conducted in an idiom of very secular origin – are mirrored by the availability of his electronic presence all over the globe. The picturesque pomp of its ceremonial, the confident assurance of its slogans – all seem to have been devised with a view to effective presentation on the screen. Of course, this is only half the story: if the media are the message, the media limit the message too. The pictorial presentation of the Church is attractive because it seems to circumvent the problem of time and of what time brings. Pictures have no past to jar with the present, they are a continuous performance that has only its own rules and needs only to be looked at, and the tension between past and present gives way to an appearance of homogenisation. But problems do not go away like that, they seem to do so only because a visual medium is not competent to deal with them. Articulation of language, analysis of verbal argument and verbal inheritance cannot be captured by television; they can of course be present, but only – if I may so put it – as guests of a medium that is alien to them, because it is essentially pictorial.

And that, of course, brings us to the first of the ways in which Newman's canonisation would be all too appropriate. What I have claimed to be beyond the capacity of television to capture – articulate and prolonged argument and analysis – is precisely the kind of thing I have found wanting in what Newman writes about concrete inference in the *Grammar of Assent*. I have given many texts from that book already, but I add one more because of its unhappy felicity at proving my point:

> [Religion] has never lived in a conclusion, it has ever been a message, a history, or a vision... Christianity is a history supernatural, and almost scenic... (p. 96; IV.3).

Alas, could there be an apter saint?

I have seen one unhappy appropriateness because of what I discerned in the *Grammar of Assent*. The other I trace to something we saw in the *Apologia* – what I called Newman's 'argument to infallibility'. Earlier in this essay, I noted both the force of the argument for Newman, and his distress at things he saw in the Church of Rome, to which the argument had led him (pp. 122-3), and the juxtaposed texts at the end of the preceding essay bear witness to the distress. In particular, those juxtaposed texts concern themselves with the *centralisation* of the Church in Newman's day, so that the freedom possessed by theologians in primitive and mediaeval times is absent (pp. 105-7). That modern media have increased this centralisation does not need to be argued, although it is worth pointing out that, once more, the limits of the medium limit the message: we should not be surprised that a centralised and pictorial medium should prove today so peculiarly apt for proclaiming the theology of Pius IX. But, as we have seen in this essay, Newman's discomforts did not remove for him the force of the argument to infallibility, and the sheer vividness and immediacy of television seem to go all too well with his desire for a palpable and real embodiment of authority, proof against all scepticism.[11] Our own time has seen all too much of what modern media can do to mind and heart. We need to tell ourselves, and to tell ourselves repeatedly, that a scepticism cured by revelation is not an adequate response to what is irrational in mankind. However, Newman's combination of discomfort with submission is clearly a useful model for the Church of Rome to point to. Perhaps as useful is his defence of Roman interventions on the grounds that they have 'no bearing whatsoever on the exercise of the reason' (*A* p. 350; see previous essay, p. 103).[12] After all, the submission makes him loyal and the discontent makes him seem moderate; what more could you want?

You will want, I hope, honesty in facing the past. If that past contains unhappy affinities between what Newman found in the Church of Rome and what he brought there, it does contain something else. The most conspicuous event in the Church of Newman's day was the First Vatican Council, with its declaration of papal infallibility. Our view of that Council has changed and is changing; and one of the reasons for the change is that Newman declined to attend it. That he was right to decline seems to me and to many beyond debate – as Aristotle said, admittedly in another context, there are some things for which there is simply no mode, time or place that is right. Newman was repeatedly snubbed and frustrated in what he undertook; all that was of a piece with the Council from which he rightly stood aloof. And his absence is still real, and still counts. So let us respect it for what it was. Today, at a time when the pattern of ecclesiastical government is slipping back to what it then was; at a time when defects in the Church as it now is are reflecting in a grotesquely magnified way deficiencies in Newman's own thought – at a time like this, to make use of his memory by bestowing on him the bauble of canonisation would be worse than bestowing on him, when it was all too late, the bauble of the Red Hat. Leo XIII is said to have attributed his gesture simply to a wish to please the Duke of Norfolk – which trivialises the action; but I had sooner popes pleased dukes than pleased themselves and their attendant ministers. They would do better to take to heart the bleakly honest words near the end of *Silas Marner*: 'It is too late to mend some things, say what they will.'

Vex not his ghost.

NOTES

1. Norman Malcolm, in his memoir of Wittgenstein, says that in 1947 Wittgenstein read but disliked the theological works of Newman (Oxford, 1958, p. 71). In 1977 I read a paper to a Wittgenstein conference, calling attention to the resemblances, some of which I am going to state here. I was informed by Professor Anscombe that Wittgenstein did not read the *Grammar of Assent*; but that, on hearing this theme in the book stated, he acknowledged the likeness to his own views. On what Malcolm had in mind, I can offer no information; but I record Professor Anscombe's recollection that Wittgenstein did not like Tract 90.

2. I owe the reference here (Newman writes simply 'an old number of a magazine of great name') to the recent edition of the *Grammar of Assent*, with introduction and notes, by I.T. Ker. I have not examined this in detail, but it seems an admirable piece of work which provides a wide and helpful assembly of information. Ker's reference here might have been extended, because the article is spread over three numbers of the volume for 1853, and the author's general position – which can be compared with Newman's account of it – is stated in the first instalment, pp. 181f.

3. I take (and much simplify) the example from J.E. Gordon's lucid and informative book *Structures* (Harmondsworth, 1980).

4. I relegate to a note for those interested the analogy drawn by Newman, in both late and early writings, between religious mysteries and limitations in mathematics. Square roots of negative numbers are 'a mystery on the side of algebra [as distinct from geometry]' and such formulae have been considered (Newman must be thinking of Argand diagrams) as attempts to express direction, which is 'really beyond the capacity of algebraical notation' (p. 49; IV.1). The analogy is more than unhappy (are theological mysteries to be overcome in the way that mathematics generalises and connects?), but Newman wrote in the same spirit thirty years earlier, in the 'Sermon on Developments' – on the very next page to the notorious footnote investigated in the preceding essay (pp. 344-6; see pp. 94f.). It is interesting to notice that Newman refers to Berkeley's *Analyst* only once in his book, and then as an example of a great man's eccentricity (p. 340; VIII. 3). He could in fact have found texts there alleging a resemblance between the faith demanded in theology and the faith demanded of those who use the differential calculus. For the record, Ker's note on the *Analyst* needs correction at his p. 219: it is hardly an 'attack on higher mathematics as leading to free-thinking'. For the record too, see how, on the very page where Newman writes these curiosities about algebra, he gives a thoroughly Fregean exposition of what counting involves!

5. Newman, *Sermon on Developments* pp. 248-9.

> And should anyone fear lest thoughts such as these should lead to...scepticism, let him take into account the...Providence of God...and he will at once be relieved of his anxiety...Why should we vex ourselves to find whether our deductions are philosophical or no, provided they are religious?...We have an instinct...we have external necessity forcing us, to trust our senses...

Hume *A Treatise on Human Nature* I.iv.7 (Selby-Bigge, pp. 268-9)

> The *intense* view of these...imperfections in...reasoning has so wrought on me...that I am ready to reject all belief...Most fortunately it happens, that...nature herself...cures me...I...play a game of back-gammon...and when...I would return to these speculations,...I cannot...enter into them any farther. Hence... I find myself...determined to live...like other people...

6. There is a similar unease over evidence in Newman's reply to Kingsley's charge on another topic, not mentioned in the former essay but discussed in chapter 4 of my book. The charge concerned the

status of the moral theologian Liguori, and I claimed there that Newman's answer uses uncritically an article on Liguori's position and misinterprets the significance of Roman documents. I add that Newman may have had second thoughts on the subject: after endeavouring in the *Apologia* to restrict the status of Liguori, he defended it shortly after completing the work (*LD* XXI p. 139).

7. Newman testified to the attainments of the classical scholar Charles Badham who (barred by religious unorthodoxy from the normal path of advancement) had been obliged to be a Birmingham Headmaster and was now seeking a post in Australia; he did not claim to provide an expert's witness (D.N.B. s.v. 'Badham'). I reserve until now the *bonne bouche*. The annotations in the folio had been condemned as forgeries, executed by Payne Collier, some years before Newman ever used the article in *Blackwood's*; and condemned, not because of any mental photography, but because pencil-marks were detected under the ink. (A recent defence of Payne Collier claims that an enemy had done this.)

8. I dealt with these topics in chapter 3 of my book; Kingsley had raised them, in objection to the social effects of Romanism.

9. It is always worth remembering that Kingsley's charges against Newman appealed to writings from his days in the Church of England quite as much as to those of his Roman days. Kingsley's suggestion that Newman was a secret papist is both absurd and unjust. What I have tried to show is that, both before and after going over to Rome, Newman's view of the human condition led to the assigning of a dominating and curative role to the instruments of divine revelation. The 'Economy' to which Kingsley objected (p. 96) is but one example of the role; it goes naturally with what I have called Newman's 'argument to infallibility'.

I now proceed to keep my promise to say something of the references given by Newman in the revised footnote he added to his account of St Clement, in the later edition of his *History of the Arians*. The note as a whole I have already discussed (pp. 96f); here I simply print the part that requires comment:

> Vide Plat. Leg. ii 8, οὔποτε ψεύδεται, κἂν ψεῦδος λέγῃ. Sext. Empir. adv. Log. p. 378, with Notes T and U.

First, Newman's punctuation notwithstanding, the piece of Greek does not come from Plato but from Sextus Empiricus (fl. c. 200 A.D.). The reference to Plato is to Book II of the *Laws*, 663B-664E, where the speaker commends a proposition as, even if not true, a lie in a good cause. The reference to Sextus Empiricus, in a civilised form, would be to *Adversus Logicos* I, §§42-3: the wise man 'never lies, even when he says what is false' (that is the phrase given in Greek). Newman must have used the edition of 1718 by Fabricius: footnote T there allows the wise man to say what is false sometimes; note U draws an analogy with doctors, who smear with honey the rim of the bowl containing a bitter draught. I wish I could decide what the texts are meant to show. Perhaps that Clement's permission to lie in the cause of religion was shared by pagans? It seems an odd palliation, given what the early Church said about paganism. Newman moreover, as we saw when first examining the note (p. 97), goes on to give a reference to what he writes of economy and equivocation in the *Apologia*. Are then Plato and Sextus Empiricus invoked as throwing light on those topics? That would be odder – and darker. The *Laws* (or so I hope) is not a proper model for any Church; and analogies with medical deceptions always end up by allowing truth, for its own sake, not to be a virtue.

10. For instance, amid all the labour involved in writing the *Apologia,* Newman bore the administrative burden of the Oratory School and of responsibility for the pastoral work of the Oratorians, was engaged in negotiations (once more, eventually frustrated) for the establishment of a Hall at Oxford for Catholic students, and was exposed to an incessant stream of enquiries from those who sought his spiritual advice. 'Excuse my extreme occupation', he writes to one correspondent, 'I write this during dinner-time' (*LD* XXI p. 107; the whole volume merits examination).

11. I cited in the previous essay a letter from Newman to a friend in which he complains of the repressive activities of 'a particular school in the Church, which is dominant' (p. 106). The letter complains too of 'the acting authorities at Rome', but also has a sentence worth noticing here: 'To be the slave of Christ and of his Vicar, is perfect freedom; to be the slave of man is as bad in the mind as in the body'. (*LD* XXI pp. 48-9). How Newman made sense with all this, I do not know. But sense is not always what is needed by *Realpolitik*.

12. I write 'perhaps' because some Roman documents make Newman look dangerously liberal – they demand an internal acceptance, or something. Perhaps the Bull of Canonisation could settle this delicate point?

BIBLIOGRAPHY

Preliminary note on methods of citation

The items by Newman and Kingsley that led to the *Apologia*, and the differences between the first and second editions of the work, are conveniently assembled in the edition by Ward (this is Wilfrid Ward, the son of the W.G. Ward mentioned earlier, and dissimilar in theology to him). I cite Newman's *Mr Kingsley and Dr Newman...*, Kingsley's *What, then, does Dr Newman mean?* and the *Apologia* itself (first edition) as *N*, *K* and *A* respectively. The *Grammar of Assent* I cite from the sixth (1887) edition, but (as far as I can make out) the pagination here is identical with that in the Uniform Edition of Newman's works, and appears as marginal numbers in the new edition by Ker. However, not all editions of the book preserve this pagination, so I add the chapter and section after each citation by page. The two volumes of Newman's *Letters and Diaries* used I cite by *LD* with volume number. I add that my own book on the controversy with Kingsley appeared under the pseudonym 'G. Egner'. I had used this earlier ('Gegner' in German is 'adversary' – *diabolus*, if you will), and found the name growing on me! I also make a point about the item 'FitzPatrick 1978', an article on the *Grammar of Assent* published in the *Irish Theological Quarterly*. While I am grateful for the generous space then allotted me by the Editor, I must repeat my protests made elsewhere at the illiterate nonsense manufactured in places from what I wrote, by whoever set it up in type. I was given no opportunity to correct, and I have never been quite the same since reading the result.

Asquith, M., *The Autobiography of Margot Asquith*, 2 vols (London, 1920).

Davidson, R.T. and Benham, W., *The Life of Archibald Campbell Tait*...2 vols (London, 1981).

Denzinger-Schönmetzer, *Enchiridion Symbolorum*...(Barcelona, 1963). [This gives, either in extracts or complete, the texts of Roman documents. References are made by the outer marginal numbers. Pius IX's Munich Letter is at pp. 2875-80; his 'Syllabus of Errors' is at pp. 2901-80, preceded by a prefatory note that exhibits signs of editorial embarrassment.]

Egner, G., see FitzPatrick, P.J.

FitzPatrick, P.J., *Apologia pro Charles Kingsley* (London, 1969).

——— 'A Study in the *Grammar of Assent*', *Irish Theological Quarterly* 45 (1978), pp. 155-66, pp. 217-33.

Housman, A.E., 'The Application of Thought to Textual Criticism' in his *Collected Classical Papers*, ed. J. Diggle and F.R. Goodyear, 3 vols (Cambridge, 1972) Volume 3, pp. 1058-69.

Huxley, L., *The Life and Letters of Thomas Henry Huxley*, 2 vols (London, 1900).

Kingsley, C., see Ward, W. (ed.).

Malcolm, N., *Ludwig Wittgenstein: a Memoir* (Oxford, 1958).

Newman, J.H., Advertisement to 'The Family of St Richard' [where the 'Life of St. Walburga' is given], series 2 in *The Lives of the English Saints* (London, 1844-5).

——— *Apologia pro Vita Sua*. For this, and for the pamphlets by Newman and by Kingsley that preceded it, see Ward, W. (ed.). See also prefatory note to this Bibliography.

——— *Certain Difficulties felt by Anglicans*... VIII: 'The Social State of Catholic Countries no Prejudice to the Sanctity of the Church' (London, 1900).

——— *An Essay in aid of a Grammar of Assent* (London, 1887) edited with introduction and notes by I.T. Ker (Oxford, 1985).

——— *The Arians of The Fourth Century* (London, 1833).

——— revised edition (London, 1871).

——— *The Letters and Diaries of John Henry Newman* Volume XXI: *The Apologia, January 1864 to June 1865* ed. C.S. Dessain and E.E. Kelly (Walton-on-Thames, 1971) [cited as '*LD* XXI'].

——— Volume XXIV *A Grammar of Assent January 1868-December 1869* ed. C.S. Dessain and T. Gornall (Oxford, 1973) [cited as '*LD* XXIV'].

——— '[Sermon on] the Theory of Developments in Religious Doctrine' in *Sermons, Chiefly on the Theory of Religious Belief, Preached Before the University of Oxford* (London, 1843).

——— but with the altered footnote, in *Fifteen Sermons Preached before the University of Oxford*... (London, 1872).

——— '[Sermon on] Wisdom and Innocence' in *Sermons Bearing on Subjects of the Day* (London, 1843).

Trevor, M., *Newman: The Pillar of the Cloud* (London, 1961).

——— *Newman: Light in Winter* (London, 1962) [I cite these as 'Trevor I' and 'Trevor II'].

Ward, W., *The Life of John Henry Cardinal Newman*, 2 vols (London, 1912).

_______ (ed.), *Newman's* Apologia pro Vita Sua: *The Two Versions of 1864 and 1865. Preceded by Newman's and Kingsley's Pamphlets*...(Oxford, 1931) [For methods of citation, see note prefixed to this Bibliography].

Wittgenstein, L., *Über Gewissheit/On Certainty* (Oxford, 1969).

5

DID NEWMAN ANSWER GLADSTONE?

Fergus Kerr, OP

Newman clearly believed that, with *A Letter to the Duke of Norfolk*,[1] he had refuted Gladstone's *Expostulation*.[2] He was delighted by the many letters of gratitude and congratulation which he received in the weeks after publication, from bishops, priests both Irish and English, Jesuits (including Hopkins) and Dominicans, lay people (including W.G. Ward), as well as Gladstone himself.[3] In listing the eminent clergymen among them he reveals his relief that his arguments were 'orthodox'.

It cost him three months of hard work. He returned to Birmingham at the end of September 1874, after ten days of sightseeing and walking in Yorkshire and the Lake District, to find that Gladstone, in the course of defending the place of ritual in the liturgy of the Church of England, had hit out parenthetically at the Roman Catholic Church – 'no one can become her convert without renouncing his moral and mental freedom, and placing his civil loyalty and duty at the mercy of another'.[4] Such charges had dogged Newman since 1845, but the Marquis of Ripon,[5] one of Gladstone's colleagues in the recently defeated Liberal government, had just been received into the Roman Catholic Church – all the more reason for Newman's friends, Lord Blachford[6] and Lord Emly,[7] to be angered by this casual aspersion on the patriotism of Roman Catholics in public life.

Throughout October Newman tried to write a reply to Gladstone's parenthesis but without success. The protests of others, both private and public, compelled (or encouraged) Gladstone to set his thoughts out at greater length. His *Expostulation* appeared on 5 November 1874. On receiving a proof copy from Gladstone, Newman at once started work again – 'I *could not* have answered Gladstone's parenthetic, sweeping declamation. It had no points. And Ireland became a great difficulty – But his today's pamphlet, I can answer – at least I shall try and will tell you when I fail or else go to press', as he wrote to Emly.[8] It is interesting that Newman immediately felt that

Gladstone's *Expostulation*, in contrast with the parenthesis, made it easier for him to deal with that 'great difficulty'.

Newman's main argument, communicated to Gladstone in a copy of a letter which Newman wrote to Ambrose Phillipps de Lisle before he had seen Gladstone's pamphlet and relying on the London newspaper reports of its content, was not found convincing. This could not surprise anyone today, since Newman urged only that, in his interpretation of 'Pastor Aeternus', Gladstone erred by taking the text at face value – 'Theological language', however, 'like legal', so Newman wrote,[9] 'is scientific, and cannot be understood without the knowledge of long precedent and tradition, nor without the comments of theologians'. He instances Fessler's authoritative book[10] – 'Even now Bishop Fessler has toned down the newspaper interpretations (Catholic and Protestant) of the words of the Council, without any hint from the Council itself to sanction him in doing so'. Obedience to the Pope, so Newman concludes, will have 'important limitations' – '*in the writings of theologians*' (my emphasis).

Could such an argument have removed Gladstone's fear of 'Vaticanism'? Acton, to whom Gladstone showed Newman's letter to Phillipps de Lisle, reported to Newman that Gladstone 'did not feel the full force of the argument you employ' – 'but', as he goes on to say,[11] 'I think it is one he would feel the force of if it was put more fully before him'. Thus Acton encouraged Newman in the work that he had already begun. How far, however, did Newman develop or supplement his argument? Does Newman's *Letter* belong to the category of toning down newspaper interpretations of papal supremacy and, if so, did he really refute Gladstone?

Gladstone began, somewhat disingenuously, with an apology for the 'seeming roughness' of his offensive parenthesis. He wanted only to show that the 'alarm at the aggressive activity and imagined growth of the Roman Church in this country', although 'groundless', helped to 'disturb and perplex the public mind in the consideration of our own religious difficulties' (*Exp*., p. 5). A Royal Commission had been grappling with these difficulties since 1867, and they were supposed to have been dealt with by the Public Worship Regulation Act earlier in 1874. (The imprisonment of four 'ritualist' priests between 1877 and 1882 so discredited the Act that it lay dormant until repealed by the Ecclesiastical Jurisdiction Measure of 1963.) Gladstone does not properly explain why this public perception (mistaken, as he thinks) of the advance of the Roman Catholic Church in England should so confuse Anglicans. His concern originally, so he claims, was limited to 'the question whether a handful of the clergy are or are not engaged in an utterly hopeless and visionary effort to Romanise the Church and the people of England' (*Exp.*, p. 6). The 'Romanising' liturgical practices of a few Anglican clergymen hardly warrant his immediately raising the question of anybody's civil allegiance – or so it might seem today. But, as Newman noted so enigmatically, Ireland was perhaps the great difficulty. Gladstone refers to his five million Roman Catholic fellow-countrymen – 'nearly one sixth of the inhabitants of the United Kingdom' (*Exp.*, p. 46). Gladstone the theologian no doubt wanted to keep Anglican worship 'English'; Gladstone the politician knew that four million dubiously loyal British subjects lived in Ireland. It was their loyalty to the State that had been placed in doubt once again, by the doctrine of papal infallibility.

Fears about the loyalty of the Irish lie at the root of Gladstone's *Expostulation* – as Newman notes (*Letter*, p. 179):

> The main question which Mr Gladstone has started I consider to be this: – Can Catholics be trustworthy subjects of the State? Has not a foreign Power a hold over their consciences such that it may at any time be used to the serious perplexity and injury of the civil government under which they live?

Indeed, Gladstone claims that his concern is not with *theological* controversy (*Exp.*, p. 9):

> Indeed, with theology, except in its civil bearing, with theology as such, I have here nothing whatever to do. But it is the peculiarity of Roman theology that, by thrusting itself into the temporal domain, it naturally, and even necessarily, comes to be a frequent theme of political discussion.

That remark reveals his ecclesiological presuppositions. Gladstone thinks that conflicts between Church and State need not arise unless Church leaders make claims as exorbitant as the Roman Catholic Church appears to him to do (*Exp.*, p. 10):

> All other Christian bodies are content with freedom in their own religious domain. Orientals, Lutherans, Calvinists, Presbyterians, Episcopalians, Nonconformists, one and all, in the present day, contentedly and thankfully accept the benefits of civil order; never pretend that the State is not its own master; make no religious claims to temporal possessions or advantages; and, consequently, never are in perilous collision with the State.

Admitting that the *Kulturkampf*, then at its most violent stage, had brought Church and State into conflict, though professing not to be competent to have an opinion on the particulars of the case, Gladstone maintains that the Vatican Council is 'primarily responsible for the pains and perils, whatever they may be, of the present conflict' (*Exp*., p. 48).

Newman sends Gladstone straight back to 1833: 'The Tracts for the Times were founded on a deadly antagonism to what in these last centuries has been called Erastianism or Caesarism' (*Letter*, p. 198). Indeed, the Roman Catholic Church's independence of the State was 'the luminous fact which more than any other turned men's minds at Oxford forty years ago to look towards her with reverence, interest, and love' (ibid.). Newman turns on Gladstone with all the passion of his magnificent rhetoric (*Letter*, p. 197):

> Go through the long annals of Church History, century after century, and say, was there ever a time when her Bishops, and notably the Bishop of Rome, were slow to give their testimony in behalf of the moral and revealed law and to suffer for their obedience to it? ever a time when they forgot that they had a message to deliver to the world, – not the task merely of administering spiritual consolation, or of making the sick-bed easy, or of training up good members of society, or of 'serving tables' (though all this was included in their range of duty), – but specially and directly, a definite message to high and low, from the world's Maker. Whether men would hear or whether they would forbear? The history surely of the Church in all past times, ancient as well as medieval, is the very embodiment of that tradition of Apostolical independence and freedom of speech which in the eyes of man is her great offence now.

Newman ignores the many times and places in which the Roman Catholic Church has betrayed the 'political and social traditions' which it has inherited from 'that free-spoken dauntless Church of old' (*Letter*, p. 198). But this anti-Erastian note sounds as relevant as ever in many countries today (even in England). Although he dearly wants to clear his fellow Catholics of the charge of divided allegiance, Newman refuses to do so at the price of allowing the Church to moderate its message to please the State – 'collisions can take place between the Holy See and national governments' (*Letter*, p. 237).

On one point Newman could never have moved Gladstone. His conception of himself as an Englishman and an Anglican (his father, 'that overpowering Liverpool tycoon',[12] had made the break from Scotland and Calvinism) ensured that, for Gladstone, 'the Church and people of England' were one and the same thing. Even in his most Tractarian days, he seems never to have been tempted to secede to Rome. To leave the Church of England was, for Gladstone, equivalent to leaving the English nation. Political realities showed him its impracticality, but he never repudiated the vision of Christian nationhood which he expounded in his first (and arguably his best) book, *The State in its Relations with the Church*.[13] Even there, at that early date, he seems less than fully convinced about the appropriateness of the Anglican establishment in Ireland.

'My mission is to pacify Ireland': everyone knows the story of Gladstone's first words when he realised that he was to become Prime Minister.[14] Within days he was at work on a draft of the Irish Church Bill, which was passed in the House of Commons on 23 July 1869. Three or four years earlier nobody imagined that the Church of Ireland could be so decisively disestablished and disendowed. Gladstone's second measure to wean the Irish from Fenianism, the Irish Land Act, became law in 1870, although he was prevented from accompanying it by the liberation of some Fenian prisoners ('those who can be regarded as purely political offenders').[15] His intentions are plain in such words as these:

> What we have to do is to defy Fenianism, to rely on public sentiment, and so provide (as we have been doing) the practical measures that place the public sentiment on our side, an operation which I think is retarded by any semblance of *severity* to those whose offence we admit among ourselves to have been an ultimate result of our misgovernment of the country. I am afraid that local opinion has exercised, habitually and traditionally, too much influence in Ireland, and has greatly compromised the character of the empire. *This* question I take to be in most of its aspects an imperial question.[16]

A question of security, as we might say today. Gladstone's attempt to complete his programme for the stabilisation of Ireland with the Irish University Bill was defeated on 11 March 1873 by only three votes, but Cardinal Cullen's vehement opposition to the scheme evidently influenced so many of the Irish Catholic members even of Gladstone's own party that he was forced to offer his government's resignation. Archbishop Manning, who supported Gladstone throughout, wrote to him afterwards as follows: 'This is not your fault, nor the Bill's fault, but the fault of England and Scotland and three anti-catholic centuries'.[17]

That seems a more profound judgment than Gladstone's own – or Newman's for that matter. That Gladstone felt aggrieved seems clear. His government had done all it could 'to give Ireland all that justice could demand, in regard to matters of conscience and of civil equality' (*Exp.*, p. 59), and, 'under the great head of Imperial equity', nothing remained except better provision for higher education –

> But the Roman Catholic prelacy of Ireland thought fit to procure the rejection of that measure, by the direct influence which they exercised over a certain number of Irish Members of Parliament, and by the temptation which they thus offered – the bid, in effect, which (to use a homely phrase) they made, to attract the support of the Tory opposition. Their efforts were crowned with complete success (*Exp.*, p. 60).

Gladstone supposes that the intervention of the Irish Bishops was made possible by 'the great change... in the position of Roman Catholic Christians as citizens' which he deems to have 'reached its consummation', as he goes on to say, 'by the proceedings or so-called decrees of the Vatican Council' (*Exp.*, p. 57). He does not offer any evidence for a connection, direct or indirect, between the Bishops' hostility to the Irish University Bill and the definition of papal infallibility.

Newman does not resist this invitation to ridicule Gladstone – 'this step on the part of the bishops showed, if I understand him, the new and mischievous force which had been acquired at Rome by the late acts there' – leading, allegedly, to 'the daring deed of aggression in 1873, when the Pope, acting (as it is alleged) upon the Irish Members of Parliament, succeeded in ousting from their seats a ministry who, besides past benefits, were at that very time doing for Irish Catholics, and therefore ousted for doing, a special service' (*Letter*, pp. 181-2). Newman's irony, whilst scoring off Gladstone's injured pride in his administration's services to Ireland as well as exploiting his failure to demonstrate any 'interposition of Rome' (*Letter*, p. 184) in the defeat of the Irish University Bill, deflects attention from the serious issue. From his first sight of the draft of the Bill he knew that the Irish Bishops could not honourably accept it – why did Gladstone not consult him rather than Manning (one almost hears him whisper)? In any case, the Irish Bishops have an interest which has as much right to be represented in the House of Commons as the railway interest or the brewers. Finally, 'they spoke not simply as Catholic Bishops, but as the Bishops of a Catholic nation':

> It seems to me a great mistake to think that everything that is done by the Irish Bishops and clergy is done on an ecclesiastical motive; why not on a national? but if so, such acts have nothing to do with Rome. I know well what simple firm faith the great body of the Irish people have, and how they put the Catholic Religion before anything else in the world... but who can deny that in politics their conduct at times – nay, more than at times – has had a flavour rather of their nation than of their church? (*Letter*, pp. 185-6).

Thus Newman simply denies that Irish episcopal opposition to the Bill was grounded on pastoral or theological considerations – a denial that Cardinal Cullen's famous pastoral letter would itself suffice to refute.[18] Newman's explanation for the Bishops' opposition seems much less perspicacious than Manning's. It does nothing to clarify Gladstone's admittedly inadequately stated problem: did the Vatican Council embolden bishops to confront the State on behalf of the Church? His denial that the Irish Bishops acted *as bishops* is couched in what some readers might feel to be typically anti-Irish English political rhetoric (unconsciously so, of course). More interestingly, it perhaps already reveals Newman's strange lack of interest in the function of the episcopate in the Church.[19]

As we have already seen, Newman allowed that 'collisions can take place between the Holy See and national governments' (*Letter*, p. 237) – but that it was with the Holy See, rather than with the local Bishops, that he saw the possibility of conflict indicates how profoundly ultramontane his ecclesiological sympathies were. He could, of course, also show how deeply ambivalent he was about the papacy. Consider, for example, what he wrote to Lady Simeon in November 1870:[20] 'The present Pope cannot live long – he has lived too long – but, did he live Methuselah's age, he could not in his acts go beyond the limit which God has assigned to him – nor *has* he, though he wished it'. He was admittedly trying to comfort her, but his own rancour surely shows through in such private remarks. Compare the mellifluous sycophancy in the following passage, written just over four years later (*Letter*, p. 193):

> It [the Vatican Council] was an extraordinary gathering, and its possibility, its purpose, and its issue, were alike marvellous, as depending on a coincidence of strange conditions, which, as might be said beforehand, never could take place. Such was the long

> reign of the Pope, in itself a marvel, as being the sole exception to a recognized ecclesiastical tradition. Only a Pontiff so unfortunate, so revered, so largely loved, so popular even with Protestants, with such a prestige of long sovereignty, with such claims on the Bishops around him, both of age and of paternal gracious acts, only such a man could have harmonized and guided to the conclusion which he pointed out, an assembly so variously composed.

Newman was, of course, a master of irony; but it is hard to believe that he wrote that encomium with tongue in cheek.

Gladstone speaks of 'the wonderful change now consummated in the constitution of the Latin Church' as involving the 'degradation of its Episcopal order', a sign of which was that the Pope, not the Council, endorsed the document – 'and the humble share of the assembled Episcopate in the transaction is represented by *sacro approbante concilio*' (*Exp*., pp. 32-4). Despite the pernickety detail with which Newman criticises so many of Gladstone's assertions, particularly about the *Syllabus*, he never adverts to this point. Gladstone speaks of 'that spirit of centralisation, the excesses of which are as fatal to vigorous life in the Church as in the State' (*Exp*., p. 33), something of which Newman often complained elsewhere, especially in letters; but here, in the *Letter*, where he is supposedly expounding the correct interpretation of papal claims, we find no anxiety at 'that concentration of the Church's powers' (*Letter*, p. 209). On the contrary, we are offered some lyrical pages, of dubious historical value, to show that 'that which in substance was possessed by the Nicene Hierarchy, that the Pope claims now' (*Letter*, p. 208). The rights, prerogatives, privileges, and duties ascribed to the Bishops in the ancient Church, are now all concentrated in the Pope.

Consider this (*Letter*, pp. 210-11):

> Say that the Christian polity now remained, as history represents it to us in the fourth century, or that it was, if that was possible, now to revert to such a state, would politicians have less trouble with 1800 centres of power than they have with one? Instead of one, with traditionary rules, the trammels of treaties and engagements, public opinion to consult and manage, the responsibility of great interests, and the guarantee for his behaviour in his temporal possessions, there would be a legion of ecclesiastics, each bishop with his following, each independent of the others, each with his own views, each with extraordinary powers, each with the risk of misusing them, all over Christendom... It would

> be an ecclesiastical communism: and, if it did not benefit religion, at least it would not benefit the civil power.

Divine providence has brought it about, however, that the exercise of the apostolic powers once given to the Bishops 'should be concentrated in one see' (*Letter*, p. 211). The choice lies between 'episcopal autonomy', which means 'ecclesiastical communism', and the see of Peter – 'With him alone and round about him are found the claims, the prerogatives, and duties which we identify with the kingdom, set up by Christ' (*Letter*, p. 208). He is 'a thousand bishops in himself at once' (*Letter*, p. 212).

Newman is often cited as a precursor of the ecclesiology of the Second Vatican Council. In some respects he may well be so; but he was not an exponent of the doctrine of the One Church as a communion of local churches. Indeed, on the evidence of the *Letter*, he had no understanding of the relationship between papacy and episcopacy. In the aftermath of 1870 he did little to redress the balance in favour of the episcopate. 'To believe in a Church is to believe in the Pope' (*Letter*, p. 208) – a conclusion which, for a Roman Catholic, is unexceptionable – provided that the other Bishops are not reduced to papal vicars or rendered superfluous (as they seem to have been for Newman) by the development of the papacy. It would be difficult to be more ultramontane.

Newman needed this emphasis on the papacy to circumvent Gladstone's embarrassing reminder that the Roman Catholic Relief Act of 1829, and all that had taken place in the next forty-five years down to Gladstone's own Irish legislation, depended on episcopal assurances that the definition of papal infallibility was absolutely impossible. Newman simply asserts that, at the time (1826), 'the clergy, both of Ireland and England, were educated in Gallican opinions' (*Letter*, p. 189). The Bishops then (he goes on to say, very significantly) could never have imagined that a majority of their order would one day find it their duty 'to relinquish their prime prerogative, and to make the Church take the shape of a pure monarchy' (ibid.). But the representatives of the British government who sought to reassure themselves concerning Roman Catholic beliefs about papal supremacy were wrong to consult English and Irish Catholic authorities:

> If they wanted to obtain some real information about the probabilities of the future, why did they not go to headquarters? Why did they potter about the halls of Universities in this matter of

> Papal exorbitances, or rely upon the pamphlets or examinations of Bishops whom they never asked for their credentials? Why not go at once to Rome? (*Letter*, p. 190).

For Gladstone, of course, the consultation with local Catholics that took place in the 1820s seemed entirely proper. One course of action was to look at the arrangements then in the Austrian empire (Josephinism, as it was to be labelled) –

> But there were also measures taken to learn, from the highest Roman Catholic authorities in this country, what was the exact situation of the members of that communion with respect to some of the better known exorbitancies of Papal assumption (*Exp*., p. 25).

It was reasonable to consult 'the leaders and guides of Roman Catholic opinion nearest to our own doors' (*Exp*., p. 29). To this Newman answers that, 'considering the state of theological opinion seventy years before', it is indeed 'marvellous' that 'all but a few out of so many hundred Bishops' concurred in 'the theological judgment, so long desired at Rome' – and he concludes this part of the argument as follows (*Letter*, pp. 193-4):

> For myself, I did not call it inopportune, for times and seasons are known to God alone, and persecution may be as opportune, though not so pleasant as peace; nor, in accepting as a dogma what I had ever held as a truth, could I be doing violence to any theological view or conclusion of my own; nor has the acceptance of it any logical or practical effect whatever, as I consider, in weakening my allegiance to Queen Victoria; but there are few Catholics, I think, who will not deeply regret, though no one be in fault, that the English and Irish Prelacies of 1826 did not foresee the possibility of the Synodal determinations of 1870, nor can we wonder that Statesmen should feel themselves aggrieved, that stipulations, which they considered necessary for Catholic emancipation, should have been, as they may think, rudely cast to the winds.

And with these words he passes from 'the mere accidents of the controversy' to 'its essential points'.

It is with perceptible relief that Newman passes to the essential points – but should Gladstone have been satisfied with the argument so far? He has been ridiculed for alleging that the Vatican decrees enhanced the Irish Catholic hierarchy's influence on the opposition to the Irish University Bill in 1873. He has been told that they were not acting as bishops, in any case, but as Irish nationalists. Newman agrees that Catholic emancipation, a lóng and difficult process, undertaken almost entirely in order to stabilise Ireland, in the aftermath of the Napoleonic wars, had as its premise guarantees by English and Irish Bishops that traditional claims for papal jurisdiction no longer had the power to divide Catholic allegiance. But what English and Irish Bishops believed at the time was irrelevant – inquiries about what Catholics believe should always be addressed to 'headquarters'. It is a pity that the English and Irish Bishops in 1826 lacked the foresight to allow for the Vatican Council. One quite understands that politicians who risked a good deal to bring about Catholic emancipation should 'feel themselves aggrieved'. But the doctrine of papal authority defined in 1870 has no bearing on anyone's civil allegiance in any case – let us get on with showing *that*.

Why exactly was Ireland a 'great difficulty' for Newman when he first tried to refute Gladstone's aspersions on Catholic loyalty? Why was Gladstone's *Expostulation* so much easier to answer than the original parenthetical remark? Was it that, in the *Expostulation,* Gladstone raises so many other questions that Newman felt able to dismiss 'the mere accidents of the controversy' in this cavalier way? How far does his exposition of the 'essential points' confirm that the 'mere accidents' may be so smoothly dismissed?

The structure of the *Letter* is as follows. Newman first sketches the anti-Erastianism of the 'ancient Church' (pp. 195-205). Fidelity to the Gospel will often bring the Church into conflict with the State. Next, he describes how, providentially, authority in the Church has gradually been concentrated in the hands of the Pope – the extraordinary doctrine to which we have already alluded (pp. 206-22). Newman then tackles the question of 'divided allegiance' (pp. 223-45), allowing that allegiance to Queen Victoria and to Pope Pius IX might pull him in contrary ways – 'in which in this age of the world I think it never will' (p. 243) – and labouring to produce examples, 'extreme and utterly improbable cases' (p. 240), which by their fancifulness are intended to show how unlikely obedience to the Pope would ever conflict with allegiance to the Crown. Indeed he finds great difficulty in tracing *any* papal impact on people's lives (*Letter*, p. 228):

> What interference with our liberty of judging and acting in our daily work, in our course of life, comes to us from him? Really, at first sight, I have not known where to look for instances of his

actual interposition in our private affairs, for it is our routine of personal duties about which I am now speaking.

It was, of course, easier in 1874 than it has been since 1968[21] to argue that 'the amount of the Pope's authoritative enunciations has not been such as to press heavily on the back of the private Catholic' (p. 231). Newman is engaged, understandably, in minimising the importance of papal teaching – 'the weight of his hand upon us, as private men, is absolutely unappreciable' (p. 229). In practice, that is to say, at least 'in this age of the world', Gladstone did not need to fear papal impositions on the conscience of any of his Roman Catholic acquaintances. But this argument does not go to the root of the problem. In much of the *Syllabus*, not to mention the social teaching inaugurated by Pope Leo XIII, there was surely a good deal to trouble the conscience of many Catholic politicians and industrialists. In the last decades of the twentieth century one might welcome much greater pressure on the private and public conscience from the Pope and his representatives on human rights, nuclear deterrence, and much else besides abortion and population control. Newman's reassuring marginalisation of papal moral teaching no doubt pacified Gladstone; it contributes little towards a deeper understanding of how people's social conscience and political options might be pulled in contrary ways by Church and State.

We then have the famous chapter on 'Conscience' (pp. 246-61):[22]

> Conscience is the aboriginal Vicar of Christ, a prophet in its informations, a monarch in its peremptoriness, a priest in its blessings and anathemas, and, even though the eternal priesthood throughout the Church could cease to be, in it the sacerdotal principle would remain and would have a sway (*Letter*, pp. 248-9).

Conscience is thus a kind of internal Prophet-Monarch-Priest, informative, peremptory, and a source of blessings and anathemas, the mirror image of an ultramontane pope. But Newman's notion of conscience, at least as expounded here in the *Letter*, is far from perspicuous.[23] Newman is generally taken to have defended 'the duty of obeying our conscience at all hazards' (p. 259) as Catholic doctrine; but he does not mean 'at *all* hazards' since he has already maintained that 'infallibility...could block the exercise of conscience' (p. 257). But then it turns out that 'conscience cannot come into direct collision with the Church's or the Pope's infallibility' because conscience bears on *conduct*, 'something to be done or not done', whereas the Church's infallibility 'is engaged on general propositions, and in the condemnation of particular and given errors' (p. 256). This anticipates Newman's insistence that papal infallibility bears on the domain of *thought* but not on that of *action* (p. 341). But even where infallibility is not involved obedience to the Pope should be the norm:

> Unless a man is able to say to himself, as in the Presence of God, that he must not, and dare not, act upon the Papal injunction, he is bound to obey it, and would commit a great sin in disobeying it. *Prima facie* it is his bounden duty, even from a sentiment of loyalty, to believe the Pope right and to act accordingly. He must vanquish that mean, ungenerous, selfish, vulgar spirit of his nature, which, at the very first rumour of a command, places itself in opposition to the Superior who gives it, asks itself whether he is not exceeding his right, and rejoices, in a moral and practical matter, to commence with scepticism. He must have no wilful determination to exercise a right of thinking, saying, doing just what he pleases, the question of truth and falsehood, right and wrong, the duty if possible of obedience, the love of speaking as his Head speaks, and of standing in all cases on his Head's side, being simply discarded. If this necessary rule were observed, collisions between the Pope's authority and the authority of conscience would be very rare.

As in the case of 'ecclesiastical communism' as the alternative to papal monarchy, Newman's rhetoric blinds him to the third possibility: we need neither 'commence with scepticism' nor love finding ourselves always on the head's side.

Newman then turns to the Encyclical of 1864 and the *Syllabus Errorum* (pp. 262-98) and gleefully trounces Gladstone for his amateurish approach to these texts:

> At Rome the rules of interpreting authoritative documents are known with a perfection which at this time is scarcely to be found elsewhere. Some of these rules, indeed, are known to all priests; but even this general knowledge is not possessed by laymen, much less by Protestants, however able and experienced in their own several lines of study or profession (*Letter*, pp. 294-5).

Whether Roman documents need quite as much professional decoding as Newman makes out we need not stop to consider. The havoc he wreaks with Gladstone's untutored hermeneutics, in what is also the longest section of the argument, certainly encourages the reader to remember Newman's *Letter* as a refutation of the *Expostulation*, root and branch. But Newman's diverting attention to Gladstone's blunders also diverts attention from the serious inadequacies of his own ecclesiology as well as from his persistent refusal to deal with 'the mere accidents of the controversy', as he calls them: the political effects (as we might rather say) of papal ascendancy in the strongest Church in the world. The rest of Newman's *Letter* (pp. 299-340) deals with the Vatican Council itself. He deplores the way in which the definition of papal infallibility was achieved but insists that it did not invalidate the Council – 'right ends are often prosecuted by very unworthy means' (p. 299). He offers a good, clear summary of his theory of the development of doctrine (pp. 308-15). He argues that the condemnation of Pope Honorius in no way compromises the doctrine of papal infallibility (pp. 315-17). He mentions the Petrine texts, in less than two pages, much of them taken up with a quotation from Butler's *Analogy*, preparing for the following claim (p. 319):

> What has the long history of the contest for and against the Pope's infallibility been, but a growing insight through centuries into the meaning of those three texts, to which I just now referred, ending at length by the Church's definitive recognition of the doctrine thus gradually manifested to her?

Gladstone shows no interest in Honorius or the Petrine texts. It does not seem necessary for Newman to touch on them even as barely as he does.

At last Newman reaches what must have seemed to him the main point: he begins to set out the 'important limitations' on the newly defined doctrine:

> To co-operate in this charitable duty has been one special work of (the Church's) theologians, and rules are laid down by herself, by tradition, and by custom, to assist them in the task. She only speaks when it is necessary to speak; but hardly has she spoken out magisterially some great general principle, when she sets her theologians to work to explain her meaning in the concrete, by strict interpretation of its wording, by the illustration of its circumstances, and by the recognition of exceptions, in order to make it as tolerable as possible, and the least of a temptation, to self-willed, independent, or wrongly educated minds (pp. 320-1).

This seems wishful thinking; it would certainly be interesting to know how often Newman thought that any such process had occurred. He then outlines the conditions required for a judgment that would be a proper exercise of the papal prerogative of infallibility, relying on

Fessler's book, apparently even for the clinching quotation from the Swiss bishops' pastoral letter. Such papal definitions are 'of rare occurrence' (p. 338); but, typically of theologians then and since, Newman does not discuss particular examples or even try to show how the definition of the doctrine of the Immaculate Conception of the Blessed Virgin Mary conforms to his theory.

Finally, in his concluding remarks (pp. 341-7), Newman refers to Gladstone's fears that the definition of papal infallibility must greatly enhance papal authority *tout court* –

> but his prerogative of infallibility lies in matters speculative, and his prerogative of authority is no infallibility in laws, commands, or measures. His infallibility bears upon the domain of thought, not directly of action, and while it may fairly exercise the theologian, philosopher, or man of science, it scarcely concerns the politician (pp. 341-2).

Yet Newman realised that the domains of thought and of action cannot be so easily demarcated:

> Moreover, whether the recognition of his infallibility in doctrine will increase his actual power over the faith of Catholics, remains to be seen, and must be determined by the event; for there are gifts too large and too fearful to be handled freely (p. 342).

That final ominous phrase, of course, would quite unnerve any Protestant reader who might have had his fears abated by Newman's elaborate circumscription of the exercise of this 'fearful' gift. But it also does not meet Gladstone's central difficulty –

> Will it be said, finally, that the Infallibility touches only matters of faith and morals? Only matter of morals! (*Exp.*, p. 36).

In fact Gladstone, rightly, places the emphasis on the *third* chapter of the constitution 'Pastor Aeternus':

> Surely, it is allowable to say that this Third Chapter on universal obedience is a formidable rival to the Fourth Chapter on Infallibility. Indeed, to an observer from without, it seems to leave the dignity to the other, but to reserve the stringency and efficiency to itself. The Fourth Chapter is the Merovingian Monarch; the third is the Carolingian Mayor of the Palace. The fourth has an overawing splendour; the third an iron gripe [*sic*] (pp. 38-9).

Gladstone's colourful language should not conceal from the reader that he has grasped the essential point – as he goes on to show:

> Little does it matter to me whether my superior claims infallibility, so long as he is entitled to demand and exact uniformity. This, it will be observed, he demands even in cases not covered by his infallibility; cases, therefore, in which he admits it to be possible that he may be wrong, but finds it intolerable to be told so. As he must be obeyed in all his judgments though not *ex cathedra*, it seems a pity he could not likewise give the comforting assurance that they are all certain to be right (p. 39).

Gladstone's irony is a heavier weapon than Newman's; but the point to notice is that Newman's *Letter* concentrates on explaining papal infallibility, thus sidestepping Gladstone's principal objection to the Vatican Council. Newman counters this objection only by insisting that infallibility bears upon the domain of doctrine, not that of conduct, and then by leaving it to the future to show whether the recognition of papal infallibility in doctrine would increase papal power over the lives of Roman Catholics. In effect, Gladstone saw the inevitability of what would later be called 'creeping infallibility' – 'that system, political rather than religious, which in Germany is well termed Vaticanism'.[24] Newman, in his reply, directs attention to related but subsidiary matters – 'essential points' which distract the reader from 'the mere accidents of the controversy': it would be better to say – minor academic points which divert attention from the real effects of the Vatican Council on the Roman Catholic Church and on its policies in various social and political circumstances then and since.

The controversy between Gladstone and Newman thus remains of great interest. Gladstone's commitment to 'the Church and people of England' and Newman's Roman Catholic ecclesiology would always have made understanding between them almost impossible. On the other hand, both Newman and Gladstone badly wanted to minimise the possibility of conflict between Church and State. Newman's apparent lack of interest in the episcopate, let alone in the effects on it of the definition of papal supremacy, together with his insistence on obedience to the Pope, show how profoundly ultramontane his doctrine was. Oddly enough, however, his ultramontane conception of the internal structure of the Church is not accompanied by much expectation of conflict with the State. In this Newman was very different from Manning, for whom the Church would (and should) often find itself militantly engaged in defence of the poor.[25] Newman assumes, with Gladstone, that 'civil disobedience' (as we should say) on the part of Christian people should be an extremely rare occurrence. Neither of them has anything substantial to offer Christians who think that theology should have a bearing on their civil allegiance and, furthermore, that divided allegiance may be a healthy sign. On the main issues that Gladstone raises Newman takes evasive action. No doubt we may conclude that the Marquis of Ripon would remain a loyal subject of Queen Victoria;[26] it remains far from clear to what extent the civil allegiance of Roman Catholics (in Ireland then and now, not to mention Poland, Nicaragua, the Philippines and a dozen other places) might be affected by a strong papacy. Finally, exactly what papal domination of the Church might mean, Newman, perhaps understandably, leaves for another occasion.[27]

NOTES

1. *A Letter addressed to His Grace the Duke of Norfolk, on occasion of Mr Gladstone's Recent Expostulation*, by John Henry Newman, D.D., of the Oratory (London, 1875); reprinted in *Certain Difficulties felt by Anglicans in Catholic Teaching Considered*, Volume II (London, 1879), pp. 171-378, cited in the text as *Letter*.

2. *The Vatican Decrees in their bearing on Civil Allegiance: A Political Expostulation*, by the Right Hon. W.E. Gladstone, M.P., (London, 1874), cited in the text as *Exp*. See *Newman and Gladstone: The Vatican Decrees*, with an introduction by Alvan S. Ryan (Notre Dame, Indiana, 1962), which reprints both pamphlets.

3. See *Letters and Diaries*, Volume XXVII, pp. 192-252 *passim*.

4. W.E. Gladstone, 'Ritualism and Ritual', *Contemporary Review* (October 1874), pp. 663-81, p. 674 for the offending passage.

5. G.F.G. Robinson (1827-1909), son of a Prime Minister, Secretary for War 1863, Lord President of the Council in Gladstone's administration 1868-73, received into the Roman Catholic Church 7 September 1874.

6. Frederic Rogers (1811-89), Newman's closest Oxford friend, who never became a Roman Catholic, Permanent under Secretary for the Colonies 1860-71.

7. William Monsell (1812-94), Roman Catholic 1850, MP for Limerick 1847-74, Irish landowner, held office in Liberal governments, Postmaster-General 1871-3, when misapplication of Post Office funds forced him to resign and he was awarded a peerage.

8. *Letters*, XXVII, p. 153.

9. Ibid., pp. 152-3.

10. J. Fessler, *Die wahre und die falsche Unfehlbarkeit der Päpste* (Vienna, 1871), translating which, at Newman's request, contributed, or so Newman believed, to the early death of Ambrose St John on 24 May 1875.

11. *Letters*, XXVII, p. 153.

12. M.R.D. Foot's phrase, *Gladstone, Politics and Religion*, edited by Peter J. Jagger (London, 1985), p. 35.

13. See Perry Butler, *Gladstone: Church, State and Tractarianism. A Study of his Religious Ideas and Attitudes, 1809-1859* (Oxford, 1982).

14. John Morley, *The Life of William Ewart Gladstone* (London, 1903), Volume II, p. 252.

15. J.L. Hammond, *Gladstone and the Irish Nation* (London, 1938), p. 112.

16. Morley, Volume II, p. 297, quoting a letter written in September 1870 to Earl Spencer, Lord-Lieutenant of Ireland at the time.

17. Hammond, p. 125.

18. 9 March 1873.

19. The Preface to the third (1877) edition of *The Via Media of the Anglican Church* identifies authority in the Church with the papacy.

20. *Letters*, XXV, p. 224; cf. p. 231: 'It is not good for a Pope to live 20 years'.

21. The papal encyclical 'Humanae Vitae' issued on 25 July 1968 condemned all forms of birth control except the 'rhythm method'.

22. In which Harold Laski famously found 'perhaps the profoundest discussion of the nature of obedience and of sovereignty...in the English Language', *Studies in the Problem of Sovereignty* (London, 1917), p. 202.

23. See David Nicholls, 'Gladstone, Newman and the Politics of Pluralism', in *Newman and Gladstone Centennial Essays*, edited by James D. Bastable (Dublin, 1978), pp. 27-38.

24. Gladstone's phrase in his *Vaticanism: An Answer to Replies and Reproofs* (London, 1875), p. 7.

25. See V.A. McClelland, *Cardinal Manning: His Public Life and Influence, 1865-1892* (Oxford, 1962).

26. Gladstone nominated Ripon as Viceroy of India in 1880.

27. The 1877 Preface to *Via Media*.

6

IMPEDED WITNESS: NEWMAN AGAINST LUTHER ON JUSTIFICATION

Joseph S. O'Leary

The great controversy about justification, already on its last legs in Newman's *Lectures on the Doctrine of Justification* (1838),[1] is rather like a radio programme called 'What are They Talking About?' which beguiled the dim nights of pre-television Ireland. It begins in mid-air with high talk of sin, a topic now decentered or recontextualised by the supervening question of meaning, as developed in philosophy since Nietzsche and in literature since Kafka. Discussion of meaning has united the Churches in what may be an ecumenism of exhaustion,[2] permitting a wider, subtler approach to what had been stylised under the rubrics of sin and grace. To turn back to the issue of justification is to re-enter, it seems, a sectarian echo-chamber. The voices of Paul, Augustine and Luther no longer have immediate authority, for the imposing frameworks they presume us to share with them strike us as dated 'technologies of salvation'[3] not immediately transferable to our culture. We have come to realise that Christian tradition is not a single channel broadcasting system, but is dispersed in local transmissions bearing loose analogies to one another. Its unity is that of an open-ended project, irreducibly pluralistic from the start, and marked by an epochal and cultural heterogeneity – or incommensurability – that foils synthesis. Even dogmas – Augsburg and Trent on justification – turn out to be wandering rocks, provisional attempts at clarity within selective, distorting receptions of the scriptural heritage. Dogmatic theology, then, can no longer subsume history, and must be content with a merely hermeneutic role, putting strategic questions to past discourses in view of present concerns.

For a strategic rather than archival rehearsal of Newman's *Lectures*, a promising point of attack may be the metaphysical framework of his thought – his role as a champion against Luther of Aristotelian logic and patristic ontology. Beneath the explicit claims and counter-claims of Luther and Newman, we may tune in to their tacit dispute about the appropriate texture of theological speech and writing, which, in its confusions and inconclusiveness, resonates with our own continuing unease about the relations between theology and metaphysics. Though Newman's foreground themes are ethics, holiness, faith and the sacraments, orchestrated with so many scriptural allusions that the work has been called 'basically an exercise in biblical theology',[4] yet the recurrent stress on metaphysical realism and logic is so strong that it seems to hamper the free exfoliation of those spiritual and biblical themes. That is what most divides him from Luther, whom he chiefly scolds for lack of logic and a deficient sense of (ontological) reality. Yet at times his voice seems to falter, suggesting that in some corner of his mind he may be of Luther's party without knowing it.

One of the things that makes a critique of such texts strenuous is the prevalence of those big words which our ancestors took for granted and which still have power to lure us into oblivion of what they mask. The first step of a metaphysical theology is that which defines 'love', 'faith', 'grace', 'sin' as unitary phenomena – whereas the historical pluralism of their usage reveals that they are labels for highly diverse ensembles of situations and experiential patterns. The richness of such terms in their primary usages calls for sensitive quasi-literary appreciation, not definition within a theoretical super-structure. Luther enjoys an almost Pauline plasticity in the use of these big words, but the freedom with which he retrieved biblical language was later inhibited by anxiety to identify the 'formal cause' of justification. That phrase is the key concept of the *Lectures*, and Newman is never more self-consciously Aristotelian than when explaining – with a judicious blend of the logical and the empirical – what he means by it (pp. 343-6). We shall see that this logical and ontological approach, in which Bellarmine tutored him,[5] has a cramping and flattening effect on his thought and keeps him from grasping the biblical kerygma with Luther's sense of concrete immediacy. If we can unravel the net of his reasonings, we may retrieve the vitality of his witness; only we run the risk in doing so of becoming ourselves entangled with him in that net.

IS LUTHERANISM SHADOWY?

Luther, in his quest for a language adequate to the biblical kergyma, had constantly to ward off the seemingly natural metaphysical terms that presented themselves. Thus he rejected as a diabolical gloss the seemingly innocuous notion of *fides caritate formata* (faith given form by charity) since it shifts the thinking of faith from the situation of the sinner before God to the falsely objective medium of dispassionate ontological considerations (*WA* 40:1, pp. 421-8; Newman, pp. 9, 13, 21, 22). Theological confession could only be distorted when transferred to the medium of reflexive philosophical observation.[6] The violence of this rejection perhaps stemmed in part from his lack of a technique for a more serene and comprehensive undoing of such distortions through immanent criticism, such as Kant, Heidegger, Wittgenstein and Derrida have since so elaborately undertaken. The metaphysics he most objected to is that which sees human personhood as a neutral substance, receiving successively the qualities of sin and of grace – such an anthropology of substance, habits and qualities has no validity for our existence before God.[7] This is part of a wider resistance to all efforts to explicate the process of salvation in metaphysical language. His reenactment of the Pauline escape from the tangle of the Law [8] is reflected in a freeing of his speech from metaphysical constraints through constant reference to the paradoxes of redemption. Even the secure identity of the self becomes something provisional and fragile: we are constituted sinners in our alienation from God, righteous in the relation of grace, and have no independent metaphysically fixed identity.

Luther gave expression to his vision of existential brokenness and openness in striking paradoxes, which then became frozen into firm doctrines. He was led to build a system on the Gospel experience, distilling out of it fundamental principles and articles, and so handing it over to scholastic analyses and objections.[9] Here, we may suppose, is the source of the flaws of Lutheranism, at least as Newman found it, and of his impression that Protestantism was a web of shadowy principles, not convertible into practical rules (pp. 333-5). Later, the restlessness of Luther's thought was again lost in another kind of metaphysics, in which the categories of the personal, the relational and the existential were opposed in a facile and stereotyped way to ontic and objectifying conceptions. Catholic theologians have 'excused' Luther on the grounds of his inability to surpass the merely personal-existential level to grasp the metaphysical depth of sin and righteousness,[10] which is to miss the point that for Luther the enclosure of biblical existentiality within a metaphysical framework has a denaturing effect. That denaturing also marks the Reformers' own discourse on justification in terms of its efficient, material, formal or instrumental, and final causes (categories that seemed obvious and indispensable to the thinkers of that time).[11] Luther himself may still be able to elude this framework, insofar as his use of causal jargon – as when Christ is described as the form of faith or righteousness, or faith is described as formal righteousness – is marked by subversive paradox.[12] He had a clear enough idea of what he was talking about to be able to neutralise such metaphysical categories and make them subserve a Pauline vision; later the intrinsic logic of these metaphysical elements took over, shaping a scholastic Protestant orthodoxy, as the originating convictions came to be taken for granted. Newman, who never queries the necessity or adequacy of causal language, takes Luther's use of it at face value (p. 362: 'the bold, nay correct language of Luther, that Christ Himself is the form of our justification'; pp. 358-9, 12, 20, 23).

When it is most free from metaphysics, Luther's thought dwells in the horizons of the Word-event wherein faith (not yet reduced to a pallid Melanchthonian formula) surges up to receive the proclamation of grace. At this level it would be absurd to speak of a merely forensic justification or of a faith divorced from renewal. Newman comes close to that pre-systematic Luther as he appeals to the effectiveness of the divine word (pp. 67, 72, 74, 81-4, 97-100) against the surgical differentiation of justification from renewal. Similar arguments recur in contemporary Lutheran exegesis and theology,[13] where the rigidity of such theses as the *simul iustus et peccator* (righteous and sinner at the same time) are overcome by a recall to their basis in the life of faith and prayer.[14] But Newman does not bring to Luther a generous hermeneutic that could retrieve the spirit and intent of these doctrines. His reading of the Reformers is circumscribed by the ring of metaphysical definitions in which they enshrined their message. Instead of letting their sense of the effective biblical Word remould and repristinate his patristic ontology of righteousness, he measures them against that ontology and allows it to have a petrifying effect on his understanding of the biblical kerygma itself.

Lutheranism (and Luther's own 1531 *Commentary on Galatians*) might plausibly be seen as torn between the early Luther for whom 'faith' is shorthand for the whole Word-event, which comprises justification and renewal, and the later formalisation of justifying faith and sedulous differentiation of justification and renewal. This tension may sometimes provide Newman's arguments with their pound of flesh, but he gives them an extra thrust by measuring Protestant language against the yardstick of ontological reality, bluntly opposed to the merely nominal, as when he insists that Lutheran justification is 'a declaration of what neither has been, is, nor ever will be' (p. 78). This ontological emphasis deafens him to Protestant claims to be attending to a subtler existential reality. If the Lutheran constructions are sometimes strained, Newman's own account of inherent righteousness becomes no less shadowy once it exceeds its biblical warrant and resorts to metaphysical underpinnings.

It cannot be assumed that the issues are automatically translatable into terms of being and non-being. The immediate recourse to such terms forces a reduction of Protestantism to a nominalistic extrinsicism – 'that the scheme of salvation should be one of names and understandings; that we should be but said to be just, said to have a righteousness, said to please God' (p. 56). Such ontological short-circuiting of the discussion blinded Roman Catholic theologians until recently to the fact that justification for Luther is not merely a non-accounting but also a making new, whereby Christ's justice really *becomes* ours,[15] so that 'God does not declare righteous without at the same time and for the sake of that declaration beginning the renewal'.[16] Justification establishes a community between God and man, which cannot be without effect; though it is not in view of the anticipated renewal that God declares the sinner justified.[17] The shift from *peccatum regnans*, sin as ruling, to *peccatum regnatum*, sin as ruled (*WA* 8, pp. 91-5), is a profound change in the individual's relation to God, the beginning of renewal and good works. 'The Christian "possesses" *in the personal realm* a *perfect righteousness*, since it is the alien, reputed righteousness of Christ; at the same time, however, a *partial, growing righteousness* is conferred on him through God's grace *in the ontic realm*.'[18] Newman's categories make no room for such a differentiation of the personal and the ontic. He does note the theory that 'sin in the regenerate has lost its formal part, which is guilt, and has only its matter remaining' (p. 362), but remains unimpressed. The claim that the justified are still sinners, if judged by the Law, and are righteous only as they cling in faith to Christ, seems to him to evacuate the substance of salvation. Yet he remarks that those who believe 'the infection of sin to remain in the regenerate... even if they hold that it is mortal, yet that it may be through God's grace subdued, seem to have no irreconcilable difference on this point with the Romanists' (p. 367). Here is ample ground for an *entente* with Luther, correctly interpreted. It seems that it is only by a caricature of Luther that he is able to elevate the difference between the two views of salvation into one between being and non-being.

NEWMAN'S ARGUMENT AGAINST LUTHER

Let us attend now to Lecture I in which Newman tries to show the inconsistency of the Protestant view that 'faith is the one principle which God's grace makes use of for restoring us to His favour and image' (p. 5). Note that this already is misleading, tending to divorce faith as an abstract principle from the salvation it accepts. We are saved not so much *propter fidem* (on account of faith),[19] as '*fide propter Christum propitiatorem*' (by faith on account of Christ the atoner, *BSLK* p. 201) or '*propter Christum per fidem*' (on account of Christ through faith, *BSLK* p. 56). Newman focuses on the idea of faith being acceptable 'for Christ's sake', and misses the more important point that faith justifies in that it accepts the justification offered in Christ: 'the faith which justifies consists in assenting to the promise of God, in which is offered freely, on account of Christ, the remission of sins and justification' (*BSLK* p. 169). Justifying faith has no existence outside this trusting acceptance of redemption. One cannot abstract from this relationship of trust a formal quality on the believer's side which guarantees that it is a living relationship.

Newman sees Luther in the light of the postures he ascribes to contemporary Evangelicals, whom he attacks in the last Lecture on the grounds 'that they substitute faith for Christ; that they so regard it, that instead of being the way to Him, it is in the way' (p. 324). He cites 'even Luther' as a forceful voice against this subjectivism (pp. 331-2), though that does not prevent him from blaming it on Luther in his concluding swipes (pp. 339-41). Practically, he insists, the principle of 'justification through faith' means nothing other than 'justification by Christ' (p. 335). Had he begun by recognising the Reformers' agreement with him on this point he might have launched his lectures on a more comprehensively ecumenical note.

Newman recognises that what faith *does* is to 'embrace the news of salvation through Christ' (p. 5), yet he later treats Melanchthon's teaching that justifying faith is correlative with the mercy of Christ as if it were somehow an unsaying of the *sola fides* (pp. 10, 25, 244). He reports that Protestants are always ready to say what justifying faith is not, but that their positive accounts of it tend to slippery rhapsody: 'that it is a spiritual principle, altogether different from anything we have by nature, endued with a divine life and efficacy, and producing a radical change in the soul: or more precisely [deadpan irony?], that it is a trust in Christ's merits and in them alone for salvation' (p. 6). Here he has sighted a tension in the official Melanchthonian account of justifying faith, which is both simple trust and 'a divine power whereby we are made alive and whereby we conquer the devil and death' (*BSLK* p. 209).

The Reformers' way of resolving that tension is to attribute what is powerful in faith to the power of Christ which it embraces. This cannot be thought out in Aristotelian terms as the addition of some quality to the soul's act of faith. Instead a shift to a new way of thinking is required, and it is this shift which Newman persistently refuses to make. Newman reports the classical Protestant response as follows: 'Faith, it appears, is to be defined, not by its *nature*, but by its *office*, not by what it *is*, but by what it *does*. It is trust *in Christ*, and it differs from all other kinds of faith in That towards which it reaches forward' (p. 11). But such sharp distinctions of nature and office, 'is' and 'does', are surely impracticable in regard to any spiritual reality. One can conceive the 'nature' of faith in abstraction from what it 'does' only at the price of a quite unreal reification. Newman dismisses as evasive quibbling the Protestant insistence 'that Christ Himself and He alone, the Object of the faith, is that which makes the faith what it is'. 'Such a reply is evidently no real explanation of the difficulty' (p. 13). The 'difficulty' here dwelt on, if it has any reality at all, belongs to a level of secondary reflection which attempts to underpin with the security of a metaphysical theory the biblical turning to God in faith. This shift of horizon from biblical faith to an objectifying analysis of its constitution or endowments is the source of what Luther saw as metaphysical disfigurement.

Newman urges what at first sight looks like an inescapable dilemma: 'either faith is more than personal trust, and if so, that addition, whatever it is, is a joint instrument with it in our justification; or...it is nothing more, and then it is not necessarily living and operative faith' (p. 13).[20] But this opposition between faith as mere trust like that of 'the servant in the parable' (p. 8; Matt 23.26) and faith as identical with 'love, gratitude, devotion, belief, holiness, repentance, hope, dutifulness, and all other graces' (p. 7) caricatures Protestant usage. For on the one hand the *content* of faith intrinsically differentiates it from 'mere trust', while, on the other, though faith frees us to love, which is the fulfilling of the Law (Gal 5.1-18), yet faith receives Christ's freedom and justification independently of these works. When Newman reports ironically the claim that 'the mere preaching of reconciliation...has been found to act upon the soul in a remarkable way for its conversion and renewal' (p. 18; cf. p. 257) he misses the strength of this Pauline nexus of faith and renewal. How, he asks, can a mere 'fiduciary apprehension' be lively or lead to good works? Presuming that 'trust is not necessarily lively faith' he goes on to the other horn of the dilemma: 'Shall we define the justifying faith of the Lutherans to be faith which *is* lively? This is a more adequate account of it, but a less consistent one. For what is meant by lively?' (p. 8). To this disjunction between the lively and the fiducial the Reformers would reply that the trusting reception of Christ's redemption can never be less than enlivening. But Newman insists that lively faith must have something 'discriminating and characteristic' (p. 9). Again and again he asks, 'What then is the *life* of faith? What is that which makes it what it is?...what is that property in it which makes it...acceptable?' (p. 9). The power of the rhetoric depends on misapplied logic. In demanding an objectified account of 'justifying faith' Newman is thinking of faith in an abstract and unreal way as a definable quality of the substantial soul. This is as remote from the Pauline language of faith as analogous definitions of love would be from what love lyrics convey.

Newman knows that his style of analysis is objectionable to his opponents: 'We are told that such inquiries are an undue exaltation of human reason, or at least an unseasonable exercise of it' (p. 11). He does not consider the possibility that it is not so much 'human reason' as the particular type of reasoning which he is applying that is inappropriate. His question about the formal quality of lively faith in abstraction from the faith-relation is not an innocent or neutral exercise of 'human reason', but one shaped by Aristotelian metaphysics. In reply to the objection that the doctrine of justification by faith cannot appear to its advantage 'in controversy, which employs the language of the unregenerate' (p. 15), Newman insists that in that case Protestant dogmatic itself is a mistaken venture, doomed to defective definitions and illogical reasonings. Here again his Aristotelianism prevents him from first asking what counts as an adequate definition and what kind of logical stringency can appropriately be demanded. The issue of the appropriateness of metaphysical language has almost surfaced: it is not the 'language of the unregenerate' that is inappropriate but the logic of formal qualities that inevitably misses the Word-event and the relations it creates. Newman's dilemma does not score a knock-out, as the Protestant escape-routes are not entirely blocked off and, given less rigidly ontological presuppositions, could seem perfectly viable. In *Loss and Gain*[21] these inconclusive arguments are recycled as comic dialogue between Evangelical numskulls, and thus given the conclusiveness of satire.

NEGLECTED *FIDUCIA*

Throughout this argument Newman touches the topic of faith as trust very gingerly, and with a view to exposing it as an abstraction. The variety of his own approaches to the notion of faith scarcely admits of reduction to univocity, though neither is it a wallowing in contradiction. What holds the diverse treatments together is an agnostic mood that suspends too heavy an investment in any one of them. In one version, faith justifies by 'continually pleading our Lord's merits before God' and by being 'the first recipient of the Spirit, the root, and therefore the earnest and anticipation of perfect obedience' (p. 36). This sounds rather strong, but elsewhere it is reduced to the claim that faith has merely a 'sustaining' role, enabling us to hold on to the justification received. Why it should have this role at all is far from clear:

> If by "standing" be meant...being in a justified state, faith...is that which operates in keeping us in it. Why it does so, is altogether a distinct question, and one perhaps which we cannot adequately determine. But whatever be God's inscrutable reasons for thus connecting faith immediately with his evangelical gifts, so has He done (p. 233).[22]

The Lutheran answer that faith alone puts us in a position of pure, passive receiving correlative to the gratuitous divine gift (which was well expounded on pp. 18-23, but in a hostile context) is blocked off by an insistence (more Bellarminian than Tridentine perhaps, cf. *DS* 1526-7) that faith is not trust but believing assent to revealed truth, which is shared by devils and saints alike. The fiducial note can creep back only secondarily to this.

Faith's role is thus made so mysterious as to be tenuous: 'We have no reason for supposing that the supernatural providences of God are not ordered upon a system of antecedents or second causes as precise and minute as is the natural system. Faith may be as a key unlocking for us the treasures of divine mercy, and the only key' (p. 215). Lecture X culminates in a still weaker model of justifying faith as 'an *emblem* or *image* of the free grace of our redemption' (p. 244). Justification by faith becomes a mystery to be undergone, not, as it was for Luther, an intelligible solution to a concrete problem. Indeed, Newman falls behind Trent in his grasp of the necessary sequence whereby faith comes first in the process of salvation: 'faith is the beginning of human salvation, the foundation and root of all justification' (*DS* 1532).[23] To bridge the gap between faith as assent and its (now greatly diluted) role in justification Newman has recourse to another surmise: 'Faith is the correlative, the natural instrument of the things of the Spirit' (p. 214) because it apprehends what is invisible – a tepid piece of Platonism, reminiscent of Augustine, who had similar trouble in explaining why faith in the Word incarnate should be the necessary 'way' to the 'fatherland' of the vision of God.[24]

In giving so little place to faith as *fiducia*, Newman seems to have impeded his own grasp of the liberative thrust of Luther's Pauline rhetoric. When he turns to define faith in Lecture XI, we are presented with a glowing apologia for faith as 'the evidence of things not seen'. But his rhetoric, as if aware of its irrelevance in this context and how miserably it substitutes for the fiducial strain, falters and falls flat: 'The examples of meekness, cheerfulness, contentment, silent endurance, private self-denial, fortitude, brotherly love, perseverance in well-doing, which would from time to time meet them in their new kingdom, – the sublimity and harmony of the Church's doctrine, – the touching and subduing beauty of her services and appointments...' (p. 271). The Reformers, differentiating the pregnant New Testament sense of saving faith from a weaker general usage,[25] never fall into such empty formality.

Newman was closer to them in 1825 when he used the word 'faith' in two senses: 'as a kind of knowledge when speaking of regeneration, as confession-of-no-merit when speaking of justification'.[26] In 1829 'as long as he was speaking in terms of growth in holiness, faith was seen to have an intellectual content; but once it was related to justification, it became merely fiducial'.[27] The trouble may have been the thinness of his notion of the fiducial; for the Reformers it includes and surpasses the merely noetic. Newman later claims that he never really believed in the doctrine of apprehensive faith, and deceived himself into thinking he did only because he had lumped it together with the basics of the Creed.[28] In 1838 any dalliance with the fiducial could only seem a regression to immaturity. His trust in the ontological structures of the Greek Fathers gave his faith a primarily noetic cast and ruled out any need to fall back on what seemed the inconsistent imaginings of Protestantism; it may also have ended his career as a biblical thinker by making it impossible for him to expose himself fully to the Word-event.

Luther prompts us to detect, beneath the construction of the arguments, at the level of style and tone, that Newman does not subject all his theological language, including his talk of God, to the Word-event. He shies back from the dizzying possibilities of such a strategy, unable to question the subordination of the kerygma to the metaphysical structures that encompass it. This inhibition of the Word, endemic in theology since Augustine, has only recently been recognised and partly overcome in Roman Catholic theology.[29] The Luther Newman argues with is the doctrinally insistent author of the post-Augsburg Galatians commentary, and though once or twice appreciating the kerygmatic force which still abounds in that work (pp. 23, 332), on the whole he misses, or dismisses, the preacher of the Word and sees only the constructor of the system. Newman's speech remains after all ensconced in established metaphysical and ecclesiastical structures, within which its biblical echoes can richly resound but against which it can never critically pit itself. Luther is on a quite different wavelength, dislodged from these structures by a more naked encounter with the kerygma, so that he can treat with them henceforward only as provisional and fragile means. Newman's certitude is the inner calm and joy of contemplation, Luther's depends on hearing the Word of salvation again and again. Here we are playing the latter off against the former, but both are precious in a time which whittles away all religious notions as mere delusion.

THE LOGIC OF JUSTIFICATION AND SANCTIFICATION?

Newman's critics, especially G.S. Faber, have suspected him of playing fast and loose with the logic of the relation between justification and sanctification.[30] He explains himself at the start of

Lecture III, where he sketches an argumentative frame that has the merit of allowing movement in every direction. Significantly, this is the most confusing passage in the entire work. The basic position is 'that justification and sanctification [are] in fact substantially one and the same thing' (p. 63). But if we begin to make notional distinctions, then it can be argued both (i) that 'in the order of our ideas, viewed relatively to each other, justification follow[s] upon sanctification ...we are first renewed, and then and therefore accepted' (p. 63) and equally (ii) that 'in logical order, or exactness of idea, Almighty God justifies before He sanctifies' (p. 65). That justification follows renewal is 'true in one sense, but not true in another – unless indeed those different senses resolve themselves into a question of words' (p. 63). The appearance of self-contradiction is softened when we differentiate the 'order of ideas' of (i) from the 'logical order, or exactness of idea' of (ii). (i) expresses 'the relation of the one to the other, viewed popularly and as a practical matter, as Augustine and other Fathers set it forth' (p. 64) and is thus compatible with (ii): 'I believe St. Augustine really would consider, that in the order of ideas [now, confusingly, meaning the 'logical order' of (ii)] sanctification followed upon justification, though he does so with less uniformity of expression than Luther' (p. 64).

In any case justification and sanctification belong together 'as light and heat co-exist in the sun' so it is not surprising 'that Augustine should not make a point of being logically correct, but should in familiar language speak of the Sun of righteousness, both as shining on us, in order to warm us, and as shining on us with his genial warmth, that is justifying unto renewal and justifying by renewing' (p. 64). Calvin, in criticising Osiander's doctrine that God justifies 'not merely by forgiving, but by regenerating', had professed a stricter logic: 'Though the sun's brightness is inseparable from heat, do we therefore say that the earth is heated by light, but illumined by heat?...to transfer to the one what is proper to the other, reason itself forbids' (*Inst.* III 11.6; see Newman, p. 376). Newman slips the chains of this logic, to witness in popular, homiletic language to the reality of holiness. In Scripture, he claims, 'our righteousness is but a quality of our renewal' (p. 40) and we are even encouraged to 'justify ourselves' (p. 54)[31] by our obedience, whereas Protestant logic forces one to evacuate the plain meaning of Scripture by a forced hermeneutic (Lecture V). But can he have it both ways? Is he not blurring the message that we are put right before God by the death of Christ and that it is only on this basis that our renewal and obedience are conceivable?

Newman insisted on the ecumenical impact of his refusal of one-sidedness, especially in later life. In 1874 he stressed that 'there is little difference but what is verbal in the various views on justification' (p. ix) whether Lutheran, Calvinist, Arminian or Catholic.[32] The 1838 Preface goes about proving this unity in a more aggressive style, justifying the 'severe and contentious' approach on the basis that 'no wound is cured which is not thoroughly probed' (p. vi). The irenicism of the 'merely verbal' is applied strategically to muster the forces of the *via media* against Luther and Calvin, whom Newman was to denounce as heretics in 1841 during the quarrel about the Jerusalem bishopric. Melanchthon escapes these strictures since, in Newman's view, he understood justifying faith to be a mere figure of speech (p. 181); this 'served effectually to exculpate the doctrine...from the charge of superseding good works, as showing that really and practically it had nothing to do either with faith or works, but with grace' (p. 245). Now, while it is true that Melanchthon saw faith as obliged to produce good works (*BSLK* pp. 60, 187-8) whereas Luther saw them as spontaneously generated by faith,[33] nonetheless Melanchthon excludes works from justifying just as strictly as Luther and Calvin do (*BSLK* pp. 76, 313-16). Equally unconvincing is the effort to explain away the Anglican Homilies' exclusion of sanctity from 'the office of justifying' (pp. 225, 247-50, 261-2, 304-11) – 'not the office of conveying, but of symbolizing justification' is Newman's gloss on this (p. 247)!

Luther and Calvin are almost the only theologians Newman is not able to tuck away in the loose folds of his logic. Luther's doctrine that faith justifies without love, which 'is plain enough, and no matter of words' (p. 10), and Calvin's view that the new creation is not 'involved in the essence of the justifying act' but only 'joined as a necessary accident' (p. 80; cf. pp. 360, 376), are unacceptable. In reality, even this difference is not so dramatic as it appears, for neither Luther nor Calvin denies that justification and sanctification are inseparable, nor does Newman deny the priority of justification. Even the difference with Calvin is treated as merely 'scholastic and metaphysical' on pp. 376-7. His loosened logic has teeth enough only to gnaw at the thesis that 'our holiness and works can in no sense be said to justify us in God's sight' (p. 390) and to attack the extreme view that the holiness of the regenerate 'is not really and intrinsically good, even considered as the work of the Holy Ghost' (p. 377). In the end he can only conclude that 'the modern controversy on justification is not a vital one' (p. 400), which is quite true when it is a matter of contrasting theses in the realm of serene metaphysical analysis rather than adverting to the biblical thrust in Luther that pushes beyond the unreality of the metaphysical representations.

JUSTIFICATION REDUCED TO SANCTIFICATION?

Some of Newman's expressions seem to court the danger of presenting a God who does not act but react, that is, whose justifying word is made conditional on his perception of requisite qualities in the soul of his creatures; though he generally avoids this, though he by recalling that the qualities God approves in judging us are, to begin with, his own justifying gift. When we read 'holiness is the thing, the internal state, because of which blessing comes' (p. 34) or when good works are spoken of as 'forming a concurrent cause of that imputation being ratified' (p. 95), we are brought to the brink of a commonsense rationalisation of justification as the reward of obedience. Newman's distrust of system leads him to accept uncritically the Johnsonian good sense of a Waterland, for whom sanctification 'is necessarily presupposed, in some measure of degree, with respect to adults, in their justification'.[34] The claim that justification entails renewal as its immediate consequence is the best of biblical reasoning; but to maintain that justification somehow depends on renewal as its warrant is an invitation to theological disaster. The former position chimes well with a biblical phenomenology, the latter tends to project an unreal metaphysical horizon, picturing temporal relations between divine acts, and losing grip on the realities to which it refers. To avoid all such dangers were it not better to write only in the theological passive, registering the experience of being warmed and illumined by the Sun of righteousness, but renouncing all talk of God seeing, acting, judging as conducive to misleading objectifications?

Without renewal, justification would be no more than 'a movement of the Divine Mind, and altogether external to the subject of that justification'; it would consist merely in 'Almighty God's thoughts concerning him' (p. 132). Newman summons up this spectral image of God's action only to reject it, but unfortunately it is given a theoretical validity that undermines his earlier vision of the effective divine Word. The biblical vision is bracketed by a metaphysical framework and hollowed out by being subjected to such pallid categories as omniscience – 'God sees the end from the beginning' (p. 132). Once under the sway of such representations, the biblical events of justification and sanctification have to be bolstered with ontological references. The focus of Newman's appreciation of the Christian condition becomes the soul's *substantial* righteousness. That Lecture VIII describes it as adherent rather than inherent, so that 'we really have no inherent righteousness at all' (p. 187) is an interesting concession to the Lutheran *aliena iustitia* (foreign righteousness). One wishes it had been introduced earlier and given a central place. Even this adherent righteousness is conceived as a relation to an indwelling ontological presence.

In Lecture II Newman champions the Augustinian telescoping of justification and sanctification, without adverting to the Reformers' critique of Augustine on this point.[35] They maintained that to conceive of justification as the grace that enables fulfilment of the Law occludes the proclamation of justification as the Word-event that sets the sinner in a new personal relation to Christ.[36] In Augustine, faith is the first link in a chain: it stimulates prayer for grace, grace heals the soul, this frees the will, which can then love justice, and the love of justice performs the Law.[37] The interposition of prayer and sanctification between faith and justification undercuts the immediacy of their connection in Paul. Moreover, the abstract rigidity of the Augustinian terms and their relationships contrasts with the contextual vitality of Paul's use of 'faith' and 'the Law'. It is only such ever-renewed contextualisation which gives a vital reference to Christian terms, and the effort to construct timeless accounts of the terms and their relationships is intrinsically falsifying. But the Protestant alternative to Augustine is also vitiated by metaphysical formulation which renders it obtuse to its own concrete context. Instead of maintaining the tension of the step back from the Augustinian vision to the dramatic horizons of the Word-event as retrieved in their own time, the Reformers restylised those horizons in a new metaphysical system, which lacks the strength of Augustine's, because what it intended to convey is much less amenable to metaphysical categorisation.

The impression lingers that Newman has smuggled in an inversion of the biblical sequence from sin through the cross to the blessing of holiness; now the gift of holiness comes first. The originating mystery itself is viewed as an ontological gift; it is not viewed from within, as a transition from guilt and despair to acceptance and confidence, nor is the constant reliving of that baptismal exodus, the constant rediscovery of justification as a gift claimed by faith (*WA* 6, pp. 528-9), considered a proper form of experiencing Christian freedom. Newman's stirring descriptions of regeneration present it primarily as being enabled to fulfil the Law, to attain holiness, through 'the possession of Himself, of His substantial grace to touch and heal the root of the evil, the fountain of our misery, our bitter heart and its inbred corruption' (p. 34). Holiness, grace and Baptism become ontological screens against the event of redemption. This is not an ontological arrangement for which an experiential correlative has to be cooked up by devotional exercises, but is lived as the breakthrough brought by a liberating word: 'by the mere hearing of the Gospel the Holy Spirit is received' (*WA* 40:1, p. 330).

STILL UNDER THE LAW?

If one may find healthy catholicity in Newman's refusal to sever justification and holiness, at the same time his efforts to tie the former as tightly as possible to the latter suggest a touch of the moral unfreedom of which the Reformers were such brilliant diagnosticians. The regime of holiness even threatens to become a Law blocking access to the freedom of the Gospel, precisely the situation which forced Luther to rediscover the Pauline dialectic of faith and Law. Newman counters this danger inadequately, with a Platonising gesture, a spiritualising transcendence which is a weak substitute for the leap of faith. He appeals from 'superstitious dependence' on the sacraments to their correct use: 'to lead the mind not from, but through the earthly organ to the true Author of the miracle' (p. 286; cf. pp. 314-23). The symbolic language of the sacraments is seen as an adequate antidote. It is hard to see how the Pauline message, 'You are free of the Law', could ever be experienced as liberating or even as intelligible within the circle of Newman's conceptions.

Newman, like Trent (*DS* 1569), seems to confuse Luther's freedom from the Law with amoralism (pp. 24, 28). His intense concern with the moral content of justification has an edge to it that goes beyond sober realism. One may guess from the tepidity of his youthful exercises in a Pauline mode – 'in all ages and in all countries faith will save a man and (as far as we know) faith alone. Now I will tell you what faith is: – simply this: to feel ourselves to be nothing, and God everything' (March 1828)[38] – that he had never undergone with unmistakable clarity (any more than most of us have) the experience that would have put him on the Pauline wavelength – the drama of awakening from moral complacency to despairing guilt and finding that Christ's justification is the sole way out. His reception of that dimension of the New Testament is poor. His witness is rather to the 'beauty of holiness', cultivated in an ecclesiastical devotion that is more deutero-Pauline, Johannine or Augustinian than Pauline, and restrained from tasteless 'enthusiasm' (see p. 328) by a weighty sense of moral responsibility.

When he preaches the Law his words carry weight: conscience and duty are the backbone of everything – of his style, his romantic self-image, his contemplative sense of divine guidance. 'No justification without sanctification' is a theme that brings out his most characteristic writing:

> God cannot, from His very nature, look with pleasure and favour upon an unholy creature, or justify or count righteous one who is not righteous. Cleanness of heart and spirit, obedience by word and deed, this alone in us can be acceptable to God; that is, this alone can constitute our justification (p. 32).

This stress on justification by works is the most questionable element in Newman's vision, not merely from a Protestant viewpoint, but perhaps even from a Tridentine one, as we shall see. There is no need to call it Pelagian, for it does not take from our final reliance on justification by Christ's mercy: Newman is an ardent proponent of the idea of double justification, the ecumenical position most likely to reconcile Catholics and Protestants (pp. 366-82).[39]

One is made uneasy by the self-conscious character of this moral vision, as the treasuring of an inward gift. Justification in Luther unites us with Christ, not inwardly but in the entirety of our existence, and at the same time confers the freedom to rule over the world and to be at the service of the world: 'most free lord of all, most dutiful servant of all' (*WA* 7, p. 49). Perhaps Newman's Evangelical friends found his teaching depressing,[40] not because they misunderstood it,[41] but because they found justification by faith freed them for action in the world as concern for distinguishing marks of personal holiness did not.[42] The only reference to social matters in the *Lectures* is an almost caricatural reference to 'the bountifulness of her [the Church's] almsgiving, – her power, weak as she was and despised, over the statesmen and philosophers of the world, – her consistent and steady aggression upon it' (p. 272). For Luther morality is worldly, whereas faith is what overcomes the world, since it frees one from anxious efforts at self-justification so that one can act freely, creatively and energetically in, for and against the world. For Newman, however, morality is entangled in religion in such a way that goodness has constantly to be thought of in otherworldly terms; the secular good act has value only as an occasion for religious attainment. There is much to be said for Luther's reduction of morality to a secondary position after faith. It grants autonomy to the ethical conscience, which no longer has to look over its shoulder to see how it is doing in God's eyes and whether it has the credits necessary for salvation. It also frees faith to welcome the tidings of gratuitous acceptance.

NESCIENT MOODS

Let us pause to take our bearings in regard to Newman's attitude to metaphysics and logic. We are beginning to suspect that, despite his Aristotelian side, Newman is not really guided by any firm logical guidelines at all, and that his ontological realism tends to collapse into a mere commonsense insistence. We have seen that he arranges for considerable latitude in his dealings with logic, both in his discussion of how faith justifies and in his discussion of the relations between justification and sanctification. He does not allow a firm logical structure to hamper the resonance and suggestiveness of his writing. Masterful in the conduct of sustained argument, he nevertheless does not allow his books to form closed wholes, but leaves wide margins for open-ended ramifications, which in the present work become an ever thinner, ever more dispersed cobweb, impeding a firm grasp of the biblical matter. In the end one feels that his logical posturings are a cumbersome vesture for the mobile and impulsive play of his thought. He seems to feel this himself when he lapses into suspirations in a nescient mode, as when he quotes Taylor: 'No man should fool himself by disputing the philosophy of justification, and what causality faith hath in it' (p. 401).

Do we catch here, and in the similar passages already quoted, a hint of a possible Wittgensteinian Newman, who might have seen much deeper into the relativity of his language, had not respect for hallowed representations kept him back? Unfortunately, Newman's nescient moments do not launch a penetrating skepsis but suggest rather a failure of theological nerve and an irremediable cloudiness in the *via media* he is proposing. 'Let us be sure things are going wrong with us, when we see doctrines more clearly, and carry them out more boldly, that they are taught us in Revelation' (p. 341). That dismissal of theological refinements could as well have been aimed at Augustine as at Luther or Calvin; nor does the step back from the novel clarity of the latter win a retrieval of Augustine's classical pellucidity. A lack of confidence in the power of theological definitions and distinctions, as well as a latecomer's sense of the remoteness of the terms of the debate, is what keeps Newman, unlike Bellarmine, from giving his work the final incisive thrust of a single argument. Luther and Calvin broke the hold of a certain metaphysics by a logical vigilance Newman refuses to practice. Newman's refusal of system does not free him from metaphysical presuppositions but leaves him at their mercy.

His sense of the limits of logic allows him to slip into a scepticism foreign to the Fathers and to Bellarmine:

> We know nothing of the reasons of God's wonderful providences; why an Atonement was necessary, why the Son of God was the sacrifice: why that sacrifice must be applied in order to "wash away the sins" of individuals; let us accept what is given, adore God's wisdom, and be thankful and silent (pp. 204-5).

Perhaps directed at Anselm or at the remote anticipations of Anselm in Athanasius' *On the Incarnation*, this scepticism seems to underestimate the clarity of the concrete salvation-historical accounts of atonement in the New Testament, so essential to Reformation thought. Relinquishing the search for 'reasons' he returns to the biblical phenomena, but in a way that intends to discredit the Reformers' claims to a lucid apprehension of these phenomena. This is not the ancient negative theology, which came after strong speculation, nor the Protestant subjection of reason to the Word, but a modern weariness, which might have been given a critical turn, but which is instead hushed up in Anglican attitudes of piety and sobriety. The surrender of exorbitant claims of reason over revelation is not reflectively exploited in a critical rebound of the Word on his own representations, and it thus leaves him dallying with thought-forms in which his mind can never be fully at home. Instead of overcoming Luther in the direction of greater fidelity to the biblical matter (and greater contemporary credibility), Newman recalls him to acquiescence in an ontotheology incapable of further development – whereas Luther had renewed the thought of God by freeing it from metaphysical categories – and in a correspondingly static representation of the New Testament message. Similarly, the speculation on the ontology of the Resurrection and Ascension (pp. 202-22) is a rehash of patristic themes, which it does nothing to renew, while remaining far behind Luther in its engagement with the texture of Scripture. Newman's mind grew and expanded in many directions in the following half-century, but it does not seem that there was any further growth in his reflection on these 'ontological foundations'.

THE ABYSS OF THE ORIGIN

The inadequacy of Newman's commonsense realism is apparent in the way he stumbles into such homely queries as the following: how can infinite holiness declare righteous one in whom there is no holiness? Pushed far enough this would make the entire notion of redemption impossible. That the alien righteousness of Christ should substitute for ours undercuts commonsense at least at the beginning of the Christian life. Newman seems to avoid contemplating the abyss of that beginning, the strangeness of that birth, whereas Luther sees faith as a constant reliving of it. Though deploring the so-called Arminians' tendency 'to put out of sight the doctrines of election and sovereign grace' (p. 189), he himself dwells chiefly on the 'justification of the already just' (p. 154) as the normal Christian experience, in which faith justifies in much the same sense as other good works do: 'Justifying faith does not precede justification; but justification precedes faith and makes it justifying' (p. 227). 'Such is justifying faith, justifying not the ungodly, but the just, whom God has justified when ungodly;...justifying the just as being the faith of the justified' (p. 237). Here faith justifies in a secondary sense – as increasing not acquiring righteousness, *meritorie* not *formaliter* (Bellarmine, *De Justificatione* II 15). Indeed it is the muddying of the distinction between these two senses of justification that underlies much of the unease created by Newman's insistence that we are justified by works. Pusey's claim that Newman upholds the Anglican doctrine which 'excludes sanctification from having any place in justification'[43] is tenable only if we consistently interpret his language of justification by works as referring merely to the secondary realm of merits. In taking the state of the already justified Christian as the model for his understanding of justification, Newman projects a vision that overrides the basic paradox of the free justification of the sinner. A strained logic might reconcile this vision with Paul's in some abstract ontological arrangement, but at an immediate, existential level the two horizons are incompatible.

Newman's protests against the tyrannical, arbitrary, unscriptural system of Lutheranism may stem not only from a positive concern with 'the beauty of holiness' but also from a defensiveness against the scandalous leap at the origin of Christian salvation to which Luther witnessed. How tepid are Newman's accounts of that origin in Lecture III: 'God treats us *as if* that had not been which has been; that is, by a merciful economy or representation, He says of us, as to the past, what in fact is otherwise than what He says it is' (p. 67). This language tones down to the point of mere shabbiness the scandal of the justification of the ungodly. It robs sin and divine justice of their bite (which necessitates a much stronger account of the working of the Atonement than the extremely cursory references here). Despite the touching analogies with parental forgiveness (p. 68), Calvin would protest that 'any "as if" must give rise to the opinion that after all God does not take sin all that seriously'.[44] Here we have a feeble external view of the process of salvation; whereas Luther plunges us *in medias res*, confining himself to the double perspective of the terror of judgment and the joy of being declared righteous, in identification with Christ crucified; what falls outside that perspective is 'error and poison'. The lack of this perspective is reflected in Newman's surprising vagueness about the working of the Atonement in regard to guilt (pp. 204-5 as quoted above).

He wants to give justification autonomous significance despite its necessary link to the sanctification it initiates and whose fullness it proleptically imputes. He exploits well, as we have seen, the biblical vision of the effective divine Word to convey the force of justification. But for a more precise account of what is done to us when God justifies, he finds only cold banking metaphors – 'Before man has done anything as specimen, or paid anything as instalment...he has the whole treasures of redemption put to his credit' (p. 74) – or an emptily solemn juridical language which pales beside Luther's experience of being made righteous. 'It is a great and august deed in the sight of heaven and hell; it is not done in a corner' (p. 74) – this is not phenomenological; it places the act of justification in a never-never land; the quote from Athanasius (pp. 76-7) confirms this impression of remoteness. The evocation of the joy of being justified is equally abstract, piling on conventional *topoi* in place of a single concrete point of application: 'His tears are wiped away; his fears, misgivings, remorse, shame, are changed for "righteousness, and peace, and joy in the Holy Ghost;" he is clad in white' (p. 74). It is not surprising that the autonomous justification (preceding renewal, pp. 77, 85), which is thus feebly introduced, plays little role after the return, in Lecture IV, to the 'popular' view that 'justification renews, therefore...it may fitly be called renewal' (p. 86). Renewal, substantial righteousness (identified with passive justification, p. 99), becomes the focus of attention, in forgetfulness of the abyssal origin (active justification, the utterance of the divine Word). Though 'justification is imparted to us continually all through our lives' (p. 101), this is done without the drama and paradox that never ceases to mark the Christian condition in Luther; it is a secure ontological process, not the daily rediscovery of the miracle of a relationship.

A TRIDENTINE CRITIQUE OF NEWMAN?

A. McGrath suggests that Newman misunderstood the Catholic view as basing justification on 'the inherent righteousness of the individual, *achieved through moral renewal*' rather than 'the *infusion of divine righteousness* which is the *cause* of subsequent moral renewal, and is not identical with that renewal'.[45] But infused divine righteousness does not seem as sharply differentiated from renewal as McGrath suggests. Infused righteousness, sanctifying grace and the supernatural habit of charity seem to coincide as the 'single formal cause' (*DS* 1529) of justification. Trent describes justification as a gift of divine righteousness by which 'we are renewed in the spirit of our mind' (*DS* 1529) and identifies it with 'the sanctification and renewal of the inner man through a voluntary acceptance of grace' (*DS* 1528). This language telescopes infused righteousness and renewal of life – much as Newman does, when he identifies the Tridentine (Augustinian) 'righteousness of God whereby he makes us righteous' with 'renovation of spirit and the good works thence proceeding' (p. 349). He points out that the question of a real distinction between them (between 'justifying grace' and 'charity') was disputed between Dominicans and Franciscans at Trent and left open (p. 351).

However, Newman may occasionally court a dangerous confusion between justification by this supernatural principle and justification by works. He speaks of 'obedience' as 'the one condition, the one thing in us which involves acceptance on God's part, that one requisite, in naming which all we need is named' (p. 39), and he identifies righteousness with 'acceptable obedience' (p. 131). This seems to be in tension with the Tridentine view: obedience conserves and increases the gift of justification (*DS* 1574) and is a condition of salvation (*DS* 1538, 1570), but the 'one requisite' is infused divine righteousness. Citing Augustine – 'there the law is laid down externally, to terrify the unrighteous; here it is given internally, to justify them' – Newman draws the conclusion: 'that Law then so implanted is our justification' (p. 46). But Augustine, unlike Newman, makes it clear that he is referring to the infused gift of charity: 'for the law of God is charity'.[46] 'Romanists', Newman tells us, 'consider that that on which justification at once takes place...is inherent righteousness (whether habitual or of works, which is an open question)' (p. 349). But is it an open question? Bellarmine rejects the notion that inherent righteousness is 'actual' rather than 'habitual' as in contradiction with the teaching of Trent (*De Justificatione* II 15). Trent speaks of righteousness as an infused habit – 'a power which ever precedes, accompanies and follows their works and without which they can by no means be pleasing to God and meritorious to God' (*DS* 1546). Is Newman attempting to smooth out here a contradiction in his own emphases?

However, he does not feel his stress on works to be incompatible with infused divine righteousness, for the obedience he celebrates springs from 'the possession of Himself, of His substantial grace' (p. 34). Nor does he show any sense of contradicting himself when he declares that 'the possession of that grace is really our justification, and not renewal, or the principle of renewal' and that 'our righteousness is the possession of that presence [of the Holy Ghost]' (p. 137). McGrath states that 'Newman appears to believe that Protestants taught that man was justified on account of faith...and that Roman Catholics taught that man was justified on account of his works or renewal – and therefore that the *via media* consisted in the affirmation that man was justified on account of both faith and works.'[47] The following may be a better account: Newman believed that Protestants taught that man was justified by the imputation of Christ's righteousness apprehended by faith, and that Roman Catholics taught that man was justified on account of a 'new and spiritual principle imparted to us by the Holy Ghost' (p. 131) and the works proceeding from it – but that the *via media* consisted in the affirmation that we are justified 'by Christ's imputed righteousness and by our own inchoate righteousness at once' (p. 368; 'in this then I conceive to lie the unity of Catholic doctrine'; cf. p. 374), that Christ's righteousness is 'both imputed and imparted by His real indwelling' (p. 181), and that justification is ascribed to 'the presence of the Holy Spirit, and that immediately, neither faith nor renewal intervening' (p. 137; this is 'the doctrine of Scripture, which our Church plainly acknowledges', p. 138; see pp. 379-87 for evidence).

The staleness of these metaphysical constructions of justification may be gauged from the distance between the sense of 'righteousness' on which they turn and the everyday secular usage of such terms as 'justice' and 'integrity'.[48] What lends concreteness to these constructions is a myth of inner holiness as a state of soul to be preserved and deepened, a notion which has become increasingly suspect. This is enhanced by the eschatological scenario – God judging the soul – which loomed so large in Newman's imagination, but lingers in ours only as a distraction from a more concrete vision of the Christian life.

LUTHER'S EXTRA NOS

Something is missing, we increasingly feel, in Newman's confident discourse. It is that punch or bite which Luther's voice never lacks, and that comes from the *extra nos* (outside ourselves), the idea that salvation consists, not in a modification of qualities attaching to the soul, but in a total change of situation whereby the sinner is taken out of himself. It is not that the quality of sin is removed from the sinner's soul, but that the sinner is removed from sin as the Israelites from Egypt and given a new identity in Christ (*WA* 56, pp. 334-5). For Newman the *extra nos* is an imputational extrinsicism. The notion of justifying faith is reduced to a subjective quality of the mind, and the all-transforming relationship it initiates is missed: 'What do they mean, in short, when they say that an act of our minds changes our *real* state in God's sight?' (p. 361). Again we note that blunt disjunction of subjective and objective, being and non-being, which forestalls any subtler engagement.

To miss the force of the *extra nos* is to miss also the vigorously Christocentric nature of Luther's thought. Whenever Luther's ideas are about to close into a system, the closure is disrupted by a turning to Christ in faith, and this is no stereotyped gesture but has all the mobility and creativity of a loving relationship. Here Christ is not a unitary metaphysical quantity, but positively elicits an ever-surprising plurality of perspectives in the believer's thinking on him. In Newman's theological writing this personal presence of Christ is screened off by an assembly of metaphysical quantities with which Christ is identified: his divinity, his humanity, his grace, his sacramental presence in Baptism and the Eucharist, his righteousness. Similarly, it is hard for him to express God's love for the believer as a person, since it seems that the believer is loved for the sake of qualities and works he possesses. Contrast Luther: 'God accepts the works because of the person, not the person because of the works; he accepts the person before the works' (*WA* 56, p. 268). The doctrine of the primacy of justification over holiness was intended to keep clear the space for a leap of trust on the part of the believer and for a free manifestation of love toward the believer on the part of God. Neither of these realities offers much foothold for a metaphysical clarification, and are already falsified in the very lucidity of the Protestant doctrine. The opposing position, which translates into metaphysical terms with suspicious ease, makes trust on both the divine and human sides conditional on the quality of holiness, and thus brings us back under the Law.

NEWMAN'S PATHOS OF HOLINESS

If we may now add a psychological twist to our audition of Newman, we surmise that for him to surrender the primacy of holiness over justification would have spelt the sacrifice of his ideal self,[49] for its beauty and its very identity repose entirely on a certain 'myth' of sanctity (quite different from the more biblical one espoused by Luther). He sometimes allows us to eavesdrop on his intimacy: 'Make me preach Thee without preaching – not by words, but by my example and by the catching force, the sympathetic influence, of what I do – by my visible resemblance to Thy saints, and the evident fulness of the love which my heart bears to Thee'.[50] Without this impassioned self-idealisation – a happy combination of challenging self-ideal and flattering ideal self – he would not be the Newman we know; he would have lost his style, his charm, perhaps also his creativity.[51] He might even have lost his conscience, for his moral self-ideal draws its power from a narcissistic vision of perfection. This enchanting vision could not be reconciled with Luther's picture of the wart-ridden sinner who must again and again look away from self to Christ crucified, relying entirely on the imputation of Christ's *aliena iustitia*. Newman's is the saint's desire – to be beautiful before God. The identity of the self, growing and blossoming through the acquisition of attributes of virtue and holiness, is essential to him, and cements his fidelity to the substantial definition of personhood prevalent in traditional theology.

It is true that this cultivation of self – this perpetual sculpting of his own statue, as Plotinus urges (*Ennead* I 6) – proceeds within a relation to the other, to God. Yet that relation too draws much of its vitality and fascination from its narcissistic structuration. It is a circle scarcely disrupted by the paradox of Christ crucified: 'two and two only absolute and luminously self-evident beings, myself and my Creator'.[52] This experience calls out for the Platonic categories of interiority and presence and eclipses the drama of justification and renewal. Newman's contemplative sense of the presence and guidance of God always kept him within the circle of the beauty of holiness. The grievousness of obedience, of being set apart for the Lord's service, shapes mortal clay into a work of art, brings one back to one's true perfected self. Luther's electrifying identification with the biblical Word cast his life in the register of the *extra nos*, but for Newman the essential happenings are very definitely *intra nos*. Both styles of sanctity have their limits; their mutual critique, which need not be a polemic, frees us to create other styles.

It is true that Newman was an ardent preacher of the Cross, but he did not attend much to the dialectic of condemnation and justification which was the core of the Cross for Luther. Justification is subordinate to the experience of the indwelling Spirit; the Cross is the purifying pain that the Spirit operates in us; this too may seem to enjoy a precedence over justification. For Luther's dialectic of Law and Gospel Newman has a more static one of suffering and joy, and the Cross becomes a moment of metaphysical synthesis: 'It is the tone into which all the strains of this world's music are ultimately to be resolved'.[53] To view the Cross as closure rather than transition, as resolution rather than paradoxical disruption, can create a climate of paralysing masochism:

> And in the garden secretly,
> And on the cross on high,

Should teach his brethren and inspire
To suffer and to die.

This in turn chimes intimately with the metaphysics of indwelling:

And that a higher gift than grace
Should flesh and blood refine,
God's presence and His very Self,
And Essence all divine.[54]

Suffering refines flesh and blood as the mode and medium of its transformation and deification.

Newman could not see why faith should be the privileged instrument of justification, yet he has no difficulty in grasping suffering as the privileged instrument of sanctification.

> Justification is the setting up of the Cross within us... We know that in Baptism a cross is literally marked on the forehead. Now suppose...we were ordered to mark the cross, not with the finger, but with a sharp instrument [a masochistic scenario]. Then it would be a rite of blood. In such a case...you could not receive the justification without the pain. Justification would involve pain (p. 173).

This insistence on pain is correlative with the ontological image of indwelling; the liberative event of the cross becomes a metaphysical machinery of transformation. In the Gospel, pain has a secondary role, about the same level as good works; here it is made central at the expense of the leap of faith (and hope) which is the nub of the Lutheran theology of the Cross.[55] Moreover, both pain and good works are concrete and situational in the New Testament, whereas Newman's pain is an abstract and interiorised quality. The same abstraction and interiorisation marks his conception of good works and robs his ethics of concrete content. Instead, the economy of pain and transformation gives his dealings with Scripture a Platonizing and pietistic orientation.

Newman's keen sense of shame, indicating a strong defence against narcissistic humiliations, conditions both the high perfection of his literary performance and the inhibitions limiting his exposure and vulnerability. The refinement of his conscience has more to do with shame than guilt. In youth 'a vivid self-consciousness...sometimes inflicted on him days of acute suffering from the recollection of solecisms, whether actual or imagined, which he recognised in his conduct in society'.[56] Luther's moral agonies were of a different order;

can one imagine him blushing? 'So much stress is laid upon taking our *shame* away... Guilt makes us veil our eyes in the sight of God and His Angels' (p. 75).

> All through Scripture we find stress is laid on one especial punishment...of a most piercing and agonizing character, the manifestation of our shame. When we consider what our feelings are now as connected with this subject, we may fancy what an inexpressibly keen anguish is thus in store for sinners (p. 158).

The masochistic satisfaction with which Newman dwells on the sense of shame paradoxically strengthens narcissistic self-possession; the narcissistic wound is treasured as an experience of the self and so robbed of its sting. Luther provides medicine for a conviction of sin unknown to Newman, for all the subtlety of his probings of moral self-deception. As a keen moralist Newman exposes himself to a constant diet of self-humiliation, yet these self-inflicted wounds never undermine the lucidity of his self-possession, but rather reinforce it.

The image of the robe of righteousness (pp. 74, 133, 155-61, 170, 190) suggests the unbroken self-possession of the ego, a false innocence based on the repression of the anxiety the subject feels when made aware of its contingency, vulnerability and fragmentedness. He clutches at the robe almost as at a fetish.[57] The 'enjewelled robe of righteousness' is envisioned as 'a light streaming from our hearts, pervading the whole man, enwrapping and hiding the lineaments and members of our fallen nature, circling round us, and returning inward to the centre from which it issues' (p. 161). This stylisation of righteousness as the completion of a circle of self-identity removes the subject from the dynamic interplay of freedoms in history and human relationships and robs the quest for integrity of its elements of risk and uncertainty: 'we are enjoined *not* to injure or profane it, but so to honour it in our outward conduct, that it may be continued and increased in us' (p. 156; see Trent, *DS* 1531).

'My soul is in my hand' says Gerontius as he nears God's throne.[58] That is the last thing Luther would have thought of saying! Newman's self-recollection made impossible for him the terrific lurch of the *extra nos*, the adventure of finding one's only claim to identity in another, in Christ crucified. The beauty of his style, itself mirroring the enactment of transformation, holds him back from anything like Luther's identification with the Word. Newman haunts his own text to an uncanny degree; in every sentence we are conscious of his presence in addition to, and sometimes at the expense of, what he is saying. For each sentence he composed is a mirror reflecting the perfection of his ideal self. Something similar might be said of Augustine, Milton, Kierkegaard, James, or Proust. But in these the stamp of personality is a self-projection rather than a self-mirroring, whereas the 'continual motion of mind' which animates Newman's style is a rhythm of first striving to fulfil a self-ideal and then cherishing his ideal self in delighted self-recollection. Take any sentence at random: 'I shall now proceed to consider it [the gift of righteousness], under two chief designations which are there [in the New Testament] given to us; by attending to which we shall conceive more worthily of our privilege, and gain a deeper insight into the sacred text; I mean *glory* and *power*' (p. 161). First the lofty strenuous gesture of setting himself a task, labouring honourably under it, aspiring to fulfil the self-ideal; then the dwelling, in a majestic pause, on the satisfactory worthiness of the goal proposed (the self-ideal now considered as gratifying to the ideal self); finally, the reward, the moment of triumphant self-return in the cadence.

'The axial reality of the subject is not in its ego', which is rather the headquarters of illusion; 'that subject unknown to the ego, unrecognized by the ego, which Freud calls "the core of our being"' [59] is scarcely likely to emerge in Newman's self-presentation, any more than the biblical subject can emerge within a metaphysics of the substantial soul. One is more directly exposed to the truth of subjectivity with Luther than with Newman, though one can tease it out in Newman too, but as repressed. 'Literally, the ego is an object – an object which fills a certain function which we here name the imaginary function.'[60] Newman objectified himself in a most attractive form – as saint, as gentleman, as a mannered and fragrant rhetorical voice, as a living, questing mind – but we may be in touch with his true subjectivity only at those points at which that imaginary screen is displaced, disrupted or shown to be hollow. A truly puzzling question emerges when we no longer take his self-presentation at its face value: what is he really trying to say across these splendid rhetorical performances? This enigma reaches a pitch of concentration in the *Apologia pro Vita Sua*, a text apparently breathing confidence of justification. Luther repels or quickly shatters the narcissistic identification which, to the contrary, is the obligatory first stage in an understanding of Newman, one at which his admirers often remain fixated, thus becoming, albeit vicariously, worshippers of that most captivating of idols, the 'dear self'. It is an immense point in favour of Luther's theology that it is able to do more justice to 'the excentricity of the subject in respect to the ego'.[61]

THE FOUNDATIONS: INDWELLING AND OMNIPRESENCE

In Lecture VI, Newman insists on being told the cash-value of justification in terms of something identifiable here and now in the inward state of the individual soul. 'It stands to reason that a soul that is justified is not in the same state internally as if it had not been justified' (p. 130). One might query the objectifying effect of 'a soul', which assumes that personal identity is solidly constituted outside and apart from the dynamic existential relations in which alone Luther grasps it. The word 'internally' cordons off an area of individual self-possession, isolating the believer's individuality from the communal process into which we enter in being justified. The 'reason' to which such argument 'stands' is a Platonically-tinged commonsense which Luther would find inadequate to the biblical word. Newman wants an inner label marking one as justified: 'what is the state of a justified man? or in what does justification *consist*?'; 'what is that object or thing, what is it in a man, which God seeing there, therefore calls him righteous?'; 'I wish to insist that there really must be...in every one who is justified, some such token or substance of his justification'; 'a certain distinctive state of soul to which the designation of righteousness belongs'; 'the criterion within us, which God sees there...the seal and signature of his elect'; 'something present and inward'; 'something in us, not out of us' (pp. 130-2). The more one considers these phrases the more their discordance with a biblical phenomenology of Christian life becomes apparent. It is as if one were to ask: 'what is that object or thing in a person which is the token and substance of their being in love with another person?' To abstract such a reconstructed substance from the all-transforming *relation* in which one is justified is to subsume the horizon created by the Word under one governed by a metaphysics of the soul. The biblical robe-imagery does not warrant the reduction of the pneumatic to the categories of object, thing, token; in fact the production of such literal correlatives destroys its metaphorical force. These reifications shore up a metaphysical (illusory) identity of the self and impede awareness of righteousness as a dynamic and constantly renewed relation rather than a fixed, nameable quantity. Newman's empirical realism could have led him (with some help from Hume) to suspect that the human spirit is too much a function of mobile relations to allow itself to be examined 'objectively' – even in divine judgment – with a view to detecting its possession or lack of a requisite mark or criterion.

Doggedly, he pursues his question: what substantial difference does justification make? For Luther, it is not only the transcendental condition of 'Christ's righteousness imputed' (p. 131), which Newman says is 'no answer at all, and needs explanation before it will apply' (p. 133). It might be explained that the empirical offshoot of this condition, that makes justifying faith the effective beginning of renewal, consists in a changed relation to sin.[62] But Lutherans hesitate to identify the empirical effect of justification by isolating a quality of any sort; for it is essentially a relation of the whole person to the Saviour; one cannot abstract from this relation qualities in the soul either meriting justification or caused by justification. Faith is experienced as liberation for the lifelong conquest of sin. This is the 'something present and inward' Newman asks for, but that is a misleading way to describe it. To see it as 'something in us, not out of us' (p. 133) would be to miss the fact that one's whole being is set in a dynamic relationship to grace and to sin. How foreign all this is to Newman may be gauged from his dismissal of Luther's identification in faith with Christ crucified, his 'contemporaneity with Christ' (Kierkegaard): 'to say that our present state of being accounted righteous is nothing else than the fact of Christ's having obeyed the Law eighteen hundred years since...is like saying that our animal life consists in the creation of Adam' (p. 134). The parallel between life and justification as present, inner principles shows a tendency to draw on vital or organic metaphors for the spiritual, which elsewhere produces unitary idealisations of the life of the mind, the life of faith and the development of dogma.

Newman is prepared to concede that 'if it be laid down that our justification consists in union with Christ, or reconciliation with God, this is an intelligible and fair answer' (p. 134). But 'what is *meant* by union with Christ?...if we consider Scripture to be silent on this point, then we shall say that justification consists in an *unknown, unrevealed, mysterious* union with Christ' (p. 134). If that is what Protestants hold, let them maintain an appropriate silence; but if they explain that *faith* is that in which union with Christ consists, then let them stand their ground against those who argue that it is *renewal*. Let them answer the question: 'faith is acceptable as having a something in it, which unbelief has not; that something, what is it? It must be God's grace...'

(p. 136). The urge to objectify here again abstracts faith from the concrete relation of its turning to Christ. He insists that there must be an ontological foundation to both faith and renewal, first identified as grace: 'the having that grace or that presence...must be the real token, the real state of a justified man' (p. 136). Grace here is thought of as substance, not relation; its acting in us is conceived on the model of the soul's acting in the body as principle of life. Then it is identified as 'an immediate divine power or presence', 'the presence of the Holy Ghost shed abroad in our hearts' (p. 137). Here the deeper foundation, the indwelling Trinity, comes into view, at first in a warmly biblical language. But gradually we are made conscious of the brackets of a non-biblical ontology, enclosing this language.

Newman goes on to claim 'that justification actually *is* ascribed in Scripture to the presence of the Holy Spirit, and that immediately, neither faith nor renewal intervening' (p. 137). Again we suspect an inversion of the biblical sequence, threatening ontological annulment of the entire drama of justification mapped in Paul and Luther. One might turn Newman's line of questioning against himself and ask: if the indwelling presence is the something in us, not out of us, that makes us justified and holy, how do we experience it? In justification/renewal we experience only 'a supernatural quality imparted to the soul by God's grace' (p. 136); by what extra experience do we become aware of 'the grace itself, as an immediate divine power or presence' (p. 137). The experiential upshot seems to be that justification/renewal is most authentically lived as the cherishing of an indwelling presence:

> this justifying power though *within* us, as it must be, if it is to separate us from the world, yet is not...any quality or act of our minds, not faith, not renovation, not obedience, not anything cognizable by man, but a certain divine gift in which all these qualifications are included (pp. 143-4).

Three Neo-Platonic, un-Pauline traits emerge here: the recollection whereby we cherish the power within; the apophatic reverence for its incognisable nature; the sense of removal from the world. Trusting in these Neo-Platonic attitudes, Newman short-circuits the biblical experience.

Newman uses 'The Law of the Spirit of life hath made me free from the law of sin and death' (Rom 8.2) and 'It is the Spirit that giveth life' (John 6.63) as proof-texts, with a massive emphasis on the notions of life and death (p. 138). The *processes* of justification and of spiritual enlightenment, vividly dramatised in the composition of Romans and of John, are eclipsed by this foregrounding of their final moments. An undifferentiated ontological unity is imposed on the biblical notions, preventing attention to their context and its nuances. The Pauline and Johannine notions of spirit (*to pneuma*), equated with the Holy Spirit of trinitarian doctrine, are grasped in terms of substantial life, at the expense of the dialectical, existential dimensions of pneumatic contemplation. In reducing justification to indwelling, Newman would swap the Pauline perspective as constructed by Luther for the fuller and firmer ontological version of Athanasius (*On the Incarnation*), who describes a conquest of life over corruption and knowledge over ignorance, finally summarised as divinisation. But here too he takes over the conclusion at the expense of the process, making divinisation static and substantial, whereas for Athanasius it is the *event* of the communication of knowledge of God and divine life.

Righteousness as 'a definite inward gift' is opposed to 'any mere quality of mind, whether faith or holiness' (p. 139). This abrupt dualism of subjective and objective further impedes him from finding a language of *pneuma*. The ontological 'gift' is eventually mediated with the subjective by a devotional orchestration of the theme of inner presence. This gap between objective ontology and its subjective appropriation is unknown to the Greek Fathers, and indicates the restorational character of Newman's use of their language. What makes all restoration hollow is the repression of awareness it exacts; in attacking Luther it is his own modern subjectivity that Newman wants to subject to a patristic vision which cannot truly satisfy it. He tries to make the Fathers more vital by reinforcing the biblical basis of their vision, but he does not carry that process far enough, and is led to prize them as venerable rather than to interrogate them as witnesses to biblical truth. A subtle confusion between the firmness of biblical faith and a numbing fidelity to the past runs through Newman's writing. Though never a barren traditionalist, again and again he loses the thread of his best awareness, seduced by the beauty of an imagined past. He found himself amid the Fathers, felt that he lost himself amid the Reformers. Did he one-sidedly allow that pattern of return to shape his life? Had he lost himself a little more, might he not have more to say to us now? He had, it is true, a broad grasp of his age, and he 'changed often' – the conversion to Rome entailed a major counter-narcissistic immersion in a foreign element. Yet he is also always defending some unyielding core of identity, cushioned in devout precautions. What threatens it is kept at a distance.

McGrath finds proof of Newman's 'purely superficial engagement with the thought of the Reformation' in his failure to notice in Luther and Calvin a doctrine of Christ's indwelling very similar to his own.[63] But their teaching is by no means easy to interpret: it proceeds in the register of identification with Christ by faith, a Christ who remains *extra nos* even though we can become 'one person' (Luther) with him in faith.[64] Calvin might find Newman's notions of indwelling to reek of the substantial interfusion of which he accused Osiander (*Inst.* III 11.5). His 'eminent sentence, that the faithful live outside themselves, that is, in Christ'[65] gives the notion of Christ indwelling a refined and dynamic inflection foreign to Newman. He is quite aware of Calvin's teaching that 'Christ indwelling is our righteousness', but 'what is with them a matter of words I would wish to use in a real sense as expressing a sacred mystery' (p. 382). This category of 'sacred mystery' fails to capture the pneumatic quality of the Pauline, deutero-Pauline or Johannine accounts of indwelling. Luther's language of indwelling also seems to him unreal, or 'merely' spiritual, in comparison with the substantialist ontology of the Fathers: 'Since then the thought of Him is ever present in it [faith], therefore He may be said to be...*spiritually* present in it' (p. 20). In Newman, indwelling overrides the Lutheran *extra nos*. Osiander, also, thought that 'Luther's language about righteousness "outside ourselves" was a figurative concession to simple believers',[66] but the Formula of Concord corrects him by insisting that the divine indwelling does not precede but follows justifying faith (*BSLK* p. 933) and by condemning the view, shared by Newman, that 'faith does not look alone to the obedience of Christ, but to his divine nature as it dwells and acts in us, and that it is through this indwelling that our sins are covered' (p. 935). In the first edition (p. 426) Newman repeats Calvin's association of Osiander with Manicheanism, but this he subsequently retracted, admitting his kinship with Osiander: 'it is unnecessary to advance so grave a charge against him' (third edition, p. 387).[67]

The model of indwelling, 'the distinguishing grace of the Gospel' (p. 147), prevails over all others, as ontologically the most fundamental, and is in turn underpinned by axioms about the substance and omnipresence of God. The metaphysics of omnipresence becomes the ultimate bedrock of this vision. As the phenomenology of justification was diluted by its reduction to sanctification (its necessary underpinning) and both are further diluted by being recalled to a spirituality of indwelling divine presence, so this chain of metaphysical grounding finally leads to the erasure of all distinctively biblical phenomena in a cold presentation of a God, characterised above all by the necessities of his ontological constitution. 'If this notion of the literal indwelling of God within us...be decried as a sort of mysticism, I ask in reply whether it is not a necessary truth that He is with us and in us, if He is everywhere?' (p. 145). A stronger reply would have been to show that the indwelling was not a mere undifferentiated mystical piety but had a precise evangelical character; Luther and Calvin would have been indispensable references in the construction of such a phenomenology. Instead Newman falls back on 'a necessary truth' which blunts the originality of his vision and prevents him from deepening it and freeing it from devotional notions of intimate presence. Once again the powerful hold of unquestioned metaphysical ways of reasoning keeps him from the existential penetration of which he should have been capable. This failure of engagement shows up in his style, which crumbles into fustian when cut off from the springs of experience:

> His infinite and incomprehensible Essence, which once existed by and in itself alone, and then at the creation so far communicated itself to His works as to sustain what He had brought into existence,...may in the Christian Church manifest itself in act and virtue in the hearts of Christians, as far surpassing what it is in unregenerate man, as its presence in man excels its presence in a brute or a vegetable (p. 145).

This God is encased in a dead ontology, which yet co-exists with a vivid phenomenology of God's intimate presence to the soul in judgment (conscience), painfully transforming grace and sustaining love. The phenomenology was never invoked to transform the metaphysics, and so remained confined to a subjective sphere of devotion. Newman's objective discourse on God and the soul flounders in metaphysical jargon without metaphysical conviction, and only when he modulates back to the subjective does his style recover its glow. 'Two Voices are there': one subtle and engaging in its testimony to a lived holiness, the other the droning of a thrall of metaphysics. The task for Newman's readers is to free the first voice from the inhibiting intrusion of the second, and to find for it the philosophical and theological language that may allow it to resonate beyond a cocoon of subjectivism.[68]

NOTES

1. Page references are to the third edition of 1874 (London, 1900). *WA* = Weimar Edition of Luther; *DS* = Denzinger-Schönmetzer, *Enchiridion Symbolorum* (32nd edn, 1963); *BSLK* = *Bekenntnisschriften der evangelisch-lutherischen Kirche.*

2. See G. Sauter (ed.), *Rechtfertigung als Grundbegriff evangelischer Theologie* (Munich, 1989), p. 19.

3. Cf. L.H. Martin et al. (eds), *Technologies of the Self: A Seminar with Michel Foucault* (London, 1988).

4. P. Toon, *Evangelical Theology 1833-1856* (London, 1979), p. 150.

5. Thanking J.F. Christie for the gift of Bellarmine's *Disputationes*, he says; 'it has written my lectures on Justification' (*Letters and Diaries*, VI, p. 83).

6. See W. Link, *Das Ringen Luthers um die Freiheit der Theologie von der Philosophie* (Munich, 1955), p. 208.

7. See K.-H. zur Mühlen, *Reformatorische Vernunft-Kritik und neuzeitliches Denken* (Tübingen, 1980), pp. 44-66.

8. This is another of those unitary terms that are exploded by a grasp of historical pluralism. Paul's reception of the Jewish senses of the term seems disrupted by some cultural or psychological interference (see E.P. Sanders, *Paul and Palestinian Judaism* [London, 1977]; H. Räisänen, *Paul and the Law* [Tübingen, 1983]) while the patristic receptions of Paul are steeped in Hellenistic metaphysics of cosmic law and allegorical stylisations of salvation history. What are we to make today of Luther's powerful constructions, which transfer Paul to the sixteenth century and pit him against all that had then acquired the status of Law? The most that can be said, as in so many analogous cases, is that in yet another radically altered (post-Nietzschean, post-Freudian) context they remain suggestive and stimulating for our moral reflections.

9. See M. Greschat, *Melanchthon neben Luther* (Wittenberg, 1965).

10. See A. Hasler, *Luther in der katholischen Dogmatik* (Munich, 1968) II, p. 66.

11. See R. Schröder, *Johann Gerhards lutherische Christologie und die aristotelische Metaphysik* (Tübingen, 1983).

12. See K. Bornkamm, *Luthers Auslegungen des Galaterbriefs* (Berlin, 1963), pp. 93-9.

13. See H. Schütte, *Protestantismus* (Essen-Werden, 1967), pp. 392-430. Defences of Luther against Newman seem to have been ineffective and blustering, to judge from J.C. Hare's *Vindication of Luther* (Cambridge, 1855), pp. 74-100.

14. See O.H. Pesch, *Theologie der Rechtfertigung bei Martin Luther und Thomas von Aquin* (Mainz, 1967), pp. 109-22; R. Hermann, *Luthers These 'Gerecht und Sünder zugleich'* (Gütersloh, 1930) with the ecumenically significant review articles of R. Kösters, *Catholica* 18 (1964), pp. 48-77, 193-217; 19 (1965), pp. 138-62; 171-85.

15. See M. Schmaus, *Katholische Dogmatik* III/2 (Munich, 1951); cf. Newman, pp. 108-10.

16. Pesch, p. 302.

17. See Hermann as quoted by Kösters (1964), pp. 209-10.

18. H. Hübner, *Rechtfertigung und Heiligung in Luthers Römerbriefvorlesung* (Wittenberg, 1965), p. 115.

19. A. McGrath calls this an Arminian view (*Iustitia Dei* [Cambridge UP, 1986] II, p. 130). Newman does quote an Arminian author in this sense on p. 185, but the source of his view that Luther made faith the formal cause of justification is Bellarmine (*De Justificatione* II 4) and the language of the Reformers themselves (e.g. *BSLK* p. 218 and the texts quoted by Newman on pp. 135, 359). He believes that the Lutherans originally presented faith as the formal cause of justification, but then retracted this in favour of the apprehensive notion of faith (pp. 358-9). The dilemma he poses in Lecture I is more telling against the first position, but contrary to what McGrath suggests, he is well aware of the second, which tends to spoil his argument (see pp. 20-3).

20. J.A. Möhler pursues a similar argument, *Symbolik* (1832; 5th edn, 1838), ed. J.R. Geiselmann (Cologne, 1958) pp. 199-230. Newman may have consulted Möhler's work in the French translation (McGrath II, p. 234).

21. (London, 1906), pp. 137-54.

22. This question is richly discussed in Pesch, pp. 195-262.

23. Möhler (pp. 186-94) is clearer on this point. On *DS* 1532 see S. Horn, *Glaube und Rechtfertigung nach dem Konzils-Theologen Andrés de Vega* (Paderborn, 1972), pp. 226-45.

24. See Augustine, *On the Trinity*, Book IV. The early Luther still worked with this Augustinian schema: 'They wish to hear and contemplate the eternal Word, though not yet first justified and having the eyes of their heart cleansed by the incarnate Word' (*WA* 56, p.

299). For Newman's own doubts about his argument here see T.L. Sheridan, *Newman on Justification* (New York, 1967), p. 255.

25. See M. Chemnitz, *Examen Decretorum Concilii Tridentini* (1578; Berlin, 1861), p. 183; Chemnitz does not bear out the claim that for Protestants other senses of faith have 'no connection whatever, except in the accident of an homonymous term, with that faith which justifies' (p. 6).

26. Sheridan, p. 153.

27. Ibid., p. 193.

28. 'Autobiographical Memoir' in A. Mozley (ed.), *Letters and Correspondence of J.H. Newman* (London, 1903) I, p. 110.

29. See M. Bogdahn, *Die Rechtfertigungslehre Luthers im Urteil der neueren katholischen Theologie* (Göttingen, 1971), pp. 236-50.

30. See *Letters and Diaries*, VI, p. 242; E.A. Knox, *The Tractarian Movement* (London, 1933), pp. 204-5; Toon, pp. 143-4.

31. Stated thus bluntly in the first edition (p. 58), but in the third we find the softening clauses: 'so far as they are enabled to please Him by what they are and what they do, so far may they be said, through His secret grace, to justify themselves.'

32. He claims to have shown that 'the difference between Melanchthon's view and the teaching of the Tridentine Council is a matter of words' (*Letters and Diaries* XXIX, p. 354) and 'that the difference between Calvinists and Arminians is *verbal* – the former maintaining that justification is an *act of God*, but the latter meaning by it a *state of a man's soul*' (ibid., XXXI, p. 260).

33. B. Lohse, *Evangelium in der Geschichte* (Göttingen, 1988), p. 154.

34. D. Waterland, 'A Summary View of the Doctrine of Justification', *Works* VI (Oxford, 1856), p. 7. Newman acknowledges agreements with Waterland (p. 251). Newman's uncritical reliance on the later Caroline Divines is criticised by McGrath, see II, pp. 130-2.

35. See pp. 393-4. The Lutheran critique of Augustine is well stated in Link, pp. 236-70.

36. See Hübner, pp. 98-9: the earlier Luther inclines to the Augustinian understanding, but already stresses the paradoxical extrinsic nature of the resulting righteousness: 'external to us is all the good that we have, which is Christ' (*WA* 56, p. 279). Here it is not yet the kergyma, but a quasi-mystical self-transcending, that takes us *extra nos* (see O. Bayer, *Promissio* [Darmstadt, 1989], p. 59).

37. *De Spiritu et Littera* 52 (*CSEL* 60.1 p. 208).

38. Sheridan, p. 152. For a late meditation on sin see *Meditations and Devotions* (Westminster, Md., 1975), pp. 333-46.

39. See E. Yarnold, '*Duplex iustitia*: the Sixteenth Century and the Twentieth' in G.R. Evans (ed.), *Christian Authority* (Oxford, 1988), pp. 204-23.

40. See D. Newsome, 'Justification and Sanctification: Newman and the Evangelicals', *Journal of Theological Studies* 15 (1964), pp. 32-53.

41. As suggested by Sheridan, p. 216 and Toon, p. 146.

42. This surmise depends on the reputation of the nineteenth-century Evangelicals; that the justification doctrine had quite the opposite effect in the seventeenth century, emptying the everyday world of meaning and rejecting the Calvinist reinvestment in good works, is a thesis of W. Benjamin's *Ursprung des deutschen Trauerspiels* (*Gesammelte Schriften* I [Frankfurt, 1980], pp. 317-20).

43. Toon, p. 144.

44. T. Stadtland, *Rechtfertigung und Heiligung bei Calvin* (Neukirchen-Vluyn, 1972), p. 151.

45. McGrath II, p. 131.

46. *De Spiritu et Littera* 29 (p. 182).

47. II, p. 130.

48. See J.S. O'Leary, 'Integrity', *Furrow* 36 (1985), pp. 467-74.

49. On the notions of 'self-ideal' and 'ideal self' see Freud, 'Zur Einführung des Narzissmus' III (*GW* X pp. 159-70; *SE* XIV pp. 92-102); J. Lacan, *Le séminaire I: Les écrits techniques de Freud* (Paris, 1975), pp. 125-63.

50. *Meditations and Devotions*, p. 365.

51. Yet such a sacrifice might have produced a rugged 'late style' as in the cases of Yeats and T.S. Eliot; see R. Bush, *T.S. Eliot* (Oxford UP, 1983), pp. 226-37.

52. *Apologia pro Vita Sua* (London, 1908), p. 4.

53. *Parochial and Plain Sermons* VI (London, 1901), p. 85.

54. *Verses on Various Occasions* (London, 1903), p. 364.

55. On how Luther outgrew pious internalisation of Christ's sufferings to receive the message of the Cross as a liberating kerygma, see Bayer, pp. 66-70, 84-6, 106-7 etc.

56. 'Autobiographical Memoir', p. 92.

57. A fetishism protective of the ideal self, is apparent in his habit of preserving relics of his past (the pairs of spectacles etc. displayed in the Birmingham Oratory) and celebrating anniversaries. The com-

fort drawn from burying his head in the cloaks of friends (= other selves) also betokens narcissistic restoration. I am not attempting a 'psychological reduction' of the kind rightly criticised in J.L. Powell, *Three Uses of Christian Discourse in John Henry Newman* (Missoula, Montana, 1975), pp. 12-15. Such categories as narcissism etc. are not intrinsically pejorative and are indispensable, I believe, for illuminating the dynamics of Newman's creativity.

58. *Verses on Various Occasions*, p. 360.

59. J. Lacan, *Le séminaire, livre II: Le moi dans la théorie de Freud et dans la technique de la psychanalyse* (Paris, 1978), p. 59.

60. Ibid., p. 60.

61. Ibid.

62. Pesch, pp. 283-95.

63. McGrath II, p. 130. McGrath captiously suggests that Newman did not consult Luther's text at first hand (pp. 127-9). The omission in the quotation from Luther (*WA* 40:1 pp. 414-16) on pp. 300-1 does not prove dependence on an intermediary or deliberate misrepresentation. Newman's misunderstanding of Luther's analogy between faith and works and Christ's divinity and humanity is in good faith; the Luther specialist O. Modalsli makes the same mistake less guardedly: 'Luther can come close to a doctrine of justification through works – indeed he actually expresses it: *ut vere dicitur de Christo homine, quod creavit omnia, ita tribuitur etiam iustificatio fidei incarnatae seu fideli facere* (*WA* 40:1 p. 416). Faith incarnate, believing action justifies!' (*Das Gericht nach den Werken* [Göttingen, 1963], p. 40). See P. Manns, 'Fides absoluta – Fides incarnata' in *Reformata Reformanda* (Münster, 1965) I, pp. 265-312. McGrath's argument (p. 129) from verbal discrepancies between Newman's citations and *WA* 40 (rather than the text Newman used) is futile.

64. Pesch, pp. 239-45; Stadtland, pp. 118-24.

65. Quoted by Stadtland, p. 121.

66. J. Pelikan, *The Christian Tradition* 4 (Chicago, 1984), p. 151. G. Zimmermann perhaps underestimates the difference between a Greek patristic ontology of the indwelling Trinity and Luther's sense of the believer's identification with Christ *extra se* when he insists on a concord between Osiander and Luther on this point ('Die Thesen Osianders zur Disputation "de iustificatione"' *Kerygma und Dogma* 33 [1987], pp. 224-44).

67. G. Zimmermann concurs: 'Calvins Auseinandersetzung mit Osianders Rechtfertigungslehre' *Kerygma und Dogma* 35 (1989), pp.

236-56. See Toon, p. 155.

68. I note, too late to address them, three recent discussions of the *Lectures*: J. Morales, 'Newman and the Problem of Justification' in *Newman Today* (San Francisco, 1988), pp. 143-64; I. Ker, *John Henry Newman: A Biography* (Oxford, 1990), pp. 151-7; H. Chadwick, 'The *Lectures on Justification*' in *Newman after a Hundred Years*, ed. I. Ker and A.G. Hill (Oxford, 1990), pp. 287-308 (p. 292: Newman read Möhler immediately *after* correcting the proofs of the *Lectures*, vs. note 20 above). These authors' eschewal of any critical confrontation between Luther and Newman's account of him is to be regretted at a time when so painful a gulf may be felt between the Gospel and the Church.

7

INDIVIDUALISM AND THE APPEAL TO AUTHORITY

David Nicholls

> I may say: Read Newman; he is by far the best writer the Church of Rome has had in England since the Reformation. And the pupil will come back and say: But do you think his arguments sound, or his religion Catholic? I shall have to say: No; if you work it out, it is a school of Infidelity.[1]

Thus wrote the Roman Catholic historian Acton to the Anglican statesman Gladstone.

In this chapter I shall argue that a radical individualism, lying at the basis of Newman's understanding of life in general and of Christianity in particular, vitiates much of his theology and is intimately linked to a strongly authoritarian approach to religion. In Newman's early thought, life is seen as an adventure of the individual soul, temporarily inhabiting a material body, as it passes through an unreal world. Salvation consists in deliverance from this world. The model owed much to Platonic assumptions, though Newman maintained that salvation comes not by knowledge but by faith. Metaphysical individualism – which at times became solipsism – was thus complemented by moral individualism, for faith is essentially a disposition of will and desire. In his Anglican days, he emphasised the acceptance of Christian teaching on the basis of its content. Good people believe because they wish and hope that the Gospel is true; bad people disbelieve because they hope it is untrue. The good believe because, if it is true, they will be rewarded; the evil disbelieve because, if it is true, they will be punished. The reasons both give are secondary to their commitment. Newman willingly embraced the scepticism of Hume; reason is a slave of the passions.[2] Later, Newman interpreted faith as essentially the submission of the will to an external authority and the acceptance of Christianity, less because of its substantive content, than because it was the teaching of an infallible authority.

Here too the criterion is moral; submission is virtuous and rebellion is the greatest evil. Only an external and infallible authority can guarantee truth, permit certitude and maintain the unity of the Church. Without such a person or body, generally recognised and easily identifiable, the collection of individual souls who make up the visible Church would fall apart into heresy and disunity. In this view of things there remains a role for private judgment, but the Catholic position is distinguished from the Protestant, in being concerned not with a judgment about the content of revelation but about who is the accredited teacher; whose voice is to be followed?[3]

'MYSELF AND MY CREATOR'

In a celebrated remark in the *Apologia* Newman recalled how in his early life he felt isolated from the objects around him, doubting the reality of material phenomena, making him rest in the thought of only two 'absolute and luminously self-evident beings', himself and God.[4] We are reminded of Elizabeth Clephane's hymn 'Beneath the Cross of Jesus':

> And from my stricken heart with tears,
> Two wonders I confess:
> The wonders of redeeming love,
> And my own worthlessness.

This was published just four years after Newman's *Apologia* and shares much of the same spiritual ethos. This psychic individualism, this feeling, to which he referred, is related to the much wider – metaphysical, epistemological and social – individualism which characterises his writings. He was even prepared to deny the existence of space 'except as a subjective idea of our minds'.[5] His 'atomism' is reflected most vividly in his religion and stands out in his sermons. 'To every one of us,' he declared in that thin but musical voice, so graphically described by Matthew Arnold, 'there are but two beings in the whole world, himself and God.'[6]

In his sermon on 'The Individuality of the Soul' Newman spoke of the 'separate existence' of the soul. 'Nothing,' he proclaimed from the pulpit of St Mary's,

> is more difficult than to realize that every man has a distinct soul, that every one of all the millions who live or have lived, is as whole

> and independent a being in himself, as if there were no one else in the whole world but he.[7]

The preacher went on to consider a great town, with crowds of people pouring through its streets. But what is the truth? That each is his own centre and those around him are but shadows. 'He is everything to himself, and no one else is really anything. No one outside him can really touch him, can touch his soul, his immortality.' God created the soul and 'sent it into the body', where he preserves its detached existence until, 'severed from the body', it returns to him. This radical Cartesianism – where an essential soul inhabits an accidental body – makes a poor philosophical framework within which to formulate a Catholic theology. Heart does not speak to heart, people talk to each other!

With such little understanding of how people relate to each other in the context of community, it is not surprising that he believed religious conversion to be an individual phenomenon, and that people must be changed one by one. Likewise, addressing Anglicans as a Roman Catholic, he insisted that 'The Eternal God deals with us one by one'.[8] On practical matters Newman was equally individualistic. When discussing the editorship of the *British Critic* he maintained that all great things are done by concentration of authority and by the principle of individuality.[9] It is my contention that the construction of a truly Catholic theology of redemption is impossible within the framework of this radically atomistic understanding of reality.

The spirituality of Newman is closely related to this atomistic principle, which is one reason for his popularity among middle-class English people, Protestant and Catholic. 'The Christian has a deep, silent, hidden peace' he told his St Mary's congregation,

> ...He is the greater part of the time by himself, and when he is in solitude, that is his real state. What he is when left to himself and to his God, that is his true life. He can bear himself; he can (as it were) joy in himself, for it is the grace of God within him, in the presence of the Eternal Comforter, in which he joys.[10]

Rejoicing in the unreality of the material world and isolated in their spiritual cocoons, Christians have every incentive to ignore the changes taking place in the world around them. It is no coincidence that it was Manning rather than Newman who responded positively to the social and political developments in late nineteenth-century England.

In a fascinating essay, written in 1855 for the *Catholic Standard*, Newman ascribed the blunders of the British army in the Crimea to the British constitution which reflects the character of 'the Englishman' [*sic*].[11] The English are a race of individuals, suspicious of organisations and institutions, particularly of government. 'A government,' he declared, 'is their natural foe; they cannot do without it altogether, but they will have of it as little as they can. They will forbid the concentration of power; they will multiply its seats, complicate its acts, and make it safe by making it inefficient', words which might have been written by Acton or Maitland. Further examination of the text reveals, however, less of pluralism than of individualism – the seats of power are based on the individual rather than on the group. London, with all its complexity, is the production of 'individual enterprise'. British imperial expansion was the work of individuals,

> wherever we go, all over the earth, it is the solitary Briton, the London agent, or the *Milordos*, who is walking restlessly about, abusing the natives, and raising a colossus...No one can say beforehand what will come of these various specimens of the independent self-governing, self-reliant Englishman.[12]

DOGMA, MORALITY AND BELIEF

To be a Christian is to accept certain dogmas as true. 'From the age of fifteen,' we read in the *Apologia*, 'dogma has been *the fundamental* principle of my religion.'[13] This emphasis on the central role of dogmatic statements in Christianity coexisted in Newman's thought with a recognition of the limits of human language. He therefore insisted that this acceptance of dogma must be 'real' and not merely 'notional'. It must be a belief of the heart as well as of the intellect. Unfortunately Newman does not clearly distinguish between dogma, doctrine and theology, so we find him at times asserting that 'Theology is the fundamental and regulating principle of the whole Church system. It is commensurate with Revelation.' Elsewhere he seems to have equated revelation with a 'system of opinions' given to the world.[14] Most Catholic writers today would find difficulty in this apparently intellectualist formula. They would generally speak of revelation as an event, as a person or as an idea, rather than as a list of theological propositions; indeed Newman himself in his celebrated *Essay on Development* spoke of Christianity as 'an idea'.[15]

In any case Newman clearly thought that the acceptance of dogma by the individual is a necessary condition of being a Christian. This acceptance is by faith and not reason. 'Man is *not* a reasoning animal; he is a seeing, feeling, contemplating, acting animal.'[16] He poured scorn on philosophers who sit at home, working out complex metaphysical systems; 'like blind men, though they can put a stranger on his way, they cannot walk straight themselves, and do not feel it quite their business to walk at all'. The Christian faith is not a matter of logical deduction, the Gospel is not good news for the clever, for the educated or for the well-informed. 'Life is for action. If we insist on proofs for everything, we shall never come to action; to act you must assume, and that assumption is faith.'[17] But what leads some to believe and others to reject the Gospel?

For Newman faith is ultimately a moral principle. This he asserted in classical form in his brilliant *Oxford University Sermons*. People are disposed to believe what they *wish* to be true. It is clear that in these Anglican sermons Newman was assuming that people believe – or disbelieve – largely on the basis of a judgment about the *content* of revelation. Its message is welcomed by some, who are thus predisposed to believe it to be true, and rejected by others. The good person will hope that the Gospel is true and will therefore find it easy to accept. Reasonable belief is founded on probabilities; 'a good and a bad man will think very different things probable'.[18] The Gospel does not come with incontrovertible proof, because in that case,

> there is no merit, no praise or blame, in believing or disbelieving; no test of character in the one or the other. But a man is responsible for his faith, because he is responsible for his likings and dislikings, his hopes and his opinions, on all of which his faith depends.[19]

Newman – a true child of nineteenth-century England – was determined to make belief a test of the moral character of individuals and to ascribe Christian faith to the merit and virtue of believers.[20] This is particularly so in his Anglican period, but it carried over to his later thinking. Those who find it impossible to continue in allegiance to the Roman Catholic Church on the ground that its teachings are 'unscriptural' cannot do so in good faith, as a matter of conscience; rather they must have opened the Bible,

> in an unbelieving spirit, and for unbelieving purpose; they would not have opened it, had they not anticipated – I might say, hoped

> that they should find things there inconsistent with Catholic teaching. They begin in self-will and disobedience, and they end in apostasy.[21]

Their fault is a moral one. The Gospel may not be good news for the knowledgeable, but it is good news for the good. It is as though Jesus came not to call sinners but the righteous!

Newman's experience of Italy, however, did something to shake his moralistic individualism. He wrote in puzzlement of the 'simple certainty in believing' which he found among the ordinary people of Rome. 'But though they have this,' he went on,

> they show in a wonderful way how it is possible to disjoin religion and morality...the same people, who have a sort of instinctive conviction of the unseen world...have not that *living* faith which leads to correctness or sanctity of character.[22]

Their religion was less self-consciously sanctimonious and more communal than he could readily understand.

In a series of lectures, addressed in 1850 to those of his former associates in the Tractarian movement who had declined to follow him to Rome, Newman again raised this question of the relation between faith and morality. He conceded that the social state and religious conditions which obtained in Catholic countries constitute an apparent difficulty in accepting the claims of that Church. He referred with obvious fascination to 'the strange stories of highwaymen and brigands devout to the Madonna' and to the 'feeble old woman, who first genuflects before the Blessed Sacrament, and then steals her neighbour's handkerchief'. In our own day he might have taken the mafia or the IRA as his examples. These instances were ascribed to 'having faith and hope without the saving grace of divine love'.[23] Faith is 'the certainty of things not seen but revealed'.[24] Later in these lectures Newman distinguished 'formal' from 'material' faith and it is not at all clear which kind of faith these devout Catholic murderers and thieves are thought to possess. It may seem appropriate to think of their having merely material faith – believing because they have been brought up to do so. There is, however, no reason for denying that many of them may have that 'real', formal, faith which believes on the authority of God's oracle, the Church. The important point here is that Newman was prepared to recognise the possibility of belief without love, a possible separation between faith and morality, which is difficult to reconcile with the position argued in the *Oxford University Sermons*. The difference would seem to be his changing conception of faith. In the earlier writings it involved believing because one accepted the content of revelation (and a bad person is predisposed to reject it). In his later thought faith is essentially the acceptance of an infallible authority and thereby the acceptance of anything it says; this is equally possible for good and bad alike.

Newman was, of course, no Pelagian and insisted that the holiness which disposes people to believe is a gift of God, as is the 'saving grace of divine love'. Yet these are essentially gifts to the individual and are characterised by that high moral tone which we have noted. The pharisee in the Gospel story presumably believed that his virtues were gifts, for he *thanked God* that he was not as other men.

THE CHURCH AND THE BELIEVER

Newman's fervent belief in the holy Catholic Church and the communion of saints surely conflicts with the kind of religious individualism I am ascribing to him. Close attention to his ecclesiology will, however, show how his individualistic assumptions mar his theology of Church and sacraments. The object of the Church is not to proclaim the kingdom of God, to be a symbol – a kind of first fruits – of that kingdom, but rather 'to save souls'.[25] He envisaged the Church as a collection of individual believers, which is essentially held together by political bonds. The Church is a polity, with a structure of authority analogous to that of a state. As a state is held together by force so must the Church be; as God is sovereign so must the Pope be. Both political and divine analogies are employed to reinforce an ecclesiastical authoritarianism.

At times there are indeed hints of an understanding of the Church as a real community, as in his sermon on 'The Communion of Saints',[26] but more often it is regarded as a home for the soul, as a stable for the training of individuals for their race in this world and for life after death. The saints are seen more as lone rangers of the faith than as part of a great communion. The Church is a 'home for the lonely', not where he may be lonely no more, but where he may *cherish* his loneliness. It is a 'shelter, refuge, rest, home or sanctuary from the outward world'; it is a 'secret place' to which the Christian retreats, where he may 'forget the outward world and its many troubles', a 'refuge and hiding-place', which 'shuts out the world'. Lest it be thought that Newman here means by 'the world' the New Testament concept of the *cosmos* – the fallen world insofar as it is organised apart from God – he makes his meaning quite explicit, 'by the world, I mean all that meets a man in intercourse with his fellow men, whether in public or in private'.[27] We are again reminded of Clephane's hymn:

> Content to let the world go by,
> To know no gain nor loss, –
> My sinful self my only shame,
> My glory all – the Cross.

Baptism was understood by Newman and other Tractarian writers as, in essence, a transaction between God and the individual soul; hence their obsession with the doctrine of Baptismal Regeneration. Baptism was viewed as a spiritual operation performed upon a child: original sin was (more or less) removed and grace was poured in. His sermon on 'Regenerating Baptism' betrays this atomistic and basically uncatholic understanding of baptism. While he began by properly asserting that the Holy Ghost admits Christians into the Church by baptism, he continued in a puzzling way: 'in other words that each individual member receives the gift of the Holy Ghost as a preliminary step, a condition, or means of his being incorporated into the Church'.[28] Becoming a member of the Church is therefore subsequent to receiving the gift of the Spirit. In Tract 11 Newman spoke of God's having set up the Church as a society 'which (as a general rule) Christians are bound to join'.[29] This view is very similar to the popular evangelical belief that after conversion it is a good idea for Christians to 'link up with a church'. The eucharist too is viewed as first of all a channel of grace to the solitary believer, where Christ communicates his life to us 'one by one', and the priest is he 'who has power to *apply to individuals* those gifts which Christ has promised us generally'.[30]

THE CHURCH A STATE

The other pole of Newman's ecclesiology was his insistence that the Church is a political organisation. His understanding of the Church as a corporation – and with it a rejection of Erastianism – he ascribed to Whately's influence; but in these early Oriel days its unity was conceived on the model of the family rather than the State.[31] As he moved towards Rome the political analogy began to predominate. He indeed rejected the family model, as characteristic of heretical bodies in the early Church. In the *Apologia* the Church is compared to the State with respect to the tension which exists between private judgment and public authority. Newman was arguing against the picture of an absolute *magisterium* (teaching authority) laying down arbitrary definitions to a passive laity. Nevertheless his language betrays his atomistic assumptions. The Church is 'a vast assemblage of human beings with wilful intellects and wild passions, brought together into one by the beauty and the Majesty of a Superhuman Power...'[32] As 'material force is the *ultima ratio* of political society',[33] spiritual force must be the principle of Church government. The Church is an 'imperial' power, 'a sovereign State', which exercises over its members 'an absolute and almost despotic rule'.[34] It is viewed on the analogy of the State. 'Christians are either one polity or they are not', Church unity does not admit of degrees for it is seen on the model of the sovereign State.[35]

It is thus my contention that Newman's ecclesiology is vitiated by an atomism which he carried over from his evangelical days. The Church is viewed as a collection of individuals which must be held together by sovereign power. He readily agreed with Isaac Barrow that 'the state of the most primitive Church did not well admit such a universal sovereignty'.[36] With Church growth, however, came the need for a strong central authority to hold it together, for he maintained that 'a political body cannot exist without government, and the larger the body the more concentrated must the government be'. As the Church grew, the power of the Pope grew and wherever the Pope has been rejected 'decay and division have been the consequence'.[37]

Newman's essay *On Consulting the Faithful in Matters of Doctrine*, while emphasising the importance of the *consensus fidelium*, depicted the role of the laity as essentially passive; the faithful are 'consulted' in the sense of being observed (as one consults a watch). In the original article which Newman was defending, he had used the term 'consult' to mean making an effort 'to know the opinion of...' and his celebrated essay is based on the distinction between *knowing* and *asking* the opinion of the laity. Many ecclesiastics of his day would indeed have rejected even this minimal degree of attention being paid to lay opinion on the tradition. Nevertheless 'The gift of discerning, discriminating, defining, promulgating, and enforcing any portion of that tradition,' he insisted, 'resides solely in the *Ecclesia docens*.'[38]

His notion of authority as stated here resembles Lenin's idea of 'democratic centralism', with a somewhat less active participation on the part of the subjects. Decisions are made after 'consulting' the rank and file, but having been made they are imposed as official policy from the centre.

Behind all this lies a particular theory of government. Curiously, though Newman's *bête noire* was liberalism, he was himself a victim of liberal, Lockean, assumptions. A state is based upon a compromise between liberty and power, deriving its authority from people giving up their natural liberty – on the contract model. 'Those political institutions are the best which subtract as little as possible from a people's natural independence as the price of their protection.'[39] He thus fully acknowledged the danger of unlimited power in the State, and his 'minimalist' interpretation of the Vatican decrees on papal infallibility suggests a growing recognition of an analogous danger in ecclesiastical government.

AUTHORITY AND SUBMISSION

The dominant image of religious authority throughout Newman's life was that of submission to the dictates of an external authority. In the political sphere, Newman asserted that 'the greatest privilege of a Christian is to have nothing to do with worldly politics, but to be governed and to submit obediently', a privilege shared with 'the lower orders'![40] Again and again in his *Oxford University Sermons* the themes of obedience and submission recur. Later he told the Archbishop of Armagh that the authority of the civil power is based on 'sanctions so solemn and august' that unless some religious consideration arises, Christians must 'profess simple deference to its enunciations, and a hearty concurrence in its very suggestions'.[41]

As a young man, Newman had found this external authority in individual teachers, like Daniel Wilson and Keble his 'master'.[42] Later it was his bishop who was his pope. In the early 1840s he believed that, at the reformation, the authority of the Pope 'reverted to our diocesans', but as individuals; he 'did not care much for the Bench of Bishops'.[43] 'Submission' and 'acquiescence ' were, for Newman in his Anglican days, the essence of religion, while Isaac Williams, his curate, spoke for other Tractarians when he insisted that the best means for promoting Christianity in the world may be summarised in one word: 'obedience'.[44] The notion of 'reserve' in communicating religious knowledge left plenty of scope for reinforcing authority in the Church. Writing about the Thirty-Nine Articles, Newman declared 'I think they actually countenance a vile Protestantism. I do not tell people this, lest I should encourage a scoffing at authority. I submit and obey.'[45] Like the Jewish religion, Christianity is primarily a question of 'submission to a positive command'. He therefore emphasised the bondage of the Gospel rather than the glorious liberty of the children of God.[46]

Newman opposed obedience to sin; the Church must denounce rebellion 'as of all possible evils the greatest'.[47] His picture of God reinforced his authoritarianism. He believed that the unity of God was prior to his trinitarian nature. The 'first and most necessary of all religious truths is the Being, Unity, and Omnipotence of God'. He is sovereign, he can do what he will, he is unchangeable.[48] Revelation is the handing down, through an infallible oracle, of truths and commands to humans whose duty is to submit and obey. There is little place in this theology for any idea of God's co-operating with humankind – as workers together with him.

Faith then consists essentially in submission. Faith is 'assenting to a doctrine as true, which we do not see, which we cannot prove, because God says it is true'. But God speaks not with his own force, but through the voice of his messengers.[49] People are saved by faith therefore salvation comes by obedience to 'a living oracle', the Church, speaking through its established *magisterium*. Protestants can know nothing of faith because they recognise no living oracle and 'have no authority to submit to'. The image of the Church as the 'oracle' of God often recurs.[50] It connotes the enunciation of new truths and has serious implications for the understanding of the development of doctrine. Curiously Newman came much closer than did the excommunicated Tyrrell to the idea condemned in *Lamentabili* that 'revelation constituting the object of catholic faith was not completed with the apostles'.[51]

As we have seen, Newman contrasted 'material' faith with 'formal' faith. The first is the habitual acceptance of certain truths, learned perhaps from childhood and never questioned. But this has neither the character nor the reward of true faith, which is formal. It is submission to the dictates of an oracle.[52] A mere material faith was ascribed to Greek and Russian Christians, a knowledge of whose spiritual condition Newman derived from 'what travellers tell us' –

strengthened, no doubt, by antecedent probabilities! They believe passively rather than as the result of assent to the pronouncements of an infallible oracle. It is when a new definition of doctrine is made that this faulty state of mind is detected. They will tend to 'resist it, simply because it is new'.[53] This is curious because in the same lectures he insisted that later defined dogmas of the Church were 'so deeply lodged in her bosom as to be held by individuals more or less implicitly' and a few years later asserted that at the time of Athanasius and at other times 'the divine tradition committed to the infallible Church was proclaimed and maintained far more by the faithful than by the episcopate'.[54] If one of the early Fathers of the Church had been told that reluctance to accept new dogmas is a symptom of heresy, he would have raised an eyebrow. At times it almost seems that 'real' faith is, for Newman, the willingness to accept anything one is told or, as the schoolboy put it: faith is believing what you know to be untrue!

Newman's emphasis in his Anglican days on the unsystematic nature of revelation also contributed to an authoritarian approach to religion. In Tract 73, *On the Introduction of Rationalistic Principles into Religion*, he rejected the notion of revelation as a coherent system, such that a person could draw conclusions about one part from a knowledge of the rest. What is revealed is only part of a great system, most of which remains and always will remain a mystery. 'Revelation, in this way of considering it, is not a revealed system, but consists of a number of detached and incomplete truths belonging to a vast system unrevealed, of doctrines and injunctions mysteriously connected together.'[55] In his *Lectures on the Prophetical Office of the Church*, he criticised Rome for reducing religion to a system, and thereby running the risk of making something earthly an object of contemplation.[56] Even in the natural sciences harm has been done by 'excessive attachment to system'.[57] It is, he rightly pointed out, perfectly reasonable to believe, on authority, two apparently contradictory propositions, without being able to see how they can be compatible.

Yet paradoxically Newman devoted himself, for several years in his Anglican period to the elaboration of 'Anglicanism' as a theological system. He was deeply dissatisfied with the lack of coherence in the Anglican theologians of the seventeenth century and announced his desire to 'systematize' them. He also wrote of Anglicanism as a 'system of doctrine' with hiatuses which needed to be 'filled up'.[58] It was in this context that he invented the *via media* – the idea that there is a thing called Anglicanism – a coherent theological position located somewhere between Catholicism and Protestantism. As later apologists, who have tried to characterise Anglicanism in terms of a systematic theological position have illustrated, the feat may be performed only by making a judicious selection of divines from Hooker to Gore, ignoring on the one hand the powerful Lutheran, Calvinist and Zwinglian influences and the direct borrowings from Rome on the other. If the term 'Anglicanism' means anything it represents a system of Church government, within which different theological traditions may co-exist.

Not surprisingly Newman soon rejected the monster he had created, expressing his repudiation in the *Essay on Development*, written just prior to his reception into the Roman Catholic Church in 1845. There he reaffirmed his commitment to theological system, asserting that one doctrine leads to another and 'you must accept the whole or reject the whole'.[59] After becoming a Roman Catholic he used the *via media* as a blunt instrument to beat those of his friends who refused to follow in his footsteps. 'The very badge of Anglicanism, as a system', he told them, 'is that it is a Via Media; this is its life; it is this, or it is nothing.'[60] Newman the convert was impressed by the 'completeness' of the faith. The creed of the Church, he maintained,

> is so harmonious, so consistent with itself, holds together so perfectly, so corresponds part to part, that an acute mind, knowing one portion of it, would often infer another portion, merely as a matter of just reasoning.

The great truths of revelation are all connected together to form a whole; everyone can see this at a glance, to a certain degree, but to understand the full 'consistency and harmony' requires study and meditation.[61]

The argument advanced in the *Essay on Development*, for an infallible authority, I have examined elsewhere.[62] The author argued for the antecedent probability of an infallible authority on the ground that there must be some living body able to distinguish true developments from false. He saw clearly that such an authority must 'of necessity be external to the developments themselves'.[63] Yet it is also clear from the *Essay* that ecclesiastical infallibility and the universal jurisdiction of the Pope are among the doctrines which have developed. What is the criterion of legitimacy in the case of *these* developments? Newman might have replied that the *consensus fidelium* represents such a legitimating function – as he argued in the case of the Vatican definition of 1870; *securus judicat orbis terrarum*. This consensus, however, excludes about half the baptized Christians in the world. Leslie Stephen's words are perhaps apposite here: '*orbis terrarum* must not mean that part of the earth's surface which is overlooked by the spire of St Mary's, or even that wider region whose inhabitants look with reverence to the dome of St Peter's.'[64]

CONSCIENCE AND THE POPE

It would be a mistake to see Newman's idea of conscience as mitigating this syndrome of individualistic authoritarianism which I have been sketching. There have indeed been times when men or women have refused to obey civil or ecclesiastical powers on grounds of conscience, but where he stood on this issue is difficult to determine. His oft-quoted after-dinner toast – to conscience first, and to the Pope afterwards – is more ambiguous than it first appears. Clearly he did not believe that conscience is a better guide to Catholic truth than is the teaching of the Pope; that is the Protestant heresy of 'private judgment'. If the Pope defines a doctrine, such as the Immaculate Conception of Our Lady, and a Roman Catholic cannot in conscience accept it, is he right to reject it? If he is a good Catholic, he will surely submit his own private judgment to that of the Pope and accept the doctrine on authority. Even on issues when the Pope does not claim to speak infallibly he ought always to be obeyed and never criticised.[65] If a Catholic comes to the conclusion that the Church's teaching is 'unscriptural' is he or she justified in leaving the Church? As we have seen, Newman attributed such apostasy to a moral defect and presumably it cannot therefore be an exercise of conscience, but rather of 'fancy' or 'opinion' – of that 'miserable counterfeit' which goes by the name of conscience.[66]

After a valiant attempt to read Newman in a way which would make his position coherent, S.A. Grave reveals in a recent monograph a tissue of confusion and contradiction in Newman's ideas on conscience. Grave draws a clear distinction between conscience as moral sense (judging what is right and wrong) and conscience as the moral imperative of doing what we believe to be right whatever that may be. Even with the help of this distinction, which Newman himself did not explicitly draw – believing that conscience is 'a simple element' – Grave concludes that Newman's statements on the possibility of a clash between conscience and the Pope do not make sense and are characterised by 'obscurities, unrelatedness, incompleteness'.[67] The after-dinner toast – what of that? 'The inferences it might suggest,' concludes Grave, 'are not to be drawn from it. No inferences are to be drawn from it.'[68] It is, we might say, pure rhetoric.

CONCLUSION

It is my argument in this chapter that individualism and authoritarianism are intimately linked. Newman indeed seems at times to have recognised this. 'Nothing great or living', he wrote, 'can be done except when men are selfgoverned and independent: this is quite consistent with a full maintenance of ecclesiastical supremacy.'[69] The close relationship between individualism and authoritarianism is familiar to social theorists; it is noted by such Catholic writers as Alexis de Tocqueville and the remarkable Archbishop Ketteler of Mainz. By undervaluing the organic relations between members of social groups, by discouraging active participation in the life of the community, and by breaking down the power of subordinate groups and allegiances, all we have left is a great crowd of isolated and powerless individuals confronted and held together by an authoritarian government.

When individualism is linked to philosophical scepticism it provides a foundation for the appeal to an ultimate and tangible authority. If reason is not to be relied on there must be some other foundation for certitude. Sometimes – as in the case of David Hume – it is the authority of custom and habit. In the case of H.L. Mansel it was located in scripture, legitimated by miracle and the fulfilment of prophesy; with W.G. Ward it was to be found in an infallible papacy; in James Fitzjames Stephen the appeal was to some governing power which must not flinch from pronouncing on religious, moral and political issues when necessary. The *fons et origo* of this syndrome is of course Thomas Hobbes, who combined a profound scepticism and a pervasive individualism with an uncompromising authoritarianism in religion and in politics. It is the sovereign – the mortal God – who determines the prescription for the wholesome pills of religion, 'which swallowed whole, have the virtue to cure, but chewed are for the most part cast up again without effect'.[70]

George Tyrrell, the ex-Jesuit, had a strikingly different understanding of authority and of the Christian faith.

> We are not united to God singly and independently as rays which converge to a common centre and yet do not touch one another on the road, but we are first knit together into one living organic body under the Man Christ as our Head, and then with Him and through Him united to the very Godhead, whose life and beatitude flows down to the least and furthest member of that living thing.[71]

For Tyrrell authority is not a question of one person or group dictating to the rest, but is something to which all in some way contribute and in which all share; it is manifested in a true consensus. He condemned the individualism which has authoritarianism as its corollary, and denounced the oracular interpretation of papal authority as the apotheosis of this theological individualism, 'the last relic of Protestantism' which stands in the way of a truly Catholic and communal understanding of the Church. Referring to Protestant individualists he remarked 'they have many popes, we but one'.[72]

NOTES

1. Acton to Gladstone, 12 April 1896, in J.N. Figgis and R.V. Laurence (eds), *Selections from the Correspondence of the First Lord Acton* (London, 1917), p. 227.

2. 'Reason is, and ought to be, a slave of the passions, and can never pretend to any other office than to serve and obey them.' David Hume, *Treatise of Human Nature* (London, 1923), ii, p. 127.

3. C.S. Dessain et al. (eds), *The Letters and Diaries of John Henry Newman* (London and Oxford, 1961f.), xxvii, p. 162. Whether anyone in their right mind will make this latter judgment before having listened to what the voice says is another matter. Perhaps the best reason for regarding a body as authoritative is that its teachings make sense; having decided this, we listen with attention to its further pronouncements. Newman indeed went some way towards recognising this in his *Grammar of Assent*, where he maintained 'no religion is from God which contradicts our sense of right and wrong', *An Essay in Aid of a Grammar of Assent* (London, 1881), p. 419. This issue is discussed by S.A. Grave in his recent book *Conscience in Newman's Thought* (Oxford, 1989), pp. 96f.

4. J.H. Newman, *Apologia pro Vita Sua* (London, 1895), p. 4.

5. *Apologia*, p. 73.

6. J.H. Newman, *Parochial Sermons* (New York, 1843), i, p. 15.

7. *Parochial Sermons*, i, p. 48.

8. J.H. Newman, *Certain Difficulties felt by Anglicans in Catholic Teaching Considered* (London, 1895), i, p. 399.

9. *Letters and Diaries*, vi, p. 170.

10. *Parochial Sermons*, ii, p. 245.

11. Newman frequently wrote as though 'Britain' and 'England' refer to the same entity. Elsewhere he took the sentence 'England is an island' as an example of certainty. (*The Theological Papers of John Henry Newman on Faith and Certainty* [Oxford, 1976], p. 89.) Perhaps this is one of the reasons he had such a rough ride in Ireland!

12. J.H. Newman, *Discussions and Arguments* (London, 1872), pp. 336f.

13. *Apologia*, p. 49 (my italics).

14. *The Via Media of the Anglican Church* (London, 1899) i, p. xlvii; and *Discussions and Arguments*, p. 397. This identification of revelation and theology led to problems in Newman's theory of the development of doctrine, as George Tyrrell pointed out. 'Theology and revelation must be distinguished', only then can we maintain that there is no new revelation and that 'the advantage of later over earlier ages is merely secondary and protective'. (*Christianity at the Crossroads* [London, 1909], p. 32).

15. See David Nicholls, 'Developing Doctrines and Changing Beliefs', *Scottish Journal of Thelology*, 19:3, 1966, pp. 280f.

16. 'The Tamworth Reading Room' in *Discussions*, p. 294.

17. *Discussions and Arguments*, pp. 294-5.

18. J.H. Newman, *Fifteen Sermons Preached Before the University of Oxford* (London, 1909), p. 191.

19. *University Sermons*, p. 192; this theme is repeated in J.H. Newman, *Discourses Addressed to Mixed Congregations* (London, 1871), p. 226.

20. *University Sermons*, pp. 229-30.

21. *Discourses*, p. 218.

22. *Letters and Diaries*, xii, p. 24.

23. *Difficulties*, i, pp. 279, 285 and 278.

24. *Difficulties*, i, p. 273.

25. Newman to Allies, *Letters and Diaries*, xix, pp. 422 and 430.

26. *Parochial Sermons*, ii, pp. 98f.

27. *Parochial Sermons*, ii , pp. 110f.

28. *Parochial Sermons*, i, p. 606.

29. J.H. Newman, Tract 11, *The Visible Church*, (London, 1840), p. 5.

30. *Parochial Sermons*, i, pp. 292 and 385 (my italics).

31. *Apologia*, pp. 12 and 107.

32. *Apologia*, p. 252.

33. *Discussions and Arguments*, p. 355.

34. J.H. Newman, *The Via Media of the Anglican Church* (London, 1899), i, pp. xl and lxxx.

35. *Via Media*, i, p. 202n.

36. J.H. Newman, *An Essay on the Development of Christian Doctrine* (London, 1906), p. 152.

37. *Development*, p. 154. Another reading of history would suggest that the greatest schisms in the history of the Church have occurred precisely when these claims to universal sovereignty have been most stridently made.

38. J.H. Newman, *On Consulting the Faithful in Matters of Doctrine* (New York, 1961), p. 63. The perils of consulting the faithful (as well as the dangers of rhetoric) were vividly illustrated in Pope John Paul II's visit to Chile in 1987. 'The Pope asked the crowd: "Is it true that you want to reject the false god of power, of dominion over others in favour of the example Jesus gave of fraternal service?" The crowd responded with a deafening "Si". "And is it true," the Pope went on, "that you want to reject the false god of sex, of pleasure?" An equally deafening "No" filled the stadium.' (*The Independent*, 4 April 1987).

39. *Discussions and Arguments*, p. 325.

40. *Parochial Sermons*, i, p. 413; *University Sermons*, p. 143.

41. Dedication to *Lectures on the Present Position of Catholics in England* (London, 5th edition, n.d.), p. v.

42. *Apologia*, pp. 5 and 18.

43. *Apologia*, pp. 51 and 187.

44. Newman, *Via Media*, i, p. 22; and I. Williams, Tract 87, *On Reserve in Communicating Religious Knowledge*, (London, 1840), pp. 74-5. On the Tractarians' obsession with authority, see Rune Imberg, *In Quest of Authority* (Lund, 1987).

45. *Letters and Diaries*, v, pp. 70-1; quoted in Ian Ker, *John Henry Newman: A Biography* (Oxford, 1988), p. 116.

46. *University Sermons*, pp. 171-2; on this general question of reserve, see Robin C. Selby, *The Principle of Reserve in the Writings of John Henry Cardinal Newman* (London, 1975).

47. *University Sermons*, p. 51 and *Apologia*, p. 246.

48. *Via Media*, i, p. lxix; *Discourses*, p. 288.

49. *Discourses*, p. 195.

50. *Discourses*, pp. 206-7; also pp. 195f. and 280; *Apologia*, pp. 10 and 239.

51. H. Denzinger, *Enchiridion Symbolorum* (Freiburg, 1957, ed. C. Rahner), 2021 (ASS, 40, 1907, pp. 470f.); see David Nicholls, 'Developing Doctrines and Changing beliefs', *Scottish Journal of Theology*, 19:3, 1966, pp. 280f.

52. J.H. Newman, *Certain Difficulties felt by Anglicans in Catholic Teaching Considered* (London, 1895), pp. 350-1.

53. *Difficulties*, i, p. 351.

54. *Difficulties*, i, p. 394; and *Consulting the Faithful*, p. 75.

55. J.H. Newman, Tract 73, *On the Introduction of Rationalistic Principles into Religion* (London, 1841), p. 9.

56. In *Via Media*, i, p. 102.

57. *University Sermons*, p. 9.

58. Ker, *Newman*, pp. 129 and 134.

59. *Development*, 1st edition (1845) p. 154. He appears to have omitted this from later editions.

60. *Difficulties*, i, p. 374.

61. *Discourses*, pp. 193, 176 and 344.

62. 'Authority and the Development of Doctrine', *Theology*, April 1960.

63. *Development*, p. 78.

64. Leslie Stephen, *An Agnostic's Apology* (London, 1893), p. 239.

65. J.H. Newman, *Sermons Preached on Various Occasions* (London, 1891), p. 286.

66. *A Letter Addressed to his Grace the Duke of Norfolk on Occasion of Mr Gladstone's Recent Expostulation* (London, 1875), pp. 62-3.

67. S.A. Grave, *Conscience*, p. 186. I reached a similar conclusion some years ago in David Nicholls, 'Gladstone, Newman and the Politics of Pluralism', in James D. Bastable (ed.), *Newman and Gladstone: Centennial Essays* (Dublin, 1978) pp. 32f. Grave, however, takes me to task for giving a misleading impression of Newman's claim in saying that for him 'conscience is the supreme guide to action'. Grave states that in his juxtaposition of papal authority and conscience, 'the pathfinding ability of conscience' is not an issue he raised. Grave imposes on Newman a clarity of thought and expression he does not possess.

Newman regarded conscience as an individual apprehension of the Divine Law, which having been apprehended has a morally obligatory character. The Divine Law is the 'rule of ethical truth' and the 'standard of right and wrong' and is evidently 'pathfinding'. On Grave's reading, what is the meaning of the word 'conscience' in the reference to 'that subject-matter in which conscience is of supreme authority' (J.H. Newman, *Letter* p. 63)? It cannot mean what Grave calls the 'imperatival' use, for in that sense it must be obeyed in *all* matters; it must refer to the 'pathfinding' role. Again, if a 'double allegiance' to civil and ecclesiastical authorities pulled in opposite directions, Newman would listen to various opinions and take advice, but if unable to follow this, 'then I must rule myself by my own judgment and my own conscience' (*Letter* p. 53). He is evidently using 'conscience' here to include its 'pathfinding' role.

68. *Conscience*, p. 182.

69. *Letters and Diaries*, xxi, p. 331.

70. Thomas Hobbes, *Leviathan*, chapter 32 (Oxford, 1946), pp. 242-3.

71. G. Tyrrell, *Hard Sayings* (London, 1898), p. 406.

72. G. Tyrrell, *The Church and the Future* (London, 1910), p. 120n.

8

NEWMAN'S MID-VICTORIAN DREAM

Elisabeth Jay

> One of the most unique and original of the poems of the present century as well as that one of all of them which is in every sense the least in sympathy with the temper of the present century, indeed the most completely independent of the *Zeitgeist.*[1]

> Our opinions are commonly derived from education and society. Common minds transmit as they receive, good and bad, true and false; minds of original talent feel a continual propensity to investigate subjects, and strike out views for themselves; – so that even old and established truths do not escape modification and accidental change when subjected to this process of mental digestion.[2]

The creative tension between tradition and the mind of original talent sketched here by Newman in an early occasional essay, was to become central to the development and understanding of Newman's life. This essay will investigate the way in which this tension operated in *The Dream of Gerontius* (1865) so as both to impress R.H. Hutton, an influential literary and theological essayist of the day, as being 'independent of the *Zeitgeist*' and yet to gain the kind of currency and popular recognition that allowed an otherwise unadventurous Oxford Professor of Poetry, Sir Francis Doyle, to devote an entire lecture to it only three years after the poem's publication.

Newman's very articulacy in exploring and explaining his own life has often allowed his to be the pre-eminent voice in constructing and deciphering the myth of his completed life and achievement. This has had two important consequences. First, it has encouraged the study of Newman's writings as a source offering the evidence of the consistency and continuity which Newman himself was so anxious to detect in the development of his own opinions. Secondly, it has discouraged the habit of viewing Newman's life and writings as subject to specifically Victorian cultural constraints. Many of Newman's readers were never to escape the force of his self-avowedly 'childish imaginations' in 'isolating me from the objects which surrounded me, in confirming me in my mistrust of the reality of material phenomena, and making me rest in the thought of two and two only supreme and luminously self-evident beings, myself and my Creator'.[3] The tendency to regard Newman and his writings as *sui generis* has been strengthened by the image of a leader and teacher of an entire generation deliberately repudiating the spirit of the age and retreating to a life of monastic seclusion. This image itself is partly a construct of influential Victorian voices keen to marginalise and so diminish the influence of Newman's combative powers. The extent to which Newman's writings as a Catholic had been found in harmony with later developments in Catholic theology have of course intensified this habit of reading him as a man ahead of and therefore apart from his times.

Taken in conjunction these 'ways of seeing' effectively blinkered Newman studies over a long period. In particular they led readers to underestimate Newman's skill as a political tactician and rhetorical strategist. Attempts to draw attention to these qualities instantly placed the critic in the ranks of Kingsley's Protestant militia. Newman's capacity to polarise later generations of readers is in itself a tribute to the skills his hagiographers wished to deny. Newman's *Apologia*, whose second edition was pointedly re-titled *A History of My Religious Opinions*, repeatedly asserts that he is 'not writing controversially, but with the one object of relating things as they happened':[4] a carefully argued case for the defence is thus served up as objective narrative. Newman has succeeded in politicising the question of genre: by obliterating the distinction between method and object he ensures that any attempt to raise the matter of stylistic sleight of hand can be seen as the work of a self-declared enemy to his propositions. The reader has been subtly engineered into accepting or denying the validity of the work in its entirety.

To be reminded of Newman's adversarial skills is the first stage in reconstructing the public court, or courts, for which his writings were prepared. In monastic retreat Newman had more time to read and 'mentally digest' than as the harassed leader of an Anglican campaign.[5] The *Apologia* indeed begins by reconstructing his early life not so much from the self-inscription of diaries but rather as the meeting-place or palimpsest for a series of other texts.[6]

Newman's own account of his next publication, *The Dream of Gerontius*, offers active discouragement to the inter-textually inclined critic.

> *11 October 1865.* On the 17th of January last it came into my head to write it. I really cannot tell how, and I wrote on till it was finished, on small bits of paper. And I could no more write anything else by willing it, than I could fly.[7] *29 October 1865.* It was written by accident – and it was published by accident.[8]

This highly circumstantial account of the spontaneous genesis and flowing composition of the poem is reminiscent of Coleridge's apologetic proffering of his visionary poem, 'Kubla Khan'. The impression of a Romantic matrix is heightened by Newman's later placing of his poem in a volume dedicated to his lawyer friend Badeley, 'a member of a grave profession, which is especially employed in rubbing of the gloss with which '*imagination and sentiment invests matters of every-day life*'.[9] Subsequent interpretation has been inclined to see in Coleridge's account of the person from Porlock who fatally interrupted his composition, a literary fiction employed to underline the precariousness of the Romantic inspiration which forms the subject of his poem. In its denial of authorial intention and implied assertion that there were no recognisable events or influence playing a part in the poem's composition Newman's account may be seen to be equally disingenuous.

The speed with which Newman composed his poem is not in itself evidence of abnormal inspiration. The *Apologia's* complex record had been swiftly assembled in less than three months, and 'The Tamworth Reading Room', his onslaught on liberal ideology, had taken form within the space of twenty-two days in a series of seven letters to *The Times* in 1841. These prose works, of course, had a readily identifiable target and inspiration, yet the recourse to poetry as a response to the pressures of personal and public affairs had a memorable precedent in the circumstances which led Newman to write 'The Pillar of the Cloud' in 1833 ('Lead, Kindly Light').

It is difficult to know how to interpret Newman's assertion that the publication of the *Dream* was 'accidental'. Even by his standards of moving cogitation into print the lapse of time between the poem's inception on 17 January and the publication of the first part in May seems brief. At the very least he was well aware that the *Month*, which had recently become a Jesuit periodical, would prove a suitable vehicle, having published two of his own revised poems there the previous year. Newman, in fact, had very clear views about the nature and function of this magazine.

> The Catholic body in England is despised by Protestants from their (unjust) idea of our deficiency in education...I think that Protestants are accustomed to look on Catholics, as an un-English body, taking no interest in English questions...A magazine then, which without effort or pretence, in a natural way, took part in all the questions of the day, not hiding that it was Catholic to the backbone, but showing a real goodwill towards the institutions of the country, so far forth as they did not oppose Catholic truths or interests, showing that it understood them, and could sympathise with them, and showing all this in the medium of good English, would create in the public mind a feeling of respect and deference for the opinion of the Catholic body, which at present does not exist... It seems to me that, what is to be aimed at, is to lay a Catholic *foundation* of thought – and *no* foundation is above ground. And next, to lay it with Protestant bricks; I mean, to use, as far as possible, Protestant parties and schools in doing the work, as St Paul at Athens appealed to the Altar of the Unknown God.
>
> Then as to the good which such a Magazine would do to Catholic readers, I should consider it to consist in its making them what it is in itself; in creating in them that enlargement and refinement of mind, that innocent and religious sympathy in national objects, that faculty of easy intercourse with Protestants, and that power of aiding them in lawful temporal objects, which could ultimately be a means, more than any other human means, of bringing converts into the Church from all classes of the community.[10]

Moreover, Newman was not unaccustomed to seeing poetry as a legitimate polemical and educative weapon. *Lyra Apostolica* (1836), the first Tractarian anthology, carried as its epigraph the warrior Achilles' boast on re-joining the Trojan war, 'You shall know the difference, now that I am back again'. This collection of 179 poems, 109 of which were Newman's, had also first seen print in the pages of a party organ, the *British Magazine*. Newman had envisaged the poetry section of this periodical as 'an effective quasi-political engine', produced in response to stirring times which 'give opportunity for the rhetoric of poetry and the persuasion'.[11]

Why then should Newman have been so reluctant to sound a battle-cry on the occasion of the *Dream*'s publication? Although any attempt to answer this question must be speculative, a number of possible reasons occur. The *Apologia* had relived Newman's parting of the ways and though he had won much sympathy by his account (Gladstone saw the timing of the *Dream*'s publication as peculiarly apposite: 'I am truly glad that now going forth with your name it will attract the attention it deserves.')[12] it could not but have stirred the embers of residual bitterness in some Protestant circles. It would therefore scarcely be tactful to advertise a work, which on the face of it, was non-polemic in intention, as a piece of Roman Catholic propaganda, especially if the magazine in which it was destined to appear was committed to doing its work underground, operating on sensibilities rather than at the level of theological dispute.

Secular and religious poetry (in as far as such a division makes sense in talking of nineteenth-century poetry) had also moved on in the thirty years since the publication of *Lyra Apostolica*. That volume had spawned a welter of religious verses and hymns.[13] In some ways the gap between religious and secular poetry had narrowed so that the religious bias of poems no longer needed to be so clearly signposted. While the Romantic emphasis upon the poet's own psyche as the inspirational fountain had remained intact there had been a growing emphasis upon the ethical responsibility of the poet to address the serious issues of the day. Secular poetry had drawn closer to Newman's innate inclinations. Wordsworth's communings with nature and Keble's sacramental approach to nature had never really served to fire the imagination of a man who, as Sir Francis Doyle put it, 'scarcely believes in any real rose, in any actual rainbow; the stars themselves are little more than phantom lights'.[14] Tennyson's *In Memoriam* (1850), moreover, had forever problematised the devotional uses of nature: it had also firmly established poetry as an appropriate arena for the discussion of a wide range of contemporary issues. As Doyle surveyed the poetic scene in 1868 he observed, 'The poetry of abstract thought is not likely to be undervalued at present'. 'During the last thirty years', he remarked, 'there were many who had enlisted in Wordsworth's own Cumberland meditators', content to 'take Wordsworth's thought without poetry'.[15]

A cursory glance at the text of Newman's *Dream* might well seem to discountenance any attempt at placing the work within its contemporary culture. In what sense is it profitable to read a poem concerned with the transition of the Christian soul from an earthly death-bed to purgatory as a work of the mid-Victorian period? The title itself, with its use of Latinate nomenclature and the allusion to 'dream literature' would seem deliberately to distance us from the landscape of the

1860s and remove us to the mediaeval Catholic world. The poem has most often been seen as a hybrid of mediaeval descent marrying the morality and mystery play tradition with that other popular mode of dream literature. To a reader in 1865 neither genre nor chronological period might have seemed so hermetically sealed from contemporary life. Dream literature had traditionally often been used to accommodate pertinent topical commentary, whose force was lost with the passage of time. Langland's *Piers Plowman* incorporates commentary upon the social contract as it was seen to operate in fourteenth-century England. Dante's *Divina Commedia* is firmly embedded in an awareness of contemporary Florentine politics. *Alice's Adventures in Wonderland*, first published the month after Newman's *Dream* was printed,[16] serves as one obvious reminder of the way in which a Victorian author might presume on his audience's awareness of the opportunities the genre afforded for oblique commentary on events and ideas of the day.[17]

The use of mediaeval forms for implicit or explicit critique of nineteenth-century deficiencies had almost become an artistic cliché by the 1860s. In his 1839 essay, 'The State of Religious Parties' Newman had drawn attention to 'the literary influence of Walter Scott, who turned men's minds to the direction of the middle ages'. Scott's influence, Newman asserts, had been all the greater for its employment of the cardinal Tractarian doctrine of reserve.

> The general need of something deeper and more attractive, than what had offered itself elsewhere, may be considered to have led to his popularity; and by means of his popularity he reacted on his readers, stimulating their mental thrust, feeding their hopes, setting before them visions, which, when once seen, are not easily forgotten, and silently indoctrinating them with nobler ideas, which might afterwards be appealed to as first principles.[18]

The allusion to the past implicit in the poem's title may have served as a sufficient indicator of spiritual yearning for other days and other ways to a generation accustomed to Pugin's architecture and writings, Carlyle's *Past and Present* (1843), or Disraeli's *Coningsby* (1844). Yet in Newman's case any mediaeval reference remains superficial. If he looked to the past for inspiration it was to the early Church. The death-bed setting of the poem's opening seems to have encouraged the belief that the choice of the name Gerontius was a generic allusion to the Greek word for old age, but a classical scholar such as Newman would never have produced so hybrid a form. The source seems rather to have been the fourth-century Bishop Gerontius of Nicomedeia whom the Church authorities attempted to depose on account of the scandal caused by his recounting the tales of his strange dreams. Contemporary readers, less well-versed than Newman in the history of the early Church, looked obdurately for the parallels with mediaeval dream literature. Gladstone saw fit to invoke the ghost of Dante in his search for suitable hyperbole with which to praise the *Dream*: 'I own that to me it seems the most remarkable production in its own very high walk since the unapproachable Paradiso of Dante, and his less but not very much less wonderful Purgatorio.'[19] R.W. Church in his review of the poem for the *Guardian* had made a similar comparison: 'Of course our thoughts go back to Dante; for it is the one attempt, since the Divina Commedia, by any competent arm, to bend his bow'. Newman's cryptic rebuttal, which seems more than a modest reluctance to stand comparison with '*il miglior fabbro*', humorously puts aside the comparison partly because, as I shall suggest later, his primary literary models were to be found elsewhere.

> One thing made me blush, if an old man can blush – that about the bow of Dante. I will tell you the parallel which struck me myself. Do you recollect the story of humdrum and bashful Tom Churton? how at some great Ashmolean gathering he gently breathed into something that looked like a wind instrument – and what followed?[20]

Moreover, widely read though Dante was in nineteenth-century England he was not the major stimulus in the eschatological interests which resurfaced with periodic intensity during the period. The otherworldliness of Newman's concern in the *Dream* was a subject of immediate interest in the year of its publication. Newman had himself belonged to a twice-weekly study group in Oxford set up in 1829 to respond to a current wave of enthusiasm for prophetical speculation which held many Christians in a state of fervent millenial expectation. Although this particular wave of popular enthusiasm receded, die-hard Evangelical eschatologists continued their work undeterred and re-aligned their prophetical sights upon a millenium to be inaugurated at the next preferred date of 1866-7.[21] Risible though such numerologically-based calculations might seem both to us and to many nineteenth-century commentators,[22] the provision of a specific date seemed to have served as a focal point for a new wave of eschatological interest. The introduction to Geoffrey Rowell's book, *Hell and the Victorians*,[23] reveals that, although an interest in the after-life might be seen to be a distinguishing feature of the nineteenth century as a whole, there is in fact a significant cluster of books, other than the strictly Evangelical, published between 1865 and 1867 which display a strong interest in eschatology. The fillip that such a date gave to serious intellectual consideration of the question of immortality might be gauged by the formation of the Metaphysical Society in 1869, a society whose very name proclaimed it to be part of the reaction against the materialism which many contemporaries had identified as the prevailing force of the previous decade. This impression of Newman's *Dream* as part of a specifically English Victorian debate receives considerable reinforcement from his advice to Ambrose St John not to show the poem to anyone in Rome where the conditions of authorship would not be understood and 'prosaic minds may find heresy'.[24]

This account of the poem's conditions of authorship may so far have seemed to privilege cultural constraints to the virtual exclusion of the personal. Previous accounts of the poem have often stressed the intimations of mortality that Newman felt so strongly during his controversy with Kingsley, as an important factor in his choice of subject matter.[25] It is not in fact necessary to have recourse to Keble's definition of poetry to see the *Dream* as 'the expression of an overflowing mind, relieving itself, more or less indirectly and reservedly, of the thoughts and passions which most oppress it'.[26] The speculative jump between the life and the impersonal format of the *Dream* finds a more accessible bridge in the imagery and form of its literary predecessor, the *Apologia*. Linda Peterson has drawn attention to the repeated use of 'the figures of deathbed and bier' in the *Apologia* as a crucial strategy in Newman's presentation of his rebirth into Catholicism by means of negotiating a transference from the Protestant to the Catholic model of spiritual autobiography.[27] The penultimate chapter of the *Apologia* begins,

> From the end of 1841, I was on my death-bed, as regards my membership with the Anglican Church, though at the time I became aware of it only by degrees... A death-bed has scarcely a history; it is a tedious decline, with seasons of rallying and seasons of falling back; and since the end is foreseen, or what is called a matter of time, it has little interest for the reader, especially if he has a kind heart. Moreover, it is a season when doors are closed and curtains drawn, and when the sick man neither cares nor is able to record the stages of his malady. I was in these circumstances,

> except so far as I was not allowed to die in peace, except so far as friends, who had still a full right to come in upon me, and the public world which had not, have given a sort of history to those last four years.[28]

Here Newman deliberately repudiates an entire Evangelical tradition of death-beds in which the dying figure, by affirming his own assurance of salvation provides a valuable witness to the bystanders. These bystanders, in Newman's figuration, are dismissed as morbidly inclined gossip-mongers, or, at the very least, of availing themselves of rights of friendship that Newman no longer wishes to avail himself of, since his business is now solely with God in the communion of the Catholic Church. His grand dismissal of death-bed scenes, it emerges, by the end of the *Apologia*, is yet another rhetorical strategy designed to enable him to set up a death-bed of his own choosing. The dedication of the book to his fellow Oratorians is a reading of Newman's last will and testament where friends from various stages of his earthly pilgrimage are drawn up before Newman's Judgment Seat to gain a place in the Book of his Life only if they have displayed 'true attachment' or 'never been disloyal to me by word or by deed'. The last sentence of the *Apologia* ends with a prayer which suggests that the re-uniting of this whole company 'into One Fold and under One Shepherd' may have to await eternity.[29] Necessarily retrospective the *Apologia* leaves the reader at a moment of transition. Newman's new life, he has already told us in the opening paragraph of the last chapter, cannot be accommodated within this work.

> From the time that I became a Catholic, of course I have no further history of my religious opinions to narrate. In saying this, I do not mean to say that my mind has been idle, or that I have given up thinking on theological subjects; but that I have had no variations to record, and have had no anxiety of heart whatever. I have been in perfect peace and contentment; I never have had one doubt. I was not conscious to myself, on my conversion of any change, intellectual or moral, wrought in my mind. I was not conscious of firmer faith in the fundamental truths of Revelation, or of more self-command; I had not more fervour; but it was like coming into port after a rough sea; and my happiness on that score remains to this day without interruption.[30]

Entry into the community of the Catholic Church and accepting its corporate authority has effectively silenced the personal voice. By the end of the *Apologia* Newman is in search of new beginnings: from the death of the self he must look forward to an after-life in the communion of saints. The *Dream* begins where the *Apologia* left off. The death-bed scene has been appropriated by the Catholic tradition so that the passing soul becomes the focal point and the bystanders or 'Assistants' only of interest in so far as they fulfil their liturgical role of offering up prayers for the dead. The typical and essentially passive figure of Gerontius replaces the intensely personal agonies of the dramatic protagonist of the *Apologia*.

That is not to deny entirely the individual voice in the *Dream.* Such dramatic tension as does exist at Gerontius' death-bed derives in part from the counterpointing of Gerontius' fears of ultimate dissolution and non-being against the reassurance offered by the rhythmical chanting of the Litany of the Saints performed by the Assistants. The act of corporate worship is modified so that ten out of thirteen lines (II. 29-41) end with the invocation 'pray for *him*' (my italics) thus producing an assertion of a continuing identity which can be meaningfully prayed for. Yet the identity is never personalised. The poem, indeed, goes on to provide a formal metrical distinction between the individual as a member of the spiritual communion and a sense of the personal. Gerontius has his existence as an individually identifiable soul confirmed by his capacity to play his part in the corporate liturgy of credal affirmation: ('Firmly I believe and truly/God is Three, and God is One'). These firm rhythms disintegrate only as Gerontius envisages the loss of the personal physical identity which provides our earthly guarantee of individuality. The ensuing sense of panic, dissolution and invasion by disease and scepticism has to be purged away so that Gerontius may be re-absorbed into the long line of those who lived by faith 'in things not seen' enumerated in Hebrews 11. Only as he is slowly divested of spatial and temporal sensations, or, more strictly, of the compulsive desire to reassure himself by a frenzied exercise of these senses, can he become more truly himself (II. 170-200).

His transition from terrestrial identity to spiritual essence is marked by the dropping of part of that identity, his name. From now on in the poem this part becomes that of 'Soul'. Next the soul loses the human capacity for freedom of choice and sin. 'You cannot now/Cherish a wish which ought not to be wished', remarks the Angel. The potential for dramatic opposition has then to be transferred to the Demons whose staccato rhythms threaten the Angel's measured exposition as they re-assert all that the Soul has discarded: the fear of physical disintegration (II. 450-7), and 'The mind bold/And independent,/The purpose free' (II. 440-3). Gerontius, the Angel now assures him, has now become 'a disembodied soul' (I. 529), who gradually relinquishes the last vestiges of individuality as he sheds the desire for a voice: 'Yet rather would I hear thy angel voice,/Than for myself be thy interpreter.' (II. 716-17) Gerontius is finally heard only as one of a chorus of souls in purgatory who by repeating Psalm 90, traditionally ascribed to Moses, confirm the message of Hebrews 11 by conferring upon themselves a place in the continuous line of Judaeo-Christian history.

Since the poem relies so heavily on the Catholic liturgy and stresses the subordination of the individual to the wider communion of saints, why then should Newman have feared that his poem might be interpreted as 'plain heresy' in Rome?

Here, I think, one has to go back to Newman's views on the nature and function of the *Month* which he had suggested should aim to

> lay a Catholic *foundation* of thought – and *no* foundation is above ground. And next to lay it with Protestant bricks; I mean, to use, as far as possible, Protestant parties and schools in doing the work, as St Paul at Athens appealed to the Altar of the Unknown God.

Contributions should be designed to take specific account of the needs of English Catholics in a Protestant country. If Catholics in England had been distrusted on account of their divided loyalties and their ill-educated sectarianism, fresh ways must be sought to 'create a tradition' which should convince a Protestant audience of common roots while ensuring that the roots, if dug up for inspection, were distinctively Catholic. Newman's reading of his own life-history was, of course, an inestimable advantage to him here: he argued that he had been born into a particular system, the English Church, which, on further investigation, he had discovered to be derived from a Catholic foundation.[31] Indeed the determination to plan the *Apologia* in a way which insisted upon the organic growth of his development seems to have given its counter-image of abrupt amputation a peculiar and horrific prominence in Newman's mind at this period.[32]

The Dream of Gerontius was Newman's own attempt at the instant creation of an English Catholic tradition built with Protestant bricks. The poem's rootedness in Catholic liturgy is indisputable yet, as Geoffrey Rowell has pointed out, there were several eschatological traditions available to Catholics in England at this time.[33] Foreign

Catholic missionaries, directing their revivalist preaching to lapsed Irish Catholics, tended to rely heavily upon the crude deterrent of stoking hell's fires. Such minatory teaching was ill-suited to 'that enlargement and refinement of mind' Newman wished to inculcate in English Catholics and was especially inappropriate in a period when broader intellectual debates were so self-consciously ethical. Purgatory provided just that latitude within which Newman found the possibility of meliorating harsher Catholic teaching and where he could offer to Protestants an imaginative negotiation between the promises of heaven and the pains of hell. Yet how could a doctrine so distinctively Catholic as purgatory be made attractive to Protestants, even Protestants yearning for an eschatological *via media*? Where did Newman find his Protestant bricks?

Just as the *Apologia* had effected a transition from Protestant to Catholic literary forms so the *Dream* perceives a fruitful area for development. English Protestantism had provided two religious myths so powerful that it is impossible to overestimate their importance in trying to understand nineteenth-century literature: Bunyan's *Pilgrim's Progress* and Milton's *Paradise Lost*. *Pilgrim's Progress, Part I* ends, not with Christian's briefly glimpsed entry through the Gates of Heaven, but with Ignorance being bound hand and foot by the two 'shining ones'.

> Then they took him up, and carried him through the air to the door that I saw in the side of the Hill, and put him in there. Then I saw that there was a way to Hell, even from the Gates of Heaven, as well as from the City of *Destruction*. So I awoke, and behold it was a Dream.[34]

Gerontius is another such pilgrim as Christian, a seeker after Christian truth, but by no means a saint. Newman's modest disclaimer of comparison with Dante falls into place when Bunyan's central place in the English imagination is recalled. The title-page of Bunyan's *Pilgrim's Progress* requires little adaptation to serve as a description of Newman's *Dream*: 'THE PILGRIM'S PROGRESS FROM THIS WORLD TO THAT WHICH IS TO COME, DELIVERED UNDER THE SIMILITUDE OF A DREAM WHEREIN IS DISCOVERED, THE MANNER OF HIS SETTING OUT, HIS DANGEROUS JOURNEY, AND SAFE ARRIVAL AT THE DESIRED COUNTRY.' Moreover, the Author's Apology, prefixed to *Pilgrim's Progress*, bears comparison with the methodological account of the poem the Angel sees fit to deliver to the Soul.

By Metaphors I speak; Was not God's Laws,
His Gospel-Laws, in olden time held forth
By Types, Shadows and Metaphors?...
The Prophets used much by Metaphors
To set forth Truth; Yea, who so considers
Christ, his Apostles too, shall plainly see,
That Truths to this day in such Mantles be.
'Author's Apology', II. 8-10, 27-30

Nor touch, nor taste, nor hearing hast thou now;
Thou livest in a world of signs and types,
The presentations of most holy truths,
Living and strong, which now encompass thee...
And thou art wrapp'd and swath'd around in dreams,
Dreams that are true, yet enigmatical;
For the belongings of thy present state,
Save through such symbols, come not home to thee.
And thus thou tell'st of space and time and size.
Of fragrant, solid, bitter, musical,
Or fire, and of refreshment after fire;
As (let me use similitude of earth,
To aid thee in knowledge thou dost ask) –
As ice which blisters may be said to burn.
Dream of Gerontius, II. 525-8, 536-46

Such a juxtaposition, of course, also points up the distance travelled metrically between Bunyan's couplets and the Angel's magisterial blank verse pronouncements. Both the syntax and the diction of Newman's *Dream* recall T.S. Eliot's dictum that Milton had 'done damage to the English language from which it has not wholly recovered'.[35] Newman's Angel derives his authority not so much from liturgical or biblical sources as from adopting the register in which Milton's angels sought to educate Adam. Catholic doctrine is being enunciated through a Miltonic mask. Not only are nineteenth-century readers lulled into acceptance by the sheer familiarity of these cadences, but Milton's rhetoric provides just the right touch of archaism to detach the Angel's teaching from the world of nineteenth-century polemic and lend the poem the air of rootedness in and understanding of 'the institutions of the country' which Newman has seen as the only way of securing respect for English Catholics.

Having laid his Protestant bricks upon a Catholic foundation, what had Newman built? When Francis Doyle gave his lecture upon the *Dream* the matter of genre clearly puzzled him. Doyle toyed with the idea that the *autos sacramentales* or allegorical religious plays of the Spanish priest Calderon (1600-81) might possibly have influenced Newman. It is possible that Newman had read the third volume of D.F. M'Carthy's translations of *The Dramas of Calderón* (1861) which contained an example of these plays, but as Doyle then honestly admitted he felt that Newman's poem was directed at the meditative reader rather than intended for an audience. Newman was not, of course, dramatically ignorant. As part of his campaign to provide an education for the children of Catholic converts comparable to that received by their Protestant peers he had produced an expurgated edition of Terence's *Phormio* for the boys of the Oratory.[36] He was undoubtedly pleased by the devotional implications when he wrote to a friend shortly after the poem's publication, 'I am greatly honoured by the good Nuns of Notre Dame having got their children to act it'.[37] The children may have enjoyed the name-calling incantations of the demons,[38] but might have found the delivery of the Angel's Miltonic periods a sterner challenge. Like much Victorian poetry the *Dream* does invite oral performance. On the one hand it may seem to look back to the tradition of Milton's *Comus* where education is wrapped in tableau, verse and song, or to religious plays which enjoy a close relationship with the drama of the liturgy. On the other hand, Newman is consciously availing himself of the aural drama to be derived from metrical variety, a mode to which the Victorian reading public had been most fully awakened in Tennyson's *Maud: A Monodrama* (1855).

In extract form the work received instant popular currency when the Anglican editors of *Hymns Ancient and Modern* selected the verse spoken by the Fifth Choir of Angelicals ('Praise to the Holiest in the height') for inclusion in their Appendix of 1868, thus securing the type of foothold in a national institution which Newman felt to be so essential for the growth of Catholicism in England.

Newman's poem or verse drama may have struck Hutton as atypical of its period by virtue of its deliberate archaism and its apparent eschewal of contemporary reference in favour of the concerns of eternity; nevertheless it arose from, and perhaps contributed to, the literature of its period. Tennyson had long ago had in mind the composition of an idyll concerning the legend of the San Graal, but, as late as 1859, he had written to the Duke of Argyll: 'As to Macaulay's suggestion of the Sangreal, I doubt whether such a subject could be handled in these days, without incurring a charge of irreverence.'[39]

Indeed, according to another account he gave, he had composed a poem on the subject of Lancelot's quest for the Grail in his head but had not bothered to commit it to paper and so it had 'altogether slipt out of memory'. By September 1868, however, Tennyson clearly felt that the times were more propitious. In 1864 Robert Hawker, the Tractarian Vicar of Morewenstow in Cornwall, had published *The Quest for the Sangraal*, a long blank verse poem which Tennyson much admired.[40] Yet Tennyson's own rendering of the Grail legend was distinctive. He himself felt it to be 'one of the most imaginative of my poems'. 'The Holy Grail' contains the heart of Tennyson's Protestant vision: King Arthur, surveying his Order of the Round Table, tragically depleted by the pursuit of the quest, reminds those who remain that,

> ...the King must guard
> That which he rules, and is but as the hind
> To whom a space of land is given to plow.
> Who may not wander from the alloted field
> Before his work be done; but, being done,
> Let visions of the night or of the day
> Come, as they will...
>
> 'The Holy Grail', II. 901-7

Tennyson's major innovation had been to entrust the narration to Sir Percivale, 'whom Arthur and his knighthood called The Pure'. Percivale had abandoned active service and 'passed into the silent life of prayer/Praise, fast and alms', and in his monastic retreat tells his tale to a fellow monk, Ambrosius, who 'loved him much beyond the rest'. Tennyson's invention here may only involve an uncannily coincidental resemblance to Newman's history and the life-long devotion of his friend Ambrose St John, a fellow-traveller from Littlemore to the grave itself.[41] Nevertheless, 'The Holy Grail' can be read without fancifulness as one of the more moving mid-Victorian elegies for the sad depletion of the Anglican ranks effected by the secession of its bravest hopes.[42]

The circumstances attending Tennyson's composition of 'The Holy Grail' illustrate the complex nature of historical influence. There is no need to posit any direct intention on Tennyson's part to criticise Newman's choice of subject-matter when Arthur regrets that Percivale has left 'human wrongs to right themselves', but Newman's poem, as one of a cluster of eschatologically-inclined works of that decade, may well have provided the conditions that allowed Tennyson to feel that his own attitude to the Grail legend could now be handled without incurring the charges of either irreverence or irrelevance.

In concentrating upon an understanding of Newman's *Dream* as a Victorian poem it may be felt that this essay has largely chosen to ignore Hutton's reading of it as 'in every sense the least in sympathy with the temper of the present century, indeed the most completely independent of the *Zeitgeist*'. It is important to remember that Hutton penned this opinion as the Cardinal lay dying. In the quarter of a century that had passed since the *Dream*'s publication both literary and religious scenes had changed. Elgar's decision to take Newman's poem as the text of his oratorio has been variously interpreted as a courageous affirmation of his Catholicism, and as an act of defiance.[43] By the last decade of the nineteenth century the theology of the *Dream* was out of favour with 'liberal' Catholics and made far too little use of the Scriptures to please the militant Protestants who were again active in the Anglican Church. Ironically Elgar's oratorio (1890) enjoyed greater contemporary success on the Continent than it did in England. From the vantage point of the turn of the century Newman's poem seems to be a distinctly mid-Victorian *Dream*.

NOTES

1. R.H. Hutton, *Cardinal Newman* (1891), p. 244.

2. J.H. Newman, 'Poetry with reference to Aristotle's Poetics', (1829), *Essays Critical and Historical* (1872), i, p. 20.

3. J.H. Newman, *Apologia pro Vita Sua*, ed. M.J. Svaglic (Oxford, 1967), p. 18.

4. Ibid., p. 108.

5. In July 1864 a visitor to the Birmingham Oratory 'wanted to know what Newman "*did* – did I read?" He was told gravely that Newman had certainly been seen to "take out books from the Library" '. An incident quoted in I. Ker, *John Henry Newman: A Biography* (Oxford, 1988) p. 561.

6. For an excellent analysis of this process see L.H. Peterson, *Victorian Autobiography: The Tradition of Self-Interpretation* (New Haven, 1986) chapter 4.

7. *The Letters and Diaries of John Henry Newman*, eds C.S. Dessain et al., xxii, p. 72.

8. *Letters and Diaries*, xxii, p. 86.

9. *Verses on Various Occasions* (London,1868), p. iii (my italics).

10. *Letters and Diaries*, xxi, p. 423.

11. Quoted in G.B. Tennyson, *Victorian Devotional Poetry: The Tractarian Mode* (Cambridge, Mass., 1981), p. 116.

12. *Letters and Diaries*, xxiv, p. 7n.

13. See G.B. Tennyson, 'Descendants of *Lyra Apostolica*', *Victorian Devotional Poetry*, pp. 233-7.

14. F.H. Doyle, *Lectures delivered before the University of Oxford* (London, 1869), p. 97.

15. Ibid., p. 104.

16. Lewis Carroll, *Alice's Adventures in Wonderland* (London, 1865). Carroll disliked the quality of this edition, published on 4 July 1865, which was recalled. The unbound sheets were then published in New York with an Oxford imprint dated 1866.

17. For a wonderful academic *jeu d'esprit* on this subject see S. Leslie, 'Lewis Carroll and the Oxford Movement: A Paper submitted to the Historical Theology School at Göttingen University' the *London Mercury* 28 (1933), pp. 233-9, where Leslie confirms his identification of the White Queen as Newman by referring to her remark in *Through the Looking Glass* (1871): 'Why sometimes I believed as many as six impossible things before breakfast.'

18. 'The State of Religious Parties' the *British Critic* 25 (1839), p. 399.

19. *Letters and Diaries*, xxiv, p. 7n.

20. Quoted in *Letters and Diaries* xxiv, p. 42n.

21. Edward Bishop Elliott and John Cummings were the chief proponents of this date. E.R. Sandeen, *The Roots of Fundamentalism* (Chicago, 1970) p. 83.

22. For an account of the more extreme millenialist positions and the contemporary commentary see E. Jay, *The Religion of the Heart: Anglican Evangelicalism and the Nineteenth-Century Novel* (Oxford, 1979) pp. 88-97.

23. *Hell and the Victorians: a Study of the Nineteenth-century Theological Controversies Concerning Eternal Punishment and the Future Life* (Oxford, 1974), pp. 1-18.

24. *Letters and Diaries* xxiii, p. 176.

25. See G. Rowell, '*The Dream of Gerontius*' *Ampleforth Journal* 73 (1968), pp. 184-92, which identifies Wilfrid Ward's biography of Newman as the source for this approach to the poem.

26. J. Keble, *Tract No. 89: On the Mysticism attributed to the Early*

Fathers of the Church (1840), reprinted in *The Evangelical and Oxford Movements*, ed. E. Jay (Cambridge, 1983), p. 141. This is usually taken to be the classic statement of the Tractarian aesthetic. For Newman's essential sympathy with this definition of poetry see his early essay 'Poetry with reference to Aristotle's Poetics' (1829). The function of *The Dream* for a Protestant readership might be gauged from a remark Newman made in 1846 when reviewing Keble's poetry, 'Poetry is the refuge of those who have not the Catholic Church'. Quoted in I. Ker, op. cit., p. 322.

27. L.H. Peterson, *Victorian Autobiography*, p. 112.

28. *Apologia*, p. 137.

29. Ibid., pp. 252-3.

30. Ibid., p. 214.

31. Ibid., p. 186.

32. Cf. *Apologia*, p. 185 and *The Dream of Gerontius*, II. 549-53.

33. *Hell and the Victorians*, pp. 153-79.

34. *The Pilgrim's Progress*, ed. J.B. Wharey, rev. R. Sharrock (Oxford, 1960) p. 165.

35. *Selected Prose of T.S. Eliot*, ed. F. Kermode (London, 1975), p. 264.

36. I. Ker, op. cit., p. 537.

37. *Letters and Diaries*, xxii, p. 72.

38. There was considerable critical disagreement about Newman's portrayal of his demons. Doyle felt them to be 'mean and repulsive' and lacking in the intellectual *gravitas* of Milton's fallen angels (op. cit., p. 118). When the Bishop of Oxford allegedly detected in them 'the possibility of unbelief' Newman found an unlikely defender in Kingsley who wrote, 'Jean Paul Richter says somewhere, that no man believes his own creed thoroughly till he can afford to jest about it, a daring paradox, which seems to be fulfilled in Dr. Newman.' *Charles Kingsley: His Letters and Memoirs of His Life*, ed. F.E. Kingsley (2 vols, London, 1877) II, p. 270.

39. Quoted in *The Poems of Tennyson*, ed. C. Ricks (London, 1969) p. 1661.

40. For this information I am indebted to B. Richards, *English Poetry of the Victorian Period 1830-1890* (London, 1988) p. 294.

41. Tennyson is careful to emphasise that Ambrosius is no convert; he has never 'strayed beyond the cell'.

42. Tennyson said of the poem, 'Faith declines, religion in many turns from practical goodness to the quest after the supernatural and

marvellous and selfish religious excitement.' Quoted in *The Poems of Tennyson*, p. 1661.

43. The evidence for its essential catholicity is argued in G. Hodkins, *Providence and Art: A study of Elgar's religious beliefs* (Elgar Society, 1981) p. 5. In his immediate reaction to an appalling first performance and the subsequent reviews, Elgar seems to have regarded the work in the light of a final wager with God: 'I always said God was against art & I still believe it. Anything obscene or trivial is blessed in this world & has a reward... I have allowed my heart to open once – it is now shut against every religious feeling & every soft, gentle impulse *for ever*'. Quoted in J.N. Moore, *Edward Elgar: A Creative Life* (Oxford, 1984) p. 334. In later life Elgar wholly disavowed that he had ever had a religious interest in the piece.

9

DANGEROUS CONCEITS OR CONFIRMATIONS STRONG?

Valentine Cunningham

> He took weeks off to do work extraordinary in so fundamental a thinker. He wrote a couple of novels, neither of them good...[1]

Thus Owen Chadwick in his magisterial little Oxford Past Masters volume perpetuating the notion that Newman's fiction was an unworthy distraction, *parerga*, secondary writings, not central to the main works of divinity. The Puseyites, apparently, had much the same disparaging thought. Father Faber reported them as saying that in *Loss and Gain* Newman 'had sunk lower than Dickens'.[2] Doubtless they had in mind passages like those wonderfully satiric portraits of the religionists who trouble Charles Reding's last hours as an Anglican: Jack the former kitchen-boy of St Saviour's College who is now an Angel of the Irvingite Catholic and Apostolic Church, Mr Highfly the Irvingite Apostle, Zerubbabel the Jewish convert, not to mention Dr Kitchens of the Spiritual Elixir whose friends included Exeter Hall's anti-Roman polemicists Mr Makanoise and Mr Gabb. So far, though, from sinking to Dickens' level in these pages, Newman might more aptly be said to have risen to it. But Newman's particular merits as a novelist aren't the main question. The important observation to make is that Newman's methods as a novelist are not different from his methods as a preacher and apologist. A wedge cannot with any certainly be driven between his fictions, and his sermons and other apparently non-fictional texts. Both sorts of text keep exploiting fictional methods, keep offering stories, appeal to the imagination, rove nimbly about in the fields of allegory, satire and parable, and continually raise problems as to the nature of story, metaphor, rhetoric. In short, none of Newman's writing fails to be obsessively preoccupied with the nature of textuality, of words, of reading and writing, of meaning, words about words, ie. problems of interpretation.

Newman likes stories, likes reading and hearing them, likes telling them. Tales captivate him: tall stories, and not so tall ones, tales of saints, stories of miracles, secular fables, the classics and the not-so-classic fictions of the western tradition; he likes them all. His imagination is continually stirring and stirred. Repeatedly in the *Apologia* he tells how his imagination has been touched. He finds a fittingness in many of the stories traditionally told of the saints, such as those about the empty tomb of St Mary and the 'angelic choirs with their glad voices...heard singing day and night the glories of their risen Queen'.[3] And the fittingness often seems to be as much narratological as spiritual. Newman responds to the appeal of such stories not least as story. Charles Kingsley's trouble – the trouble of Protestants in general – is that he's one of those 'matter-of-fact, prosaic minds, who cannot take in the fancies of poets', and this notwithstanding the fact that Kingsley was one of the most popular fictionists of the time. He's got, Newman declares, the wrong 'intellectual build'.[4]

Newman's own intellectual build was emphatically literary. It's revealed everywhere, but one early passage in Part One of the *Apologia* will do to illustrate it nicely. As he reads Kingsley's pamphlet, says Newman,

> words have been running in my head, which I find in the Douay version thus; "Thou has also with thee Semei the son of Gera, who cursed me with a grievous curse when I went to the camp, but I swore to him, saying, I will not kill thee with the sword. Do not thou hold him guiltless. But thou art a wise man and knowest what to do with him, and thou shalt bring down his grey hairs with blood to hell".

He picks up Kingsley's reference to 'hault courage and strict honour' and brings up an apt reference to Christian duplicity in a Romance by way of riposte. Then he compares at some length Kingsley's pamphlet to a drama with a fifth act, a *coup de théâtre*, a finale. And all the while he's seeding his text with sharp metaphors of forgery, whitewash, being out of jail 'upon ticket of leave', warfare, and 'poisoning the wells' (*A* pp. 77f.). Bible story, Romance, theatre, dense metaphoricity: this is an author who thinks in terms of literature and the literary. It's no surprise to find him constantly presenting himself by literary analogues. Now, for instance, he's Hamlet, ineradicably altered by the words of a ghostly father, Augustine's '*Securus judicat orbis terrarum*; (*A* pp. 185, 203). Now his fictional surrogate Charles Reding is a fairytale knight, now he's Undine, now he's wondering if he is not Philoctetes.

By contrast, a mind like Kingsley's was unlikely to sympathise with the role of the imagination in the growth of Catholic theology. The doctrine of Purgatory, Newman explains, arose out of years of 'supposition' and 'speculation', centuries in which 'the mind of the Church' was led 'to imagine modes...by which (God) *may* solve' apparent difficulties about sins committed by Christians after baptism.[5] Newman the imaginist, a persistent supposer, a perpetual weaver of fitting stories, did sympathise.

> He toiled along the stately road which led him straight to the capital of the world. He met throngs of the idle and the busy, of strangers and natives, who peopled the interminable suburb. He passed under the high gate and wandered on amid marble palaces and columned temples; he met processions of heathen priests and ministers in honour of their idols; he met the stern legionaries who had been the 'massive iron hammers' of the whole earth; he met the anxious politician with his ready man of business at his side to prompt him on his canvass for popularity; he met the orator returning home from a successful pleading, with his young admirers and his grateful and hopeful clients. He saw about him nothing but tokens of vigorous power, grown up into a definite establishment formed and matured in its religion, its laws, its civil traditions, its imperial extension, through the history of many centuries; and what was he but a poor, feeble aged stranger, in nothing different from the multitude of men – an Egyptian or a Chaldean, or perhaps a Jew, some Eastern or other – as passers-by would guess according to their knowledge of human kind, carelessly looking at him (as we might turn our eyes upon Hindoo or gypsy, as they met us), without the shadow of a thought that such a one was destined then to commence an age of religious sovereignty, in which they might spend their own heathen times twice over, and not see its end.

That's Newman's rather gripping pulpit story of St Peter 'the first Pope' advancing 'towards the heathen city, where, under a Divine guidance, he was to fix his seat'.[6]

Newman tells a good story. He invents plausibly. Discussing, for example, the troubling matter of theologically sanctioned equivocations, he refers to Boswell's story of Dr Johnson's dismissing a murderer's right to truthful directions should he ask you which way someone he's pursuing has gone:

> As to Johnson's case of a murderer asking you which way a man

> had gone, I should have anticipated that, had such a difficulty happened to him, his first act would have been to knock the man down, and to call out for the police; and next, if he was worsted in the conflict, he would not have given the ruffian the information he asked, at whatever risk to himself. I think he would have let himself be killed first. I do not think that he would have told a lie.[7]

Newman's constant practice is to put words into people's mouths. The whole atmosphere of his Oxford life leading up to his conversion to the Roman Church is conversational. The *Apologia*'s constant note is of incessant conversation – tutorials, arguments, dialogues, friends talking, talking as they walk or sit. And in his sermons, apologies, essays, fictions and autobiography Newman falls repeatedly, and as if at the compulsion of some deep prejudice, pleasure and necessity, into dialogue. *Loss and Gain* is a fiction consisting largely of dialogue, of debate. *Doing*, action, in that novel come down mainly to *saying*: '"Go Home?" cried Bateman; "why, we have just done dinner, and done nothing else as yet; I had a great deal to say"' (Part II, chapter 19). It may seem, on the face of it, one thing to compose fictional dialogues, or to concoct an imaginary entrance exam interview (as in the 'Elementary Studies' section of *The Idea of a University*), or in the same volume to put words into the mouth or mind of a representative unorthodox 'teacher' of the day ('The teacher, then, whom I speak of, will discourse thus in his secret heart...'),[8] and rather another to put words into the mouth of Charles Kingsley in an invented dialogue with Newman. But both are central to a pervasive fictionalising method.

> Mr Kingsley begins then by exclaiming, – 'O the chicanery, the wholesale fraud, the vile hypocrisy, the conscience-killing tyranny of Rome! We have not far to seek for an evidence of it. There's Father Newman to wit: one living specimen is worth a hundred dead ones. He, a Priest writing of Priests, tells us that lying is never any harm.'[9]

But, no, Kingsley did not exclaim that. Newman is taking a poetic or polemic licence, and Kingsley rightly objected to having words 'put into my mouth' in 'an utterly imaginary conversation'.[10] And to object to that is to object to a regular practice that is central to Newman's method. And saying what people might have said is a very close neighbour to Newman's even more widespread practice of claiming to know what the words they actually used really meant. Kingsley accused Newman of preaching a 'Romish' sermon while still appearing publicly to be an Anglican. 'Romish' was doubtless a deliberately vague smear. But Newman disallows any such vagueness. Kingsley 'means by "Romish" not "savouring of Romish doctrine" merely, but "the work of a real Romanist, of a conscious Romanist"' (*A* p. 88). But this claim to have cracked Kingsley's intentions in using the word and the hardening up of its soft edges to mean 'the work of a real... conscious Romanist' is at the least dubious, and at best a piece of intense hermeneutic arrogance.

And such arrogance is pervasive, as the manipulative pressure is constant. Newman will try to make words mean just what he thinks they ought to mean. His whole rhetorical push is dedicated to convincing readers of whatever particular reading he has decided on. 'What does Dr Newman mean?' Characteristically Newman reads the question catachrestically (*katachresis*: the rhetorical figure of wrenching, distortion; *abusio* in the Latin rhetoric books). Newman won't take it as 'What does Dr Newman *mean*?' but as 'What does *Dr Newman* mean?' The ego of the hermeneute is straightaway asserted. But then that ego is everywhere pronounced. Of course a question about the meaning of texts, of meaning, gets inextricably entwined into the meaning of a selfhood that feels threatened, for Newman's hermeneutics are always profoundly at the service of an ego of extraordinary dimensions. 'He asks what I *mean*; not about my words, not about my arguments, not about my actions, as his ultimate point, but about that living intelligence, by which I write, and argue and act.' The slide from meaning of words to meaning of self is managed with consummate smoothness and the usual self-centred arrogance. The fact that the extraordinary autobiographical performance of the *Apologia* eventuated from this deliberate wrenching of Kingsley's question encourages us, no doubt, to forgive the manipulation. But even if we are pleased that Kingsley got more than he bargained for, we should never forget that Newman's reading of Kingsley's demand is not what Kingsley meant by it.

Newman's most impressively flagrant manipulations, dodges, slides and sidesteps, his slick feints and manoeuvres commonly occur when, as in the extended response to Kingsley, Newman feels his back being forced up against some wall. A classic case is the article now published as the pamphlet *On Consulting the Faithful in Matters of Doctrine*. What did Newman mean by the word *consult* in his original polemical gibe against the tardily non-consultative English Bishops, that even 'in the preparation of a dogmatic definition, the faithful are consulted, as lately in the instance of the Immaculate Conception'? Forced to defend himself, Newman claims that he meant *consult* not in its technical 'Latin' sense, *consult with* or *take counsel*, but in the 'English' sense, 'in its popular and ordinary use', its conversational use ('as it were conversing') – as one might consult a watch, barometer, sundial, or the pulse of a patient. And of course Newman was correct when he went on to point out that many English words originally derived from Latin have broken free from the Latinate root meanings: *amiable* is not *amabilis*, *crime* not *crimen*, *prevent* not *praevenire*, and so on.[11] In the *Apologia* Newman would again make this point, correctly observing in the place where he's trying to defuse the discussion of equivocation in the work of St Alfonso that Kingsley so gleefully referred to, that *censura* is not what English means by *censure*, just as *Apologia* does not correspond altogether to *apology* (*A* p. 355). It is a linguistic case that Stephen Dedalus, in Joyce's *A Portrait of the Artist as a Young Man*, who's a devotee of Newman's 'cloistral silver-veined prose', endorses as a prime difficulty in any critical discussion:

> One difficulty, said Stephen, in esthetic discussion is to know whether words are being used according to the literary tradition or according to the tradition of the marketplace. I remember a sentence of Newman's in which he says of the Blessed Virgin that she was detained in the full company of the saints. The use of the word in the market place is quite different. *I hope I am not detaining you.*

And to bring the point comically home, the Dean whom he's addressing is made to misunderstand. He replies politely, 'Not in the least'.[12]

But none of this truly applies to *consult*. Newman says that it was 'not merely sharp writing' to adduce his list of Latin-English variables in aid of his defence of *consult.* But, of course, it was precisely sharp writing. *Consult* is not a Latin word; it's an English one carrying a range of meanings, Latinate and popular. And among its quite ordinary, even popular meanings, was something like 'consult with' or 'take counsel'. And to the unbiased reader, unappraised of Newman's later advice to take it in only a very restricted sense, that is how the original paragraph invites us to read *consult.* The Bishops were being chided for being more autocratic than the Vatican in their refusal to refer, and by clear implication, defer to the expertise in educational matters of laymen. It is second thoughts, under pressure from the authoritative episcopal frown, that set Newman off seeking to bend language and meaning. Newman is inconsistent, however. When he uses the word *consult* later on in the piece, it seems clearly to denote deference to the opinions of others: 'Surely, in plain English, most considerable deference was paid to the "sensus fidelium";...their testimony was taken, their feelings consulted'. But still Newman persists in claiming that the word's range can be arbitrarily restrained and plain meanings and reader's responses simply dictated to: consult is not, as 'I have already said...to be taken in its ordinary Latin sense' (*On Consulting*, pp. 70, 71). And one can't help noticing the little jig that *ordinary* has enacted: in the space of less than twenty pages it has slid from 'ordinary (i.e. non-Latinate) use' to 'ordinary Latin sense'. But that deft slide is symptomatic of Newman's apparent conviction that words can and will do just what he, their user and interpreter, wishes them to, and his faith that the reader will be prepared to condone whatever assertions Newman cares to offer as to real meanings.

Newman's explanation of *consult* did not convince the hierarchy. He was compelled to try again. But his tactic is just the same in the compensatory Note that he added to the third edition of his *Arians of the Fourth Century* (1871). The Vatican had stuck at three points, three words, in the *Consulting* piece: the 'temporary *suspense* of the functions of the Ecclesia docens'; the 'failure' of 'the *body* of Bishops'; the occasional compromise of '*general* councils'. And in each case Newman does not climb down, but plays with words. In the matter of *suspense*, 'I did not say "suspension", purposely' (but what difference does that make?). Furthermore, 'in matter of fact I used the word "general" in *contrast* to "ecumenical", as I had used it in Tract No. 90' (but this private restriction scarcely appears in the original context). As for *body*, it becomes another case of *consult:* the word is covered in a gratuitous heap of lexical flummery as Newman once again kicks dust into the reader's eyes by diverting and irrelevant talk of the distinction between English *body* and Latin *corpus*:

> Here, if the word 'body' is used in the sense of the Latin 'corpus', as 'corpus' is used in theological treatises, and as it doubtless should be translated for the benefit of readers ignorant of the English language, certainly this would be a heretical statement. But I meant nothing of the kind. I used it in the vague, familiar, genuine sense of which Johnson gives instances in his dictionary as meaning 'the great preponderance', or, 'the mass' of Bishops, viewing them in the main or the gross, as a *cumulus* of individuals.

So foreigners and translators as well as ordinary readers got it wrong, and Newman's sense is the only genuine one. The word can be restricted to a vague and familiar meaning if Dr Newman says it must, even if that familiar sense turns out to need learned reference to Dr Johnson (followed by references to Hooker and Clarendon), and an excursion into the French of Tillemont and the Greek of St Gregory, as well as that resort to the Latin word *cumulus*. This is dangerous overkill, and arrogant special pleading.[13]

No wonder Newman felt challenged by Kingsley's charge that he went in for personal equivocation and belonged to a Church that practised and praised it. In the *Consulting* piece, and deploying some well-known examples of equivocation that were to recur in the *Apologia* (doctors misleading patients, St Athanasius saving his skin by misleading some pursuers on the Nile, and so on) Newman dismissed the charge of equivocation on the grounds that what was rather in question was *aequivocatio*. 'I do not see that there is in any of these instances what is expressed by the English word "equivocation"; but it *is* the *aequivocatio* of a Latin treatise' (*Consulting*, p. 59). Actually, Newman's cases rather look as if they are both. But Newman's faith is continually pinned on such plays of words. And, since he's given to this kind of equivocation all the time, it's no surprise at all to find him equivocating, taking a serious and repeated equivocal stand, in the case of the meaning of the word *equivocation* itself.

What is the *aequivocatio* sanctioned in the moral theologians and philosophers, and how does it differ from equivocation, he asks in the Appendix of the *Apologia*, skilfully juggling the words *equivocation* and *aequivocatio* until you can scarcely tell the one from the other? In the first place he declares that *aequivocatio* is not equivocation. *Aequivocatio* is defined as the legitimate playing upon words. Alternatively *aequivocatio* is *evasion*. But then, shortly afterwards, we're informed that 'it is very difficult to draw the line between these evasions [as in Parliament, or in the case of Athanasius on the Nile] and what are commonly called in English equivocations'. And then, again, we learn that *equivocation* is also playing upon words ('Playing upon words, or equivocation'). Newman goes on to say that the English do not admire equivocation, and nor does he. 'For myself, I can fancy myself thinking it was allowable for me to lie, but never to equivocate.' But the definition of his theologically sanctioned *aequivocatio* has collapsed into this more dubious equivocation. What's more, it looks as if Newman has been busily equivocating all the time, and that in fact equivocation is responsible for that collapse. Certainly, if equivocation is playing upon words for doubtful purposes then the paragraphs Newman has just conducted us through could scarcely provide more vivid instances of it. And in fact this kind of play is avowed as a kind of principle with Newman, following St Alfonso:

> St Alfonso certainly says that a play upon words is allowable; and, speaking under correction, I should say that he does so on the ground that lying is not a sin against justice, that is, against our neighbour, but a sin against God; because words are the signs of ideas, and therefore if a word denotes two ideas, we are at liberty to use it in either of its senses... (*A* p. 361).

Meaning – the meaning of Dr Newman, of Dr Newman's words, of Church history – is commonly in the texts of Newman a matter of choosing between interpretations; it's an affair of variant readings and re-readings, and of variant stories of those readings. Newman's writings are a palimpsest of readings and re-readings and re-readings of readings. Newman is always re-reading his own writings. The *Apologia* presents his life, his meaning, as a long interpretative engagement with his personal history of successive acts of interpretation, his life lived as a reader and interpreter. The text of that life, like the life itself, comprises a palimpsest or archaeological site where readings are layered one upon the other, variously inscribed, erased, rewritten, written over, or even just occasionally simply reinstated:

> As a boy of fifteen, I had so fully imbibed it [pure Protestantism], that I had actually erased in my *Gradus ad Parnassum*, such titles, under the word 'Papa', as 'Christi Vicarius', 'sacer interpres', and 'sceptra gerens', and substituted epithets so vile that I cannot bring myself to write them down here. The effect of this early persuasion remained, as what I have already called it, a 'stain upon my imagination'. As regards my reason, I began in 1833 to form theories on the subject, which tended to obliterate it (*A* p. 187).

And he proceeds to quote his earlier self in the matter of Rome, opinions he has long obliterated, but which show him starting to separate the Roman Church from his early Protestant designation of Antichrist. Newman's selfhood is grounded in the reinterpretability of texts, in so to say their potential for word play. And this potential is why Church history is a palimpsest. At least this is what has enabled the 'development' of Catholic doctrine as an orthodox process. Like 'Dr Newman', as his meaning is revealed in the *Apologia,* the essence of Church history derives from the interpretative possibilities offered by word play, the variability of meaning, the copiousness of the mysteries and allegories in the Scripture, the multivalent ambivalences of metaphor and figure in the sacred writings which lay there waiting for the glossers and commentators to come along and mine their rich interpretative possibilities.

Literalists, the eschewers of mystery, allegory, hidden meanings, second senses, the equivocations of figurativeness, have, according to Newman's repeated reading of Church history, been heretics. Newman's 'Development' essay is insistent that literalism is the mark of Paulicians and the Nestorians. The Nestorians are presented as forerunners of Protestants, especially Protestants like Kingsley. They were 'English', he says, in their intellectual predilection. They were immune to 'that fulness of meaning, refinement of thought, subtle versatility of feeling and delicate reserve or reverent suggestion, which poets exemplify' and which characterise 'sacred composition' viewed in correct Catholic fashion. They tended to 'abstain from allegory' and eschew 'the mystical interpretation'. They ended up by rebutting Christianising allegorical readings of the Old Testament; indeed in the last resort they denied inspiration altogether. They were in fact early versions of nineteenth-century German and rationalising biblical critics. Orthodoxy, at least in Newman's reading of it, has relied precisely on 'subtle versatility' in the text, and on the interpreter's playing along with the text's versatile potential for word play. Arians and Nestorians 'denied the allegorical rule of Scripture interpretation' (*D* p. 375: notice that a *possibility* has been hardened into a *rule*). Whereas the Church's 'most subtle and powerful method of proof, whether in ancient or modern times, is the mystical sense, which is so frequently used in doctrinal controversy as on many occasions to supersede any other' (*D* p. 339). It is 'absolutely impossible' for doctrinal truths 'to remain in the mere letter of Scripture, if they are to be more than mere words, or to convey a definite idea to the recipient' (*D* p. 151). Doctrinal truths are presented in multivalent texts, sacred writings abundant with mysteries, metaphors, allegories, the copia of figure, and so demanding comment, explication, the marginal gloss, the perpetual supplementation of the interpretative tradition and institution. The Reformation shook off 'that vein of postilling and allegorizing on Scripture, which for a long time had prevailed', and betook itself 'unto the literal sense' (*D* p. 342). And look where it got the Reformation: straight on to the pathway of error and heresy. If you want to be blessed by Scripture, to receive it as sacrament, you have to receive it according to its 'mystical or sacramental principle' of interpretation, to recognise the divine hermeneutical economy of allegory, second senses, hieroglyph, encryptedness (*A* p. 151).

> It is in point to notice also the structure and style of Scripture, a structure so figurative and indirect, that no one would presume at first sight to say what is in it and what is not. It cannot, as it were, be mapped, or its contents catalogued; but after all our diligence, to the end of our lives and to the end of the Church, it must be an unexplored and unsubdued land, with heights and valleys, forests and streams, on the right and left of our path and close all about us, full of concealed wonders and choice treasures (*D* p. 162).

And if biblical textuality on Newman's view comes down on the Catholic side, so also does his reading of the Bible's metatextual self-consciousness. Scripture 'nowhere recognises itself' on the Protestant model as an inspired set of literal truths, he declares, for nowhere does it 'assert the inspiration of those portions which are most essential'. But it does provide numerous metatextual anticipations of 'the development of Christianity, both as a polity and as a doctrine'. The parable of the grain of mustard seed, full of hidden, secret potential for great growth, is just one self-referential emblem of textual copiousness, interpretative potential, and pleromatic expansiveness. A figure illustrates, a figure carries, the developmental life of the text; the metaphorical plenitudes of Scripture are ripe for interpretative expansion; metaphor is reality, becomes reality; what is really present in it is the presence of the real, real presences. Which is why Newman can write as he does about St Mary in the *Development*. There he will quote a great wash of traditional metaphors from the Fathers and Saints. 'These are oratorical expressions', he admits; 'but we use oratory on great subjects, not on small' (*D* p. 411). And oratory clearly includes *oratio,* rhetoric, metaphor. Mary's reality is expressed and apprehended through the vast array of metaphors Church history has laden her with. And not, by any means, just Mary. The Kingsley literalism is disgusted by what the notion of metaphor as a potentia of realities, real presences, can lead Newman and his friends to in the matter of other saints, like Walburga:

> 'But the most remarkable and lasting miracle, attesting the holy Walburga's sanctity, is that which reckons her among the saints who are called "Elaeophori", or "unguentiferous", becoming, almost in a literal sense, olive-trees in the courts of God. These are

> they from whose bones a holy oil distils. That oil of charity and gentle mercy which graced them while alive, and fed in them the flame of universal love at their death, still permeates their bodily remains'. After quoting the names of male saints who have possessed this property, the author goes on to detail how this holy oil fell, in drops, sometimes the size of a hazel-nut, sometimes of a pea, into the silver bowl beneath the stone slab. How, when the state of Aichstadt was laid under an interdict, the holy oil ceased, 'until the Church regained it rights,' and so forth, and so forth; and then returning to his original image, metaphor, illustration, proof, or whatever else it may be called by reasoners such as he and Dr Newman, he says that the same flow of oil or dew is related this to this female saint and that – 'women whose souls like that of Walburga, were touched with true compassion; whose bosom, like hers, melted by divine love, was filled with the milk of human kindness...'

Thus Kingsley in *What, Then, Does Dr Newman Mean?*, quoting the Tractarian 'Life of St. Walburga' (*A* pp. 45f.), and proving what a gulf separated his view of the life of metaphor from that prevailing in Newman's more Catholic circles.

But, clearly, Kingsley was not the only one worrying about the interpretative copiousness of figure, of text, that sustains so many of Newman's readings and is the nub of his defence of Catholic doctrinal development. The anxiety of John Henry Newman himself appears at every turn. His pausing equivocally at the stumbling block of equivocation is one symptomatic case in point. The list of Latin English variants that he gives in the *Consulting* essay is full of self-referential cheek. It's a kind of leading with the chin. He defies you to notice what it says. But it also indicates what might be in Newman's mind as well as in the mind of an antagonist, as to the condition of his writing activity: '*Scriptor egregius* is not *an egregious* writer...*retractare dicta* is not *to retract what he has said*; and, as we know from the sacred passage, *traducere* is not necessarily *to traduce*.' No one compelled him to mention traducing in a context of sacred passages, but it came up anyway. Not dissimilarly, one place in the *Apologia* has Newman even admitting to speaking catachrestically (*A* p. 219).

Just so, there is considerable wobbling in Newman's texts over the question of interpretive supplementation. On the one hand, Newman is quite clear that Scripture needs the supplement of tradition, the elucidatory helps and custodianship of the Church. Tract 90 undoes the applicability to Scripture of the phrase *Rule of Faith*; it finds no support for Scripture as a self-sufficient interpretative unit.[14] A book, the Book the Protestants so revere, cannot, Newman argues in the *Apologia*, stand by itself against the anarchic living intellects of the day, which is why the Bible in Protestant, especially German, custody is in process of dissolution. Making the Bible stick up for itself as a lone maintainer of religious truth is to make it 'answer a purpose for which it was never intended' (*A* p. 280). On the other hand, Newman is also wary of the Protestant charge of Catholicism's illegitimate supplementation, the worrying possibility of alien addition, imported otherness, and so of interpretative catachresis that no act of supplementation can altogether shake off. And he wavers. Now supplement and interpretation are offered as separate and distinct: the teaching of the Church is 'partly the interpretation, partly the supplement of Scripture' (*A* p. 166). Now they become one in 'an Apostolical Tradition' that is 'supplementary to and interpretative of Scripture'.[15] The ambivalences of supplement are, of course, famously central to the deconstructive arguments of Jacques Derrida. So are the dualities of Plato's *pharmakon* – now poison, now medicine. Scripture on Newman's view is a pharmacopia of multivalence. It is, he declares, in discussing the mystical sense, 'deservedly compared by St Basil to a dispensary which supplies various medicines against every complaint' (*D* p. 339). But are these potions all benign? The curious place in the Appendix of the *Apologia* where equivocation is discussed quotes St Clement as describing equivocation as 'a necessary medicine', a *pharmakon* that has all the Derridan ambivalence inscribed in it. For Origen says 'a man, "when necessity urges", may avail himself of a lie, as medicine, that is to the extent of Judith's conduct towards Holofernes', and 'Cassian says, that the use of a lie, in order to be allowable, must be like the use of hellebore, which is itself poison, unless a man has a fatal disease upon him' (*A* p. 367).

Clearly the problems and dangers of Scripture's interpretability remain present, however forthrightly Newman practises his own particular word plays and avows the virtues of Catholic interpretative history's patrolling of the arcane, the hidden, the invitingly glossable. Often, a very thin line seems to be all that distinguishes orthodox from heretic, the practitioners Newman lauds and the heretical interpreters he derides. The *Apologia* is a lengthy set of reminders to Newman that once he saw little fault with whole schools of Anglican theology that his later position found highly unacceptable. And just over the shoulder of this would-be orthodox reader prance the wild hordes of noisy heretics, the manifestly mistaken, the ready readers Catholicism consigns to unorthodoxy. Newman chides and mocks in fiction and polemic the throngs of 'Baptist, Independent, Irvingite, Wesleyan, Establishment-man, Jumper and Mormonite',[16] but the likes of his brother Francis, a busy convert like John Henry, one who skidded along a primrose ecclesiastical pathway through Plymouth Brethrenism and beyond, must have seemed at least occasionally too close for comfort. Newman's own troubles with the English Bishops and the Roman propaganda indicate that in some orthodox and Catholic opinion 'the most dangerous man in England' wasn't far from resembling his wayward and easily led blood relation.

Imagination, however useful to interpreters, was no unalloyed endowment. Modern science appeals distractingly, Newman suggests in *The Idea of a University*, to the imagination of Christians (*Idea* p. 400). The pleasure of the imagination is what sight offers, as opposed to faith: the world,

> assails their *imagination*. The world sweeps by in long processions, its principalities and powers, its Babel of languages, the astrologers of Chaldaea, the horse and its rider and the chariots of Egypt, Baal and Ashtoreth and their false worship; and those who witness, feel its fascination; they flock after it; with a strange fancy, they ape its gestures, and dote upon its mummeries...[17]

Likewise, story is not a simple good. Protestants, and the likes of Kingsley, and those undergraduates in *Loss and Gain* who solemnly discuss a report that the Pope has repented on his deathbed and so died 'a believer' (a nice parody of Protestant tract material), have their stories too. Sometimes, also, Newman reminds himself that he has in the past, at any rate, recognised the danger of allegory and secondary meanings: 'As to allegorising, I say that the Alexandrians erred, whenever and so far as they proceeded "*to obscure* the primary meaning of Scripture, and *to weaken the force of historical facts* and express declarations"' (*A* p. 348). Just so, Newman will occasionally avail himself of a literalist argument if he can get at Protestants by that means. It is specious, he says in his 'Apostolical Tradition' essay, for,

> ultra-Protestants to assert that Scripture is a sufficient guide in matters of faith to the private Christian, who may put on it whatever sense he thinks the true sense, instead of submitting to that one sense which the writers intended, and to which the Church, in matter of fact, has testified from the first.

Now, it appears, the Church is the guardian of 'one sense', now of secondary senses, multivalence, and amplitudinous word plays.

And metaphor, figure, the tropical, remain a basic difficulty. Interpretation flourishes in and through the metaphorical, development occurs by courtesy of metaphor, in a process sanctioned by figures, stories and parables of growth potential such as that of the grain of mustardseed. In the figurative, text provides its greatest potential for reality, and indeed reality, the truth of the text and the truth of the real presence the text contains reside in the metaphoric essence of the text – the essence suspicious deconstructionists dismiss as logocentrism, or even theologocentrism. But defining the nature of the transaction between logos and flesh, the word and the real, envisioning the nature of the real textual presence especially as it applies to the contentious nature of the eucharist, is elusive and hard. The Transubstantiation section of Tract 90 is as thorny and slippery as any part of that notoriously suggestive, hintful, indirect document. Newman says there that Anglicans don't resist all prospect of the transformation of bread into 'body', only 'the shocking doctrine that "the body of Christ", as the Article goes on to express it, is *not* "given, taken, and eaten, after an heavenly and spiritual manner, but is carnally pressed with teeth".' What seems to be being advocated in the Tract's labyrinthine layering of quotation upon quotation, is a figurative or tropical apprehension: a resistance to Bellarmine's view that 'Christ's body is chewed, *is attrite or broken with the teeth*, and that not tropically, *but properly*', and a support to those who maintained (against St Odo, in whose hands the broken bread of the sacrament was said to have shed real blood into the chalice, or St Wittekundus who saw a real child entering communicants' mouths) 'that the bread and wine, after consecration, do remain in their former substance, and are not Christ's true body and blood, but a figure of it.'

The literalist position – and on this occasion Catholics are literalists – is supported by tales (coinages of 'dull inventors' of miracles Taylor called them; the 'Grecian liars' of Ussher). But then, at length, it emerges that after all, despite Newman's apparent support for the Protestant tropical, figurative reading of this sacrament, he is going on strongly to maintain the literalist Catholic view of 'a real super-local presence in the sacrament', and not a purely figurative presence. Quoting an earlier pamphlet written in defence of the Catholic real presence, Newman recognises that his position might seem dubious: 'It seems at first sight a mere idle use of words to say that Christ is really and literally, yet not locally, present in the

Sacrament; that he is there given to us, not in figure but in truth, and yet is still only on the right hand of God.' He even professes a tentativeness in his conclusion: 'I am not proving or determining anything... I am but pointing out one way of reconciling' an apparent contradiction. But it's obvious that Newman does really think that he's determined the matter. It's equally obvious that he has done no such thing. The issue between the figurative and the real in this great central example of the problem remains unresolved. For all Newman's effort the nature of the reality of the real presence remains a puzzle: the relationship between rhetoric, oratio, figure and reality stays in question.

It is very noticeable that Newman's most potent attempts to bring home, to make tangible or apprehensibly real, the real presence, occurs in fiction, in two central places in *Loss and Gain*: Willis' ecstatic explanation, in Part II, chapter 20, of the Mass as no 'mere form of words – it is a great action, the greatest action that can be on earth', and Reding's first Mass (Part III, chapter 10), in which he repeats the liturgical invocation Willis had gone on to quote:

> A cloud of incense was rising on high; the people suddenly all bowed low; what could it mean? The truth flashed on him, fearfully yet sweetly; it was the Blessed Sacrament – it was the Lord Incarnate who was on the altar, who had come to visit and to bless his people. It was the Great Presence, which makes a Catholic Church different from every other place in the world; which makes it as no other place can be, holy...as he threw himself on the pavement, in sudden self-abasement and joy, some words of those great Antiphons came into his mouth, from which Willis had formerly quoted: 'O Adonai, et Dux domus Israel, qui Moysi in rubo apparuisti; O Emmanuel, Expectatio Gentium et Salvator earum, veni ad salvandum nos. Domine Deus noster.'

And, to repeat, these moments occur in a fiction, in a text, in the medium of figure, rhetoric, metaphor. Whatever Newman might wish to argue about going beyond mere Protestant figurativeness into the reality of the Catholic's real presence, nonetheless the metaphoricity, or textuality, of the word remains stubbornly present, even necessary.

So Newman's writings unfold a curiously complex set of positions. Often he is to be caught playing fast and loose with words and textuality, being wilfully equivocal. At other times it's as if words, textuality, were playing fast and loose with him. At such times he appears to be in a genuine quandary, desiring and straining to make definition stand still, to mirror in little the work of the great Councils of the Church that have through the ages sought to pin down doctrines, dogmas, canons, and for his part failing to do so. And at the heart of that failure stand the central logocentric issues of metaphoricity, textuality, word, real presence – the perennial subjects of theological speculation, conciliar debate, and literary criticism.

Newman's equivocation, his casuistical skill, his opportunistic polemical arbitrariness – about imagination, story, supplement, literalism, but also about private judgment (disclaimed everywhere, then reclaimed in a wash of metaphors of reformatories, training schools and moral factories in the *Apologia*, p. 286), and intention ('we have no duties towards' the framers of the Thirty-Nine Articles declared Tract 90, a claim repeated in the *Apologia*, p. 197; but Catholics submit to 'that one sense which the writers' of Scripture 'intended': 'Apostolical Tradition'), and the genres of Scripture (according to *The Idea of a University*, now *sui generis* and quite different from 'human literature': 'Duties of the Church Towards Knowledge', p. 231; now, in many respects, rather like the 'profane' classics – Job's a kind of Greek drama, and so on, 'Literature', p. 289) – Newman's slippery contradictoriness melds, disconcertingly for his attempts at fixity, definition, certainty, into some of the persistent basic irreconcilabilities of language, the blend of poison and medicine, so to say, offered in the linguistic pharmacy.

Liberalism, modernistic freedom in politics and theology, the freedom from restraint of interpretation, were for Newman a terrifying bottomlessness. He speaks of the danger of being led into 'a bottomless liberalism of thought' (*A* p. 293). The Anglican Articles, misty and ambiguous, were also bottomless. Charles Reding 'can't get at the bottom of the Church of England's doctrine' on outward calling, and this is 'so on many other subjects' (Part III, chapter 5). But, for all Newman's repeated claim that joining the Catholic Church was at last to touch bottom and that Roman authority offered to all its flock a rock-bottom as solid as the rock of St Peter, it's apparent that Newman's own delight in the equivocations of word play keeps opening for readers a series of linguistic trap-doors that if not looking into bottomlessness at least reveal rather disconcertingly dark depths, and that this argumentative habit, coupled with the persistent irresolubility of some familiar logocentric problems (in particular the figure-reality difficulty) confronts Newman's readers rather often with a dizzying bottomlessness rather resembling what deconstructionists have heralded as the linguistic and textual *mise en abîme*.

The frightening prospect of bottomlessness seems to have unsettled Newman most around the great moments of crucial transition. Charles Reding has a serious moment of pre-conversion panic. 'Perhaps his convictions were, after all, a dream; what did they rest upon? He tried to recall his best arguments, and could not' (III.6). And as Newman contemplates the momentous life to death transition in *The Dream of Gerontius* he famously expresses an experience of what nineteenth-century believers knew, after Swedenborg, as vastation:

As though my very being had given way
As though I was no more substance now,
And could fall back on nought to be my stay

And drop from out this universal frame
Into that shapeless, scopeless, blank abyss
That utter nothingness, of which I came.

Such a prospect might be thought one logical consequence of thinking signs were arbitrary – as logical, indeed, as the movement of thought that links Saussure's declaration of *l'arbitraire du signe* and and the high ground of post-modernist deconstructionist scepticism. 'What are words but artificial signs of ideas?' said Charles; 'they are more musical but as arbitrary. There is no more reason why the sound "hat" should mean the particular thing so called, which we put on our heads, than why "abul-distof" should stand for 1520' (*Loss and Gain*, II.14). And Reding is right, but only up to a point. And as endless discussions of Saussure have shown, it all depends what you think of as following on from this arbitrariness. In Newman's case, the persistent equivocation, the attempts at making signs mean just what he wishes them to mean, might be thought of as a direct echo of the faith in arbitrariness of signs. If so, it does as it were then seem to have a certain appropriateness that he should have to endure, if only momentarily, Gerontius' nightmare of nothingness.

There is a very striking moment in the 'Development' where Newman, talking once again about his constant preoccupation, the chain of probabilities that seem to lead to an implied certainty, quotes *Othello* in support. '"Trifles light as air", the poet tell us, "Are to the jealous, confirmations strong, As proofs of Holy Writ".' It's not peculiar that Newman should quote Shakespeare, should adduce fiction in aid of his theology, because he does so all the time. But it is peculiar that Iago should be quoted, Iago the evil cheat and trickster, as he dwells on the tricky multivalence of Desdemona's handkerchief. Filtered through the *jalousie* of Othello's jealousy as incited by Iago, the handkerchief, Iago declares (*Othello*, III. iii. 327ff.), can be manipulated to mean anything Iago wishes. With Iago presiding over its meanings it can switch from being as beneficent as Holy Writ to something quite poisonously opposite ('Dangerous conceits are in their nature poisons'). That Newman should not be horrified at Iago's gloating manipulative hold over the sign or text of the handkerchief is, I think, significant and revealing. His quotation at this point is like a friendly handshake offered to Hermes, the thief and trickster who presides as the ancient pagan deity of interpreters and is nowadays widely welcomed as the presiding genius of deconstructionist readings. And, in fact, as Newman's paragraph continues, so the impression of an extremely unholy alliance mounts.

> Did a stranger tell us in a crowd to mind our purses, we should believe him, though in the sequel he turned out to be a thief, and gave us warning in order to gain them. A single text is sufficient to prove a doctrine to the well-disposed or the prejudiced (*D*, Chapter III, Section I, p. 179).

Iago, a thieving stranger who greatly resembles Iago ('Put money in thy purse'), a Scriptural proof text: what is contemplated here as the ways of interpreters with signs and texts and readers in general, and with 'Holy Writ' and the 'proofs' of faith in particular, seems to let some very strange felines out of the bag. No wonder, then, perhaps, that Charles Reding, when he's having doubts about truth, is made to feel that he might be Philoctetes, the mighty bowman who was however afflicted in the foot by a perpetually suppurating, stinking wound which exiled him from human company. Philoctetes belongs to that significant clutch of literary characters who have feet problems, walk with a limp, are permanently lame and crippled (they range from Jacob to Oedipus to Samuel Beckett's huge family of crippled pilgrims), and who are taken by the literary critical tradition as types and figures of the doomed writer, reader and interpreter, whether in Edmund Wilson's classic meditation on the Philoctetes myth re-read Freudianly in *The Wound and the Bow*, or in Jacques Derrida's vision of the reader committed to an endless post-modernist wrestle with the bottomlessness of meaning, the endless circulation of tantalising signs and texts, in *La Carte Postale*.

> He recollected some lines in the Ethics of Aristotle, quoted by the philosopher from an old poet, where the poor outcast Philoctetes laments over his own stupid officiousness, as he calls it, which had been the cause of all his misfortune (*Loss and Gain*, III. 6).

NOTES

1. Owen Chadwick, *Newman* (Oxford, 1983), p. 14.

2. Quoted by Meriol Trevor, in introduction to *Loss and Gain* (London, 1962), p. vii.

3. 'On the Fitness of the Glories of Mary', *The Kingdom Within: Discourses Addressed to Mixed Congregations* (Denton NJ, 1984), p. 374.

4. *Apologia pro Vita Sua* (London, 1959), Part I, p. 70. All my references to the *Apologia* are to this edition, designated *A* in the text.

5. *An Essay of the Development of Christian Doctrine*, ed. J.M. Cameron (Harmondsworth, 1974), pp. 417-19. All my references to the 'Development' are to this edition, which reprints the text of 1845, designated *D* in the text.

6. 'Prospects of the Catholic Missioner', *The Kingdom Within*. ed. cit., pp. 241-2.

7. *Apologia*, Appendix, pp. 372, 365.

8. 'A Form of Infidelity of the Day', *The Idea of a University* (London, 1927), p. 387. All quotations from the *Idea* come from this Impression.

9. 'A Correspondence – Mr Kingsley and Dr Newman', *Apologia* p. 24.

10. 'What, Then, Does Dr Newman Mean?', *Apologia*, p. 60.

11. *On Consulting the Faithful in Matters of Doctrine*, ed. John Coulson (London, 1986), pp. 54-7.

12. *A Portrait of the Artist As A Young Man*, chapter 5. Dedalus' allusion is to 'The Glories of Mary for the Sake of Her Son', *The Kingdom Within*, ed. cit., p. 358.

13. *On Consulting the Faithful,* ed. cit., pp. 115ff.

14. *Tracts for the Times*, No. 90, *Remarks On Certain Passages in the Thirty-Nine Articles*, 4th edition (Oxford, 1841), p. 8.

15. 'Apostolical Tradition', *Essays Critical and Historical* (London, 1901), I, p. 115.

16. 'Private Judgement', *Essays Critical and Historical* (London, 1901), II, p. 340.

17. 'Contest Between Faith and Sight', Sermon VII, *University Sermons*, ed. D.M. MacKinnon and J.D. Holmes (London, 1970), p. 132.

CONTRIBUTORS

Valentine Cunningham is Dean and Senior Fellow in English at Corpus Christi College, Oxford. He has written widely on modern literature and is author of *Everywhere Spoken Against: Dissent in the Victorian Novel* (Oxford, 1975) and *British Writers of the Thirties* (Oxford, 1988).

Patrick Joseph FitzPatrick is Reader Emeritus in Philosophy at the University of Durham and a Roman Catholic priest. He has written, among other things, *Apologia pro Charles Kingsley* (London, 1969). He still teaches at Durham.

Elisabeth Jay is Senior Lecturer in English at Westminster College, Oxford. Her publications include *The Religion of the Heart* (Oxford, 1979); *The Evangelical and Oxford Movements* (Cambridge, 1983) and *Faith and Doubt in Victorian Britain* (London, 1986).

Fergus Kerr, OP is Honorary Fellow of New College, Edinburgh and novice master of the English Dominicans. He has lectured and written on modern philosophy and theology and is author of *Theology after Wittgenstein* (Oxford, 1986).

David Nicholls is Vicar of Littlemore. After teaching in the West Indies, he was Chaplain and Fellow of Exeter College, Oxford. He has written widely on nineteenth-century theology and politics, and is author of *The Pluralist State* (London, 1975) and *Deity and Domination* (London, 1989).

Peter Nockles is Assistant Librarian at John Rylands Library, Manchester. He did research at Oxford and his thesis on Anglican High Churchmen of the early nineteenth century is shortly to be published by CUP. He has published several articles on nineteenth-century church history.

Joseph S. O'Leary is a Roman Catholic priest from the diocese of Cork and lectures at Sophia University in Tokyo. He studied in Maynooth, Rome and Paris and has taught in the USA and Philippines. He is author of *Questioning Back: the Overcoming of Metaphysics in Christian Tradition* (Minneapolis, 1985).

Valerie Pitt is Emeritus Professor and former Head of Humanities at Thames Polytechnic. Previously, she was Fellow of Newnham College, Cambridge, and is author of *Tennyson Laureate* (London, 1962). She wrote the minority report of the Chadwick Commission on Church and State.

INDEX

Abbott, E.A., 37f, 44f, 57f, 71
Acton, Lord (J.E.E.D.), 71, 100, 123, 136, 194, 197
Anselm, 171
Aquinas, T., 5
Aristotle, Aristotelianism, 10, 153f, 160f, 170
Arnold, M., 14, 119f, 125, 195
Arnold, T., 37, 53, 63
Athanasius, 171, 173, 185, 240
Augustine, 5, 22, 40, 162, 164, 167, 169, 171, 175, 181, 190
authority, authoritarianism, 10, ch. 7
Avis, Paul, 31, 42, 55

Bagot, R., 36, 56ff
Barberi, D., 18f
Bellarmine, R., 154, 161, 171f, 175, 247
Benjamin, W., 191
Bible, 125f, 156, 163, 166ff, 173, 176, 179, 182, 184f, 198, 234, 242ff
Birmingham Oratory, 5
Brendon, Piers, 36
Brilioth, Y., 55
Bunyan, J., 225ff
Butler, J., 8, 22, 148
Byron, G., 18

Calvin, J., 165, 171, 173, 186ff
Chadwick, O., 233
Church, R.W., 15, 29f, 37, 41, 62, 220
Churton, E., 48, 49, 60f, 62f, 70
civil allegiance, 137, 139ff, 145, 151
Clephane, E., 195, 201
Coleridge, S.T., 21, 216
conscience, 146, 169f, 178, 207
Copeland, W., 32, 60, 62, 68
Cross, F.L., 54

Dante, 219f
Dawson, C., 30
Derrida, J., 155, 245, 251
Doyle, F.H., 214, 218, 226f

Elgar, E., 229, 232
equivocation, 240

Faber, G.S., 19, 64, 163, 233
faith, 22, 25, 27, 158f, 161f, 198ff, 204f
Faraday, M., 21
Fessler, J., 136, 149, 152
freedom (intellectual), 102f, 106f, 124f
Freud, S., 181, 191
Froude, R.H., 2, 28, 30, 32, 35, 51

Gladstone, W.E., 3, 47, 50, 65, 71, 81, ch. 5, 218, 220
Golightly, C.P., 41, 59
Grave, S.A., 207f, 212f

Hackney Phalanx, 47, 51, 60
Hampden, R.D., 36, 38, 41, 71

Hare, J.C., 72
Hawker, R., 228
Hobbes, T., 208
holiness, 167ff, 172f, 176ff, 200
Housman, A.E., 117
Hume, D., 129, 183, 194, 208
Hutton, R.H., 214, 227, 229
Huxley, T.H., 71, 88

illative sense, 3, 112f, 115f
Imberg, R., 54, 211
infallibility – of Church, 101f, 106, 122f, 127, 206
– of Pope, 20, 127f, 137ff, 143ff
Ireland, 2, 137, 139, 144f, 151

James, W., 181
Jowett, B., 13, 71, 88
Joyce, J., 238

Kant, I., 155
Keble, J., 1, 16, 19ff, 28, 30f, 36, 51, 56, 203, 221
Kierkegaard, S., 181, 183
Kingsley, C., 3, 13, 19, 22, ch. 3, 120f, 130, 215, 221, 231, 234, 236ff, 240, 242ff, 246

Lacan, J., 191, 192
Liddon, H.P., 43, 62
Locke, J., 109f, 203
Luther, M., ch. 6, 72

Manning, H.E., 5, 14, 65, 123, 139f, 150, 196
Maurice, F.D., 9
McGrath, A., 174f, 186, 189, 192
Melanchthon, P., 159, 165
Mill, J.S., 22f
Milton, J., 181, 225ff
Month, The, 216f
morality, 168ff, 180, 197ff, 225
Munich Letter, 100f, 102, 104f, 123

Newman, F., 71
Newman, J.H.,
life:
ecclesiology, 141ff, 200ff
in Littlemore, 5, 13, 24, 55, 64, 228
and Oriel College, 1, 33, 122, 201
portraits, 14f
proposed canonisation, 4f, 10, 119f, 124, 126
reception into R.C. Church, 24
works:
Apologia, 3, 7f, 14, 17ff, 24, 30, 71ff, ch. 3, 124, 127, 181, 195, 202, 215, 221f, 234
Difficulties of Anglicans, 2, 30, 199
Dream of Gerontius, 3, 180, ch. 8, 250
Essay on Development, 2, 8f, 206, 242ff, 250f
Grammar of Assent, 3, 10, 23, 27, ch. 4
History of the Arians, 97f, 130, 239
Lectures on Justification, 1, ch. 6
Letter to the Duke of Norfolk, 3, ch. 5, 207
Loss and Gain, 2, 5ff, 24, 161, 233, 248, 250
On Consulting the Faithful, 2, 202, 237f
Prophetical Office of the Church, 1, 39, 205
Tract 73, 205
Tract 90, 2, ch. 2, 247
University Sermons, 11, 120, 198, 203

Oakeley, F., 52f, 61, 64
ontology, 155f, 161, 163, 170, 184, 187
Osiander, A., 164, 186
Oxford Movement, 16, 17, 18, 21, 23, ch. 2, 138

Palmer, W., 32f, 35, 48f, 59f, 64f
Paul, 7, 13, ch. 6
Peterson, L., 221
Plato, Platonism, 162, 168, 178, 182, 184f, 194, 245
Plotinus, 178
probability, 3, 22f, 111f, 250
Proust, M., 181
Pusey, E.B., 1, 28, 30f, 52f, 56f, 60ff, 85, 172

reason, 11, 14, 111ff, 160f
rhetoric, 5ff, 208, 215, 217, 222, 233, 237, 243, 248
Romanticism, 2ff, 16ff, 23, 73, 218
Rose, H.J., 33, 39
Rowell, G., 220, 224

Saussure, F., 250
scepticism, 120f, 127, 129, 171, 208, 250
Scott, W., 4, 17, 219
Sorel, G., 10
Southey, R., 4, 17
Stephen, Leslie, 9, 207
St John, Ambrose, 152, 221, 228
Syllabus of Errors, 123, 142, 147

Tennyson, 218, 227f
Tractarians *see* Oxford Movement,
Trevor, M., 124
Tyrrell, G., 208f, 210

Vatican Council,
First, 20, 127, 138, 140f, 148
Second, 4, 119, 143
via media, 4, 38ff, 165, 171, 175f, 205f, 225

Ward, W.G., 29, 52ff, 64, 102, 123, 135
Waterland, D., 166
Watson, J., 47f, 49, 51
Wilson, Edmund, 251
Wiseman, N., 40, 51
Wittgenstein, L., 110f, 128, 155, 170
Wix, Samuel, 42, 44
Wordsworth, W., 4, 17, 19, 218

Young, G.M., 71